2012

NORTHERN
GREAT LAKES
2011

ACKNOWLEDGMENTS

We gratefully acknowledge the help of our representatives for their efficient and perceptive inspections of the lodgings listed. Forbes Travel Guide is also grateful to the talented writers who contributed to this book.

Some of the information contained herein is derived from a variety of third-party sources. Although every effort has been made to verify the information obtained from such sources, the publisher assumes no responsibility for inconsistencies or inaccuracies in the data or liability for any damages of any type arising from errors or omissions.

Neither the editors nor the publisher assume responsibility for the services provided by any business listed in this guide or for any loss, damage or disruption in your travel for any reason.

Front Cover image: ©iStockphoto.com
All maps: Mapping Specialists

ISBN: 9781936010905
Manufactured in the USA
10 9 8 7 6 5 4 3 2 1

CONTENTS

STAR ATTRACTIONS

If you've been a reader of Mobil Travel Guide, you will have heard that this historic brand partnered in 2009 with another storied media name, Forbes, to create a new entity, Forbes Travel Guide. For more than 50 years, Mobil Travel Guide assisted travelers in making smart decisions about where to stay and dine when traveling. With this new partnership, our mission has not changed: We're committed to the same rigorous inspections of hotels, restaurants and spas—the most comprehensive in the industry with more than 500 standards tested at each property we visit—to help you cut through the clutter and make easy and informed decisions on where to spend your time and travel budget. Our team of anonymous inspectors are constantly on the road, sleeping in hotels, eating in restaurants and making spa appointments, evaluating those exacting standards to determine a property's rating.

What kinds of standards are we looking for when we visit a property? We're looking for more than just high-thread count sheets, pristine spa treatment rooms and white linen-topped tables. We look for service that's attentive, individualized and unforgettable. We note how long it takes to be greeted when you sit down at your table, or to be served when you order room service, or whether the hotel staff can confidently help you when you've forgotten that one essential item that will make or break your trip. Unlike any other travel ratings entity, we visit each place we rate, testing hundreds of attributes to compile our ratings, and our ratings cannot be bought or influenced. The Forbes Five Star rating is the most prestigious achievement in hospitality—while we rate more than 5,000 properties in the U.S., Canada, Hong Kong, Macau and Beijing, for 2011, we have awarded Five Star designations to only 54 hotels, 23 restaurants and 20 spas. When you travel with Forbes, you can travel with confidence, knowing that you'll get the very best experience, no matter who you are.

We understand the importance of making the most of your time. That's why the most trusted name in travel is now Forbes Travel Guide.

STAR RATED HOTELS

Whether you're looking for the ultimate in luxury or the best value for your travel budget, we have a hotel recommendation for you. To help you pinpoint properties that meet your needs, Forbes Travel Guide classifies each lodging by type according to the following characteristics:

★★★★★These exceptional properties provide a memorable experience through virtually flawless service and the finest of amenities. Staff are intuitive, engaging and passionate, and eagerly deliver service above and beyond the guests' expectations. The hotel was designed with the guest's comfort in mind, with particular attention paid to craftsmanship and quality of product. A Five-Star property is a destination unto itself.

★★★★These properties provide a distinctive setting, and a guest will find many interesting and inviting elements to enjoy throughout the property. Attention to detail is prominent throughout the property, from design concept to quality of products provided. Staff are accommodating and take pride in catering to the guest's specific needs throughout their stay.

★★★These well-appointed establishments have enhanced amenities that provide travelers with a strong sense of location, whether for style or function. They may have a distinguishing style and ambience in both the public spaces and guest rooms; or they may be more focused on functionality, providing guests with easy access to local events, meetings or tourism highlights.

Recommended: These hotels are considered clean, comfortable and reliable establishments that have expanded amenities, such as full-service restaurants.

For every property, we also provide pricing information. All prices quoted are accurate at the time of publication; however, prices cannot be guaranteed. Because rates can fluctuate, we list a pricing range rather than specific prices.

STAR RATED RESTAURANTS

Every restaurant in this book has been visited by Forbes Travel Guide's team of experts and comes highly recommended as an outstanding dining experience.

★★★★★Forbes Five-Star restaurants deliver a truly unique and distinctive dining experience. A Five-Star restaurant consistently provides exceptional food, superlative service and elegant décor. An emphasis is placed on originality and personalized, attentive and discreet service. Every detail that surrounds the experience is attended to by a warm and gracious dining room team.

★★★★These are exciting restaurants with often well-known chefs that feature creative and complex foods and emphasize various culinary techniques and a focus on seasonality. A highly-trained dining room staff provides refined personal service and attention.

★★★Three Star restaurants offer skillfully prepared food with a focus on a specific style or cuisine. The dining room staff provides warm and professional service in a comfortable atmosphere. The décor is well-coordinated with quality fixtures and decorative items, and promotes a comfortable ambience.

Recommended: These restaurants serve fresh food in a clean setting with efficient service. Value is considered in this category, as is family friendliness.

Because menu prices can fluctuate, we list a pricing range rather than specific prices. The pricing ranges are per diner, and assume that you order an appetizer or dessert, an entrée and one drink.

STAR RATED SPAS

Forbes Travel Guide's spa ratings are based on objective evalua-
tions of more than 450 attributes. About half of these criteria assess
basic expectations, such as staff courtesy, the technical proficien-
cy and skill of the employees and whether the facility is clean and
maintained properly. Several standards address issues that impact
a guest's physical comfort and convenience, as well as the staff's
ability to impart a sense of personalized service. Additional criteria
measure the spa's ability to create a completely calming ambience.

★★★★★Stepping foot in a Five Star Spa will result in an exceptional
experience with no detail overlooked. These properties wow their
guests with extraordinary design and facilities, and uncompro-
mising service. Expert staff cater to your every whim and pamper you with the most advanced treatments and skin care lines
available. These spas often offer exclusive treatments and may
emphasize local elements.

★★★★Four Star spas provide a wonderful experience in an inviting and serene environment. A sense of personalized service is
evident from the moment you check in and receive your robe and
slippers. The guest's comfort is always of utmost concern to the
well-trained staff.

★★★These spas offer well-appointed facilities with a full complement of staff to ensure that guests' needs are met. The spa
facil ties include clean and appealing treatment rooms, changing
areas and a welcoming reception desk.

TOP HOTELS, RESTAURANTS AND SPAS

HOTELS

★★★★FOUR STAR

The American Club
(*Kohler, Wisconsin*)
Canoe Bay (*Rice Lake, Wisconsin*)
Four Seasons Hotel Toronto (*Toronto, Ontario*)
The Hazelton Hotel (*Toronto, Ontario*)
Hotel Ivy (*Minneapolis, Minnesota*)
MGM Grand Detroit (*Detroit, Michigan*)
Park Hyatt Toronto (*Toronto, Ontario*)
The Townsend Hotel (*Birmingham, Michigan*)

RESTAURANTS

★★★★FOUR STAR

1913 Room (*Grand Rapids, Michigan*)
Bourbon Steak (*Detroit, Michigan*)
Canoe (*Toronto, Ontario*)
Chiado (*Toronto, Ontario*)
The Dining Room at Langdon Hall (*Cambridge, Ontario*)
The Fifth Grill (*Toronto, Ontario*)
The Immigrant Restaurant (*Kohler, Wisconsin*)
La Belle Vie (*Minneapolis, Minnesota*)
The Lark (*West Bloomfield, Michigan*)
North 44 (*Toronto, Ontario*)
One Restaurant (*Toronto, Ontario*)
Scaramouche (*Toronto, Ontario*)
Splendido (*Toronto, Ontario*)

SPAS

★★★★FOUR STAR

Immerse Spa (*Detroit, Michigan*)
Kohler Waters Spa (*Kohler, Wisconsin*)
The Spa at the Hazelton Hotel (*Toronto, Ontario*)
Stillwater Spa (*Toronto, Ontario*)

YOUR QUESTIONS ANSWERED

WHAT IS THE BEST WAY TO TOUR THE GREAT LAKES?

The most beautiful part of the Northern Great Lakes region is, of course, the lakes themselves. To encourage visitors to get close to the water, the Great Lakes Commission created the Great Lakes Circle Tour, a mapped-out system that connects all of the Great Lakes and the St. Lawrence River. It's a scenic way to road-trip it around the gorgeous bodies of freshwater. The do-it-yourself tour offers circuitous routes around each of the five Great Lakes—Erie, Huron, Michigan and Superior and Ontario. You can adapt the tour to fit your schedule and interests, whether you just want to do a portion of a tour or go all out and complete all of them in a long 6,500-mile trek. Just make sure you pack the requisite road-trip snacks and follow the designated green-and-white "Circle Tour" signs. Also, most of the looped routes traverse through Canada, so pack your passport.

LAKE ERIE

The shortest of the routes is Lake Erie. The first leg is from Detroit to Cleveland and tallies 180 miles. Follow I-75 S to Toledo and take the I-280 exit; just south of Toledo, near Oregon, take the OH-2 exit and follow OH-2. In Sandusky, start following US-6 to Cleveland.

From Cleveland, the second leg of the trip brings you to the Pennsylvania border and clocks in 70 miles. Follow OH-2 E to US-20 to OH 531, then back to US-20 again.

The third part of the drive takes you from Pennsylvania to Buffalo, New York, and is 120 miles long. Take PA-5 to NY-5 E. To finish the tour, you'll go from Buffalo to Detroit via Ontario for 290 miles. Follow Provincial Highway 3 to Windsor, Ontario. Then cross the Ambassador Bridge into Detroit, where you'll hit a toll.

LAKE HURON

The Huron tour starts out in Ontario. For the first leg, you'll be driving for 250 miles in the Canadian state, from Sarnia to Barrie. Just take Provincial Highway 21 to Provincial Highway 26.

The next portion of the drive, which is 365 miles, takes you from Barrie to Sault Ste. Marie, Ontario. Head northeast on Ontario Rte. 400 to Trans Canada 69; at Sudbury, follow Trans Canada 17; cross the International bridge at Sault Ste. Marie, where there will be a toll.

Leg three brings you from Sault Ste. Marie to Bay City, Mich., and is 290 miles long. Follow I-75 South and cross the Mackinaw Toll Bridge. Take the US-23 exit and go South until you get to Bay City.

The last leg is 150 miles from Bay City back to Sarnia. Go on MI-25 E around the "thumb" of Michigan and down to Port Huron, Mich.; cross the Blue Water Bridge into Sarnia.

YOUR QUESTIONS ANSWERED...*continued*

WHAT IS THE BEST WAY TO TOUR THE GREAT LAKES?

LAKE MICHIGAN

The Lake Michigan route is the only one that doesn't dip into Ontario. The route begins in Chicago and takes you on an 80-mile trip to Buffalo, Mich. Follow I-94E; then in Gary, Ind., follow US-12 to I-94E.

Next, you want to go to Mackinaw City. For the 450-mile second section, follow I-96E to Holland; US-31N to Manistee; MI-22 to Traverse City; US-31 to Petoskey; MI-119 to the town of Cross Bridge; C66 to US-31; cross the Mackinaw Toll Bridge into the Upper Peninsula. Then head to Menominee, Mich./Marinette, Wis. Follow US-2 W to Escanaba, and take MI-35 to Menominee/Marinette; it will take you about 205 miles.

From Menominee/Marinette, make your way to Milwaukee in a 325-mile drive. Follow US-41 to US-43 in Green Bay; follow WI-57E to WI-42S (Door Peninsula); in Manitowoc, follow I-43S to Milwaukee. Then it's time to return to Chicago. To make the 100-mile trek, follow WI-32 to the Wisconsin-Illinois border; take IL-137 to I-94.

LAKE SUPERIOR

Start out in Duluth, Minn., to make your way to Thunder Bay. Take US-61 and CR-61 for about 200 miles. The second leg, which adds up to in 380 miles, leads you to Sault Ste. Marie. Go on Trans-Canada 17 then cross the International Bridge into the U.S. The third leg brings to you Ironwood in a 310-mile drive straight down M-28. Then, it's time to return to Duluth; just take US-2 for 110 miles.

LAKE ONTARIO

For the Ontario route, the commission decided to incorporate New York's Seaway Trail, hence the route's name: the Lake Ontario Circle Tour and Seaway Trail. The 120-mile first leg starts out in Pennsylvania and brings you to Buffalo; take PA-5 to NY-5 E. The next portion points you to Watertown, N.Y., for a 250-mile drive. Follow NY-104 north of Buffalo to NY-18 east. In Rochester, follow NY-104 east to NY-104A south of Oswego. North of Oswego, follow NY-3 to Watertown. Leg No. 3 travels to Massena, N.Y.; follow NY-12 to NY-37 east for about 120 miles. The last leg of the trip drops you off at Niagara Falls, Ontario, in 366 miles. Follow NY-37 across the bridge into Canada. Go west on Provincial Highway 2. In Hamilton, Ontario, follow the QEW to Niagara Falls.

WELCOME TO MICHIGAN

MICHIGAN HAS A MIGHTY INDUSTRIAL HERITAGE AND IS WELL-KNOWN as the birthplace of the automobile industry, but rivaling the machines, mines and mills is the nearly $13 billion tourist industry. The two great Michigan peninsulas, surrounded by four of the five Great Lakes, include a vast tapestry of lakeshore beaches, trout-filled streams, more than 11,000 inland lakes, nearly 7 million acres of public hunting grounds, and the cultural attractions of Detroit, Ann Arbor, Grand Rapids, Interlochen and other cities.

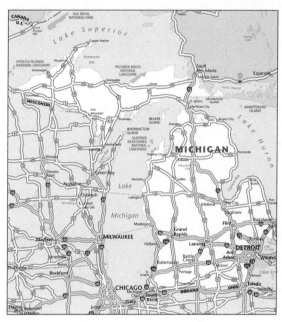

Michigan is a four-season vacationland, with tempering winds off the Great Lakes that tame what might otherwise be a climate of extremes. In a land of cherry blossoms, tulips, ski slopes and sugar-sand beaches, you can fish through the ice, snowmobile on hundreds of miles of marked trails, rough it on an uncluttered island or hunt for copper, iron ore, Lake Superior agates or Petoskey stones. One of the country's finest art museums is in Detroit, and Dearborn's The Henry Ford, which houses a museum, Greenfield Village and other sights, attracts visitors from all over the world.

While most people know Michigan as a world center for automobile manufacturing, it's also is a great spot for fresh, delicious fruit. More than two-thirds of the nation's tart red cherries are harvested here, and Traverse City hosts the National Cherry Festival each July. In addition, the state is one of the nation's leading producers of blueberries and dry, edible beans. Wheat, hay, corn, oats, turkeys, cattle and hogs are also produced in vast quantities.

Michigan's economic development has come in waves, and following the recession of 2008, the waters have been rough. First, there were trees, the basis for a great lumber industry. These were rapidly depleted. Then copper- and iron-ore mines were discovered. They are now mostly inactive, although the discovery of new copper deposits is leading to renewed activity. The automobile industry, diversified industries and tourism became successful, declined, and now could be poised for a comeback with the development of hybrid and green energy-driven cars. Today, the St. Lawrence Seaway makes Michigan's international port cities and the state's future promising.

BEST ATTRACTIONS

MICHIGAN'S BEST ATTRACTIONS

DETROIT
As Michigan's biggest city, Detroit can be gritty and downright rough in spots, but it also offers everything from top-notch art museums to big Vegas-style casinos. Locals often frequent Greektown for dinner.

HARBOR COUNTRY
People come to Harbor Country for its little lakeside towns that seem to have all of the essentials of a great getaway: beaches, beautiful scenery, cute shops and lots of wineries.

MACKINAC ISLAND
Michigan may be most well known for its cars, but vehicles are prohibited on this remote island in the Upper Peninsula. Get away from it all at this rustic escape, where most of the island is a state park.

SAUGATUCK
Dubbed the "Art Coast of Michigan," Saugatuck has a thriving arts scene. After all, it's the home of the renowned artists' residence/school Ox-Bow. But it's become a resort area, with beaches, the dunes and the river offering fun outside the galleries.

NORTHERN MICHIGAN

Northern Michigan's location along the Great Lakes makes it a prime outdoorsy destination. Skiers will want to head to resort towns like Bellaire, Cadillac and Boyne City, where downhill and cross-country skiing, snowshoeing and snow-mobiling keep you moving in winter.

See the winter in all its glory in Gaylord, known as Michigan's Alpine Village since its annual snowfall tallies more than 180 inches. Downtown Gaylord shops give the appearance of charming, Swiss-inspired chalets. Winter sports abound in Gaylord, and you'll find more than 300 miles of groomed snowmobile trails and numerous cross-country ski trails. With nearly 100 small lakes, Gaylord is also home to excellent fishing, both in summer and winter. Gaylord also boasts the best golf experience in Michigan, with two dozen award-winning courses.

For a year-round vacation spot, Harbor Springs is a picturesque town on Little Traverse Bay that boasts sandy beaches and two of Michigan's most popular ski resorts. Downtown Harbor Springs overflows with pricey but quaint shops and eateries.

A large passenger car ferry and freighters keep Ludington, an important Lake Michigan port, busy. Ludington draws vacationers because of its long stretch of beach on Lake Michigan and miles of forests, lakes, streams and dunes surrounding the town.

A popular resort nestled in a hillside overlooking Little Traverse Bay, Petoskey is known for its historic Gaslight Shopping District. These downtown shops connect to Waterfront Park, which features a walking path, playground, recreation area and marina. A bike path connects Petoskey northward to Harbor Springs and southward to Charlevoix, offering opportunities to bike, in-line skate and walk among these charming cities. Petoskey State Park and numerous local parks offer hiking trails and beaches.

Surrounded by two Great Lakes and large inland lakes, Cheboygan has long been a premier boating and fishing area. You'll also find charming Victorian shops, gorgeous spring blooms and delightful fall color. And because of heavy snowfall, winter activities abound: snowmobiling, cross-country skiing (hundreds of miles of groomed trails), snowshoeing, ice skating, hockey and ice fishing.

WHAT TO SEE

BELLAIRE
SHANTY CREEK RESORT
1 Shanty Creek Road, Bellaire, 231-533-8621, 800-678-4111; www.shantycreek.com
This popular ski resort includes two separate mountains, five quads, two double chairlifts and four surface lifts. There's also a patrol, a school, rentals, snowmaking, night skiing, a lodge, snowboarding and tubing. All in all, the resort offers 30 trails. The longest run is approximately one mile with a vertical drop of 450 feet. There are also cross-country trails (25 miles).
Thanksgiving-March, daily.

BOYNE CITY
BOYNE MOUNTAIN
1 Boyne Mountain Road, Boyne Falls, 231-549-6000, 800-462-6963; www.boynemountain.com
This mountain has triple, six-passenger, three quads and three double chairlifts. It also has a rope tow, a patrol, a school, rentals, snowmaking, a lodge, a cafeteria, a restaurant, a bar and a nursery. The longest run is one mile with a vertical drop of 500 feet. Cross-country trails (35 miles) and rentals (trail ticket; fee) are available.
Late November-mid-April, daily.

CADILLAC
ADVENTURE ISLAND
6083 E. Highway 155, Cadillac, 231-775-5665; www.cadillacmichigan.com
This family fun park includes mountain miniature golf, go-karts, batting cages, bumper boats, water slides, concessions, an arcade and a water slide.
Admission: free, ride costs vary. June-September, daily 10 a.m.-10 p.m.

CABERFAE PEAKS SKI RESORT
Caberfae Road, Cadillac, 231-862-3000; www.caberfaepeaks.com
The resort offers a quad, a triple, three double chairlifts, two T-bars, two rope

BEST ATTRACTIONS

WHAT ARE SOME OF THE BEST PLACES FOR OUTDOOR FUN?

LUDINGTON STATE PARK

When the weather gets hot, this state park offers respite with its 4,500 acres along lakes Michigan and Hamlin and the Sable River. Aside from swimming, you have your choice of water sports: waterskiing, boating, fishing and more.

NUB'S NOB

When the weather turns cold, head to this ski resort, which boasts 53 slopes and trails on three separate peaks. Nub's Nob is hailed for its great snow and snow-grooming crew, which will ensure you'll have a good time on the slopes.

tows, a patrol, a school, rentals, snowmaking, a bar, a snowboard and cross-country and snowmobile trails.
Late November-March, daily.

WILLIAM MITCHELL STATE PARK

6093 E. Highway 115, Cadillac, 231-775-7911

This state park occupies approximately 260 acres between Lake Cadillac and Lake Mitchell. It includes a beach, boat docks and rentals, interpretive hiking trails, picnicking, playground and a nature study area.

CHEBOYGAN

ALOHA STATE PARK

4347 Third St., Cheboygan, 231-625-2522

This 95-acre park includes swimming, fishing, boating, picnicking and camping.

CHEBOYGAN OPERA HOUSE

403 N. Huron St., Cheboygan, 231-627-5432; www.theoperahouse.org

This 1877 theater doesn't just offer opera. The renovated 580-seat auditorium features events ranging from bluegrass to ballet.

CHEBOYGAN STATE PARK

4490 Beach Road, Cheboygan, 616-627-2811; www.cheboyganstatepark.com

This state park is made up of more than 1,200 acres, on which you can go swimming, fishing, boating, hiking, cross-country skiing, picnicking and camping.
Daily.

GAYLORD
OTSEGO LAKE STATE PARK
7136 Old Highway 27 S., Gaylord, 989-732-5485; www.michigan.gov

Approximately 60 acres, the park boasts a beach, a bathhouse, waterskiing, boating as well as fishing for pike, bass and perch. There are also picnicking areas, a playground, concessions and camping.

Mid-April-mid-October.

TREETOPS RESORT
3962 Wilkinson Road, Treetops Village, 989-732-6711, 888-873-3867; www.treetops.com

The resort has double, two triple chairlifts; four rope tows; a patrol; a school, rentals; a cafeteria and a bar. Of its 19 runs, the longest one has a vertical drop of 225 feet. It also has 10 miles of cross-country trails and three miles of lighted trails.

December-mid-March, daily.

HARBOR SPRINGS
BOYNE HIGHLANDS
600 Highlands Drive, Harbor Springs, 231-526-3000, 800-462-6963; www.boynehighlands.com

Boyne Highlands offers four triple, four quad chairlifts; a rope tow; a patrol; a school; rentals and snowmaking. It also has four miles of cross-country trails.

Thanksgiving weekend-mid-April, daily.

NUB'S NOB
500 Nub's Nob Road, Harbor Springs, 231-526-2131, 800-754-6827; www.nubsnob.com

There are two double, three quad, three triple chairlifts; a patrol; a school; rentals and snowmaking at Nub's Nob. The longest run is one mile with a vertical drop of 427 feet. Cross-country trails and night skiing are offered as well.

Thanksgiving-Easter, daily. Half-day rates. Cross-country trails (same seasons, hours as downhill skiing); night skiing (five nights/week).

LUDINGTON
AUTO FERRY/S.S. BADGER
701 Maritime Drive, Ludington, 231-843-1509, 800-841-4243; www.ssbadger.com

Instead of driving all the way around Lake Michigan, you can drive right onto the S.S. Badger and ride across. This car ferry takes passengers and vehicles on a four-hour trip to Manitowoc, Wis. Amenities aboard the ferry include a game room, movie screenings, staterooms and food service.

Admission: round-trip fare: adults $109, seniors $99, children 5-15 $39, children 4 and under free. May-October, daily.

LUDINGTON STATE PARK
Highway 116 N., Ludington, 231-843-8671; www.ludingtonfriends.com

Approximately 4,500 acres on lakes Michigan and Hamlin and the Sable River make up this state park. Plenty of recreational activities are on hand, including swimming, waterskiing, fishing, boating, hunting, cross-country skiing and more.

May-September.

WHITE PINE VILLAGE
1687 S. Lakeshore Drive, Ludington, 231-843-4808; www.historicwhitepinevillage.org

Historical buildings re-create small-town Michigan life in the late 1800s. The village includes a general store, trapper's cabin, courthouse/jail, town hall, one-room school and more.

June-early September, Tuesday-Sunday.

PETOSKEY
LITTLE TRAVERSE HISTORICAL MUSEUM
Waterfront Park, 100 Depot Court, Petoskey, 231-347-2620; www.petoskeymuseum.org

Housed in a former railroad depot, the museum showcases historical exhibits from the area's Native American, pioneer and Victorian past.

Admission: adults $2, children 5-17 $1. May-November, daily.

PETOSKEY STATE PARK
2475 Highway 119, Petoskey, 231-347-2311

The 305-acre park has a beach, a beach house, fishing, hiking, cross-country skiing, picnicking, playground and camping.

Daily.

WHERE TO STAY

BELLAIRE
★★★SHANTY CREEK RESORT
1 Shanty Creek Road, Bellaire, 231-533-8621, 800-678-4111; www.shantycreek.com

Located on more than 4,500 acres of rolling hills, this resort offers three distinct lodges: The Schuss Village features one in a European style at the bottom of Schuss Mountain and offers guest rooms and one- and two-bedroom condos; The Summit Village gives a great view of the snow-covered lakes and forests—considered by many as some of the best views in northern Michigan; and Cedar River Village, the newest of the three, overlooks the Tom Weiskopf golf course. Onsite activities cover all seasons and include disc golf, hiking, bike trails, skiing, snowboarding and tubing. Pets are welcome with a package of treats and you'll get a map of places to take your dog on a walk. The dining options are many, from fine dining to casual post-activity choices.

640 rooms. Restaurant, bar. Beach. Ski in/ski out. Golf. Tennis. $151-250

CHEBOYGAN
★★★INSEL HAUS BED AND BREAKFAST
HCR 1, Bios Blanc Island, 231-634-7393; www.inselhausbandb.com

This pretty 6,200-square-foot home on the strait of Mackinac is five miles offshore. You'll have to arrive by ferry, plane or helicopter. Inside, the great room features a beautiful chandelier—the former helm of an old ship—a tiled corner fireplace and a floor-to-ceiling window, which overlooks the grounds. The home can accommodate up to 20 guests at a time and features three kitchens, a private library, antique furniture, Persian rugs and stained-glass accents throughout. The house is surrounded by 1,800 feet of shoreline and a mile of wilderness forests, allowing guests to enjoy various outdoor activities, such as cross-country skiing, snow shoeing, bicycling, sailing, hiking, canoeing, swimming, bird-watching and charter fishing. If you're looking for some nightlife, there is a casino 90 minutes away.

9 rooms. Complimentary breakfast. $151-250

GAYLORD

★★★GARLAND RESORT & GOLF COURSE

4700 N. Red Oak Road, Lewiton, 989-786-2211, 877-442-7526; www.garlandusa.com

This family-run resort caters to golfers with four championship courses surrounded by 3,500 acres of pristine wilderness. Lessons, practice facilities and a well-stocked pro shop enhance the experience. During the winter months, miles of cross-country trails attract skiers. You can also rent mountain bikes, fish in the Garland ponds or take a guided nature trail hike. From the main lodge to the golf cottages, villas and condos, the accommodations are comfortable, and the interiors reflect the rugged setting.

60 rooms. Restaurant, bar. Closed mid-March-April. $151-250

GLEN ARBOR

★★★THE HOMESTEAD

Wood Ridge Road, Glen Arbor, 231-334-5000; www.thehomesteadresort.com

Located in Leelanau County and on the shore of Lake Michigan, this resort sits on many acres of wooded land—the setting is private and breathtaking. You can choose to stay in a small hotel, an inn, a lodge or privately owned guest homes here. The quaint resort town of Glen Arbor is within a two-mile drive, as are the popular Sleeping Bear Sand Dunes National Park and Lakeshore.

130 rooms. Restaurant. Beach. Closed mid-March-April, November-late December. $151-250

HARBOR SPRINGS

★★★KIMBERLY COUNTRY ESTATE

2287 Bester Road, Harbor Springs, 231-526-7646; www.kimberlycountryestate.com

Just four minutes outside town, this 25-acre colonial plantation estate is wrapped in pillared balconies overlooking its swimming pool and Wequetonsing Golf Course. Rooms have English country décor, four-poster beds and fresh flowers. If you want to head outdoors, the hotel will put together a picnic lunch for a trip to the beach. When you return to the hotel in the evening, you'll be treated to wine as well as bedtime sherry and chocolate truffles.

8 rooms. Complimentary breakfast. Closed April. $151-250

PETOSKEY

★★★RENAISSANCE INN AT BAY HARBOR

3600 Village Harbor Drive, Bay Harbor, 231-439-4000, 800-362-6963; www.innatbayharbor.com

This resort is nestled on 5 acres alongside Lake Michigan. Golf is a major attraction, with 162 holes just outside the hotel, 27 of them part of the property itself. The spa soothes with a wide variety of pampering treatments, including massages, facials and hydrotherapy. The inn's suites have a classic appeal, while three-bedroom cottages offer spacious accommodations with views of the Crooked Tree Golf Club. From the photographs of Victorian cruise ships lining the walls at lakeside Sagamore's to the dark wood and leather interior at the South American lounge, this resort celebrates its history in its restaurants as well.

218 rooms. Restaurant, bar. Closed two to three weeks in April and November. $251-350

★★★STAFFORD'S BAY VIEW INN

2011 Woodland Ave., Petoskey, 231-347-2771, 800-258-1886; www.thebayviewinn.com

Built in 1866, this historic Victorian-style inn features a green mansard roof, a sun room, a library and an outdoor porch. The inn looks out over Little Traverse Bay. Guest rooms are quaint, with period furnishings and antiques, and relaxing—no televisions or telephones. Breakfast, Sunday brunch and dinner menus are offered at the Roselawn Dining Room, the inn's in-house restaurant.

31 rooms. Restaurant, bar. Complimentary breakfast. Closed April, late October-late November; Sunday-Thursday in March and early-late December. $151-250

WHERE TO EAT

CHARLEVOIX

★★★MAHOGANY'S

9600 Clubhouse Drive, Charlevoix, 231-547-3555, 800-618-9796; www.chxcountryclub.com

Inside the Charlevoix Country Club, this restaurant offers an elegant dining experience, complete with a fieldstone fireplace and handcrafted mahogany bar. Serving casual lunches on the porch and international cuisine in the dining room, this restaurant is the perfect post-game stopping place.

American. Dinner, Sunday brunch. Children's menu. Bar. $36-85

ELLSWORTH

★★★ROWE INN

6303 E. Jordan Road, Ellsworth, 231-588-7351, 866-432-5873; www.roweinn.com

This fine dining restaurant, opened in 1972, sits along the lake in Ellsworth. The focus here is on cuisine native to Michigan, and the restaurant boasts an extensive wine list, one of the largest in the state. The signature dishes include rack of lamb and pecan-stuffed morel mushrooms, but make it a point to try other offerings and the Rowe's selection of artisanal cheeses.

French. Dinner, Sunday brunch. Reservations recommended. Outdoor seating. $36-85

HARBOR SPRINGS

★★★THE NEW YORK

101 State St., Harbor Springs, 231-526-1904; www.thenewyork.com

Established in 1904, this American bistro is housed in a Victorian-style former

HIGHLIGHT

WHAT IS THERE TO DO AT SLEEPING BEAR DUNES NATIONAL LAKESHORE?

Congress designated the Manitou Islands and 35 miles of mainland Lake Michigan shoreline in the vicinity of Empire as Sleeping Bear Dunes National Lakeshore in 1970. Today, the park welcomes more than 1 million visitors per year.

To find out the origin of the unusually named park, you have to go back to an Ojibwa legend. It tells of a mother bear who, with her two cubs, tried to swim across Lake Michigan from Wisconsin to escape from a forest fire. Nearing the Michigan shore, the exhausted cubs fell behind. The mother bear climbed to the top of a bluff to watch and wait for her offspring. They never reached her. Today she can still be seen as the Sleeping Bear, a solitary dune higher than its surroundings. Her cubs are the Manitou Islands, which lie a few miles offshore.

The lakeshore's variety of landforms supports a diversity of interrelated plant habitats. Sand dune deserts contrast sharply with hardwood forests. The 71,000-acre lakeshore contains stands of pine, dense cedar swamps and a few secluded bogs of sphagnum moss. Against this green background are stands of white birch. In addition, the park supports many kinds of animal life, including porcupine, deer, rabbit, squirrel, coyote and raccoon. More than 200 species of birds may be seen. Bass, bluegill, perch and pike are plentiful, and salmon is abundant in the fall.

Explore the scenery more in depth. The Dune Climb takes visitors up 150 feet on foot through the dunes for a panoramic view of Glen Lake and the surrounding countryside. Or take the Pierce Stocking Scenic Drive, a seven-mile loop, to view the high dunes and overlooks from your car (May-October; park pass required).

Stop off at Sleeping Bear Point Maritime Museum, one mile west of Glen Haven on Highway 209, located in the restored U.S. Coast Guard Station. The museum contains exhibits on the activities of the U.S. Life-Saving Service and the U.S. Coast Guard, and the general maritime activities these organizations have aided on the Great Lakes. A restored boathouse contains original and replica surf boats and other related rescue equipment.

Check out South Manitou Island, a 5,260-acre island with 12 miles of shoreline. Formed from glacial moraines more than 10,000 years ago, the island slowly grew a forest covering. European settlers and the U.S. Lighthouse Service, attracted by the forest and the natural harbor, established permanent sites here as early as the 1830s. On the southwest corner is the Valley of the Giants, a grove of white cedar trees more than 500 years old. There are three campgrounds on the island and ranger-led tours of the 1873 lighthouse.

Nearby North Manitou Island is a 28-square-mile wilderness with 20 miles of shoreline. All travel is by foot and is dependent on weather. Camping is allowed under wilderness regulations; no ground fires are permitted. There is no safe harbor or anchorage on either of the Manitou islands, however, from May to October, the islands are accessible by commercial ferry service from Leland.

Camping is available at D. H. Day Campground (May-November) and Platte River Campground (year-round). The visitors center has information on park passes, hiking trails, cross-country skiing, campfire programs, and more.

hotel. Interesting artwork lines the walls, and the dining room looks out onto a popular downtown street, making this a great place to people-watch. Diners can also request a table overlooking Little Traverse Bay's waterfront area for a more romantic view. Locals come for the delicious seafood dishes and other delicacies made with fresh ingredients and homegrown herbs, and to partake in the award-winning wine list, which features more than 350 vintages.

American. Dinner. Closed April. Reservations recommended. Children's menu. Bar. $16-35

SOUTHWEST MICHIGAN

Vacationers head to Southwest Michigan for its beaches along Lake Michigan, resort areas like Harbor Country, wineries and theme parks.

East Lansing, home to Michigan State University, is known as the cultural and recreational center of mid-Michigan. Street festivals, outdoor concerts and 26 parks make this city a gem.

Grand Rapids, a widely known furniture center and convention city, also draws in travelers. Culture vultures come to check out the Grand Rapids Art Museum and one of Frank Lloyd Wright's restored homes. The city's most famous resident, former president Gerald R. Ford, has a museum dedicated to him here as well.

A tourist favorite is Holland, a town where Dutch settled in 1847 because its sand dunes and fertile land reminded them of their homeland. Today, much of the population is of Dutch descent, as evidenced by the mid-May Tulip Time Festival, which features millions of tulips, wooden shoemaking, dancing and Dutch delicacies. The town prides itself on being the center of Dutch culture in the United States. Gamblers hedge their bets on Mount Pleasant, home of Soaring Eagle Casino, a major tourist attraction, and New Buffalo, for its Four Winds Casino Resort.

Outdoorsy types have plenty of options. Muskegon County is in the western part of the lower peninsula, along 26 miles of Lake Michigan shoreline. Long one of the major art colonies in the Midwest, Saugatuck is now a year-round resort area. It offers swimming off the beautiful beaches, hiking and cross-country skiing in the dunes, canoeing and boating on the Kalamazoo River, yachting from marinas and a charming shopping area. A five-mile beach on Lake Michigan and surrounding lakes make sport fishing a popular summer activity in South Haven. Numerous marinas and charter boat services are available in the area. Views are stunning as the sun sets on Lake Michigan, and South Haven's charming boutiques make shopping a fun pastime. Many go to St. Joseph, or St. Joe, as it's known to locals, for Warren Dunes State Park, one of Michigan's best state parks. But Traverse City's beaches are legendary, and the views of Lake Michigan's Grand Traverse Bay are gorgeous. It's something that travelers of all stripes can appreciate.

WHAT TO SEE

BATTLE CREEK
BINDER PARK ZOO
7400 Division Drive, Battle Creek, 269-979-1351; www.binderparkzoo.org

Come here to see exotic, endangered and domestic animals in natural exhibits. The 50-acre "Wild Africa" display includes giraffes, zebras, antelope and African wild dogs. You'll see a trading village, ranger station, research camp and

HIGHLIGHT

WHAT ARE SOME OF THE BEST PLACES FOR OUTDOOR FUN IN SOUTHWEST MICHIGAN?

DUTCH VILLAGE
Michigan's homage to the Netherlands of yesteryear is appropriately in the city of Holland. You'll find authentic architecture, canals, windmills and lots of tulips, of course. You can even visit a klompen factory that makes those wooden shoes.

FREDERIK MEIJER GARDENS AND SCULPTURE PARK
Sure, you'll find plenty of plant life at this botanic garden, but the grounds also host striking larger-than-life works from renowned sculptors such as Auguste Rodin, Mark di Suvero and Magdalena Abakanowicz.

MICHIGAN'S ADVENTURE AMUSEMENT PARK
Thrill-seekers will want to get a ticket to Michigan's Adventure, the state's biggest amusement and water park. You'll especially want to conquer the Wolverine Wildcat, the largest wooden roller coaster in Michigan.

MUSICAL FOUNTAIN
Grand Haven puts on quite the show with the world's largest electronically controlled musical fountain. See bursts of color and jets of water light up the sky, all of which is synchronized to tunes as varied as "Bohemian Rhapsody" to "Apologize."

WARREN DUNES STATE PARK
This is one of Michigan's most popular state parks. People come for the three miles of Lake Michigan shoreline, the many campsites, the six miles of trails and the great views. On a clear day, you can see the Chicago skyline from atop one of the dunes.

working diamond mine alongside a panoramic African savanna. There is also a children's zoo and special events during Halloween and Christmas.
Admission: adults $12.50, seniors $11.50, children 2-10 $10.50, children under 2 free. Mid-April to mid-October, daily.

FORT CUSTER STATE RECREATION AREA
5163 W. Fort Custer Drive, Augusta, 269-731-4200; www.michigan.gov
This recreation area includes a beach, fishing, boating (launch), picnic areas as

HIGHLIGHT

WHAT ARE THE REGION'S TOP MUSEUMS?

GERALD R. FORD MUSEUM
Exhibits explore the life of the nation's 38th president, but it isn't all dusty old documents. The museum, part of the presidential library system, features the original burglar tools used in the Watergate break-in and Ford's burial site.

GRAND RAPIDS ART MUSEUM
Although it's housed in a new LEED Gold-certified building, GRAM is more than 100 years old. Inside the green building you'll see Renaissance, French and American paintings as well as visiting exhibits, like a showcase of Ox-Bow artists.

KALAMAZOO AIR ZOO
This aviation museum takes flight with more than 70 historic and restored aircraft from the World War II period, amusement park-style rides, full-motion flight simulators and a 4-D theater.

MEYER MAY HOUSE
The house isn't a museum per se, but it might as well be. It's a 1908 Frank Lloyd Wright home from the late Prairie period that's been authentically restored with architect-designed furniture, leaded-glass windows, lighting fixtures and more.

well as nature, bridle and bicycle trails. In winter, there are cross-country skiing and snowmobiling.
Daily.

KIMBALL HOUSE MUSEUM
196 Capital Ave. N.E., Battle Creek, 616-965-2613; www.heritagebattlecreek.org
This restored and refurnished Victorian home built in 1886 has an herb garden and country store. It also has displays that show the development of appliances, tools and medical instruments.
Admission: adults $5, children $3. Friday 1-4 p.m. Closed January-April.

KINGMAN MUSEUM OF NATURAL HISTORY
175 Limit St., Battle Creek, 269-965-5117; www.kingmanmuseum.org
The natural history museum features exhibits such as "Journey Through the Crust of the Earth," "Walk in the Footsteps of the Dinosaurs," "Mammals of the Ice Age," "Window to the Universe," "Wonder of Life" and "Discovery Room."

Admission: adults $6, seniors $5, children 3-17 $4, children 2 and under free. Tuesday-Friday 9 a.m.-5 p.m., Saturday 1-5 p.m.

LEILA ARBORETUM
928 W. Michigan Ave., Battle Creek, 269-969-0270; www.leilaarboretumsociety.org
This 72-acre park is filled with native trees and shrubs.

SOJOURNER TRUTH GRAVE
Oak Hill Cemetery, South Avenue and Oak Drive, Battle Creek
On the cemetery's Fifth Street is the plain square monument marking the resting place of this remarkable freedom fighter. Born a slave in the 1790s, Truth gained her freedom in the 1820s and crusaded against slavery until her death in 1883. Although uneducated, she had a brilliant mind as well as an unquenchable devotion to her cause.

WILLARD BEACH
Goguac Lake, Battle Creek
Lavishly landscaped with a wide bathing beach, this is a popular spot come summer and includes picnic areas.
June-September, daily.

W.K. KELLOGG BIRD SANCTUARY OF MICHIGAN STATE UNIVERSITY
12685 E. C Ave., Augusta, 269-671-2510; www.kbs.msu.edu
Seven kinds of swans and more than 20 species of ducks and geese inhabit the ponds and Wintergreen Lake. You can see one of the finest bird-of-prey collections in the Midwest, along with free-roaming upland game birds. There is an observation deck and educational displays. Self-guided and guided tours are offered; call in advance to make reservations for guided tours.
Admission: adults $4, seniors $2, children 2-12 $1, children 1 and under free. Tours: adults $3, seniors $2, children 2-12 $1, children 1 and under free. Daily 9 a.m.-7 p.m.

COLDWATER
TIBBITS OPERA HOUSE
14 S. Hanchett St., Coldwater, 517-278-6029; www.tibbits.org
This renovated 19th-century Victorian opera house is home to professional summer theater series, art exhibits, a winter concert series, children's programs and community events. Originally owned and operated by businessman Barton S. Tibbits, the house attracted such performers as John Philip Sousa, Ethel Barrymore, P. T. Barnum, John Sullivan and William Gillette. Tours are available.
Box office: Tuesday-Friday 10 a.m.-5 p.m. and one hour prior to show time.

WING HOUSE MUSEUM
27 S. Jefferson St., Coldwater, 517-278-2871
Originally built in 1875, this historical house museum exhibits Second Empire architectural style. The home includes the original kitchen and dining room in the basement, a collection of Oriental rugs, oil paintings, three generations of glassware, a Regina music box and furniture from Empire to Eastlake styles.
Wednesday-Sunday 1-5 p.m., also by appointment.

EAST LANSING

TRILLIUM GALLERY
107 Division St., East Lansing, 517-333-3130; www.michigan.org

This gallery showcases handcrafted artwork by Michigan artists, including glass work, jewelry, pottery and more.

WHARTON CENTER FOR THE PERFORMING ARTS
Michigan State University, East Lansing, 517-353-1982; www.whartoncenter.com

The Wharton Center puts various musical, dance, dramatic and arts-oriented performances on its stage.

GRAND HAVEN

GRAND HAVEN STATE PARK
1001 Harbor Ave., Grand Haven, 616-798-3711; www.michigan.gov

This park encompasses almost 50 acres on Lake Michigan beachfront. Spend the day swimming, fishing or picnicking there.

Daily.

HARBOR STEAMER
301 N. Harbor Drive, Grand Haven, 616-842-8950

This stern-wheel paddleboat cruises out to Spring Lake.

Mid-May-September, daily.

HARBOR TROLLEYS
440 N. Ferry St., Grand Haven, 616-842-3200; www.grandhaven.org

These trolleys take two different routes: The Grand Haven trolley operates between downtown and state park; the second trolley goes to Spring Lake.

Monday-Friday 6 a.m.-5:30 p.m., Saturday 9 a.m.-3:30 p.m.

MUSICAL FOUNTAIN
Dewey Hill, 1 N. Harbor Drive, Grand Haven, 616-842-2550; www.grandhaven.org

This is said to be the world's largest electronically controlled musical fountain. The spraying water, lights and music are synchronized, and watching the show is a long-held tradition in Grand Haven.

Admission: free. Programs June-September, evenings; May and rest of September, Friday-Saturday only.

GRAND RAPIDS

BERLIN RACEWAY
2060 Berlin Fair Drive, Marne, 616-726-7373; www.berlinraceway.com

This racetrack hosts late-model stock car, sportsman stock car and super stock car racing.

May-September, Friday-Sunday.

BLANDFORD NATURE CENTER
1715 Hillburn Ave. N.W., Grand Rapids, 616-735-6240; www.blandfordnaturecenter.org

The nature center offers more than 140 acres of woods, fields and ponds with self-guiding trails; guided tours; interpretive center has exhibits; live animals; furnished pioneer garden; and one-room schoolhouse.

Monday-Friday 9 a.m.-5 p.m., Saturday-Sunday noon-4 p.m.

CANNONSBURG SKI AREA

6800 Cannonsburg Road, Cannonsburg, 616-874-6711, 800-253-8748; www.cannonsburg.com

This ski area has a quad, triple, double chairlift; two T-bars; and eight rope tows.

Late November-mid-March, Saturday-Sunday 9 a.m.-10 p.m.

FREDERIK MEIJER GARDENS AND SCULPTURE PARK

1000 E. Beltline Ave. N.E., Grand Rapids, 616-957-1580, 888-957-1580; www.meijergardens.org

This botanic garden and sculpture park includes a 15,000-square-foot glass conservatory, a desert garden, exotic indoor and outdoor gardens and more than 60 bronze works.

Admission: adults $12, seniors and students $9, children 5-13, children 3-4 $4, children 2 and under free. Monday-Saturday 9 a.m.-5 p.m., Sunday noon-5 p.m.

GERALD R. FORD MUSEUM

303 Pearl St. N.W., Grand Rapids, 616-254-0400; www.fordlibrarymuseum.gov

Exhibits at this museum trace the life and public service of the 38th president of the United States. The museum includes a 28-minute introductory film on Ford; a reproduction of the White House Oval Office; educational exhibits on the U.S. House of Representatives and the presidency; and even the original burglar tools used in the Watergate break-in.

Admission: adults $7, seniors $6, students $5, children 6-18 $3, children 5 and under free. Daily 9 a.m.-5 p.m.

GRAND RAPIDS ART MUSEUM

101 Monroe Center N., Grand Rapids, 616-831-1000; www.gramonline.org

Collections include Renaissance, German Expressionist, French and American paintings; graphics; and a children's gallery augmented by special traveling exhibitions.

Admission: adults $8, seniors and students $7, children 6-17 $5. Tuesday-Thursday, 10 a.m.-5 p.m., Friday 10 a.m.-9 p.m., Saturday 10 a.m.-5 p.m., Sunday noon-5 p.m.

JOHN BALL ZOO

1300 W. Fulton St., Grand Rapids, 616-336-4301; www.johnballzoosociety.org

Located in 100-acre park, the zoo features more than 700 animals, the Living Shores Aquarium, an African forest exhibit and a children's zoo.

Admission: adults $7.50, seniors $6.50, children 3-13 $5.50, children 2 and under free. Mid-May-September, daily 10 a.m.-6 p.m.; October-early May, daily 10 a.m.-4 p.m.

MEYER MAY HOUSE

450 Madison Ave. S.E., Grand Rapids, 616-246-4821; www.meyermayhouse.steelcase.com

This Frank Lloyd Wright house from the late Prairie period was finished in 1908 and has been authentically restored with architect-designed furniture, leaded-glass windows, lighting fixtures, rugs and textiles. Tours begin at the visitors center (442 Madison Ave. S.E.).

Admission: free. Tuesday, Thursday 10 a.m.-2 p.m.; Sunday 1-5 p.m.

PANDO

8076 Belding Road N.E., Rockford, 616-874-8343; www.pandopark.com

Pando offers six rope tows, seven lighted runs, a patrol, a school, rentals,

SPECIAL EVENT

TULIP TIME FESTIVAL

238 S. River Avenue, Holland, 616-396-4221, 800-822-2770; www.tuliptime.org
This celebration of Dutch heritage features 1,800 klompen dancers, three parades, street scrubbing, Dutch markets, musical and professional entertainment and millions of tulips. Eight days in mid-May.

grooming equipment, snowmaking and a cafeteria. It has a run with a vertical drop of 125 feet. There's also eleven miles of cross-country trails and three miles of lighted trails.
December-March, daily.

THE PUBLIC MUSEUM OF GRAND RAPIDS
272 Pearl St. N.W., Grand Rapids, 616-456-3997; www.grmuseum.org
Located in the Van Andel Museum Center, this museum features exhibits of interactive history and natural science, including mammals, birds, furniture, Native American artifacts, a re-creation of 1890s Grand Rapids street scene and a 1928 carousel. The Chaffee Planetarium offers sky and laser-light shows.
Admission: adults $8, children 3-17 $3, children 2 and under free. Monday, Wednesday-Saturday 9 a.m.-5 p.m.; Tuesday 9 a.m.-8p.m.

HOLLAND
CAPPON HOUSE
228 W. Ninth St., Holland, 616-392-6740, 888-200-9123; www.hollandmuseum.org
This Italianate structure from 1874 was the home of the first mayor of Holland and has original furnishings and millwork.
Admission: adults $7, seniors $6, students $4, children 5 and under free. June-October, Wednesday-Saturday 1-4 p.m.; November-May, Friday-Saturday 1-4 p.m.

DUTCH VILLAGE
12350 James St., Holland, 616-396-1475, 800-285-7177; www.dutchvillage.com
The village includes buildings of Dutch architecture, canals, windmills and tulips everywhere. You can also see Dutch dancing and listen to street organs. Then have a pair of wooden shoes carved just for you.
Mid-April-late October, daily.

HOLLAND MUSEUM
31 W. 10th St., Holland, 616-392-1362, 888-200-9123; www.hollandmuseum.org
The museum features decorative arts from the Netherlands. There are also permanent and changing exhibits pertaining to local history.
Admission: adults $7, seniors $6, students $4, children 5 and under free. Monday, Wednesday, Friday-Saturday 10 a.m.-5 p.m.; Thursday 10 a.m.-8 p.m.; Sunday 2-5 p.m.

HOLLAND STATE PARK
2215 Ottawa Beach Road, Holland, 616-399-9390
This 143-acre park includes a beach on Lake Michigan and offers swimming, boating, fishing, picnicking, a playground and more.

LITTLE NETHERLANDS
1 Lincoln Ave., Holland, 616-355-1030; www.windmillisland.org

Little Netherlands is a miniature reproduction of old Holland. Watch a 20-minute film on Dutch windmills in the posthouse, see klompen dancing in summer and stop to smell the tulips.

VELDHEER'S TULIP GARDENS AND DE KLOMP WOODEN SHOE & DELFTWARE FACTORY
12755 Quincy St., Holland, 616-399-1900; www.veldheer.com

Visit the only delftware factory in the United States and take a tour. Try on wooden shoes and talk to the artisans who made them.

WINDMILL ISLAND
Seventh Street and Lincoln Avenue, Holland, 616-355-1030; www.cityofholland.com

The 225-year-old windmill De Zwaan ("the swan") is the only operating imported Dutch windmill in the United States. It was relocated here by special permission of the Dutch government, as the remaining windmills in the Netherlands are all considered historic monuments. It is still used today to grind flour.

Admission: adults $7.50, children 5-15 $4.50. April-May, July-August, Monday-Saturday 9 a.m.-6 p.m., Sunday 11:30 a.m.-6 p.m.; June, September-October, Monday-Saturday 10 a.m.-5 p.m., Sunday 11:30 a.m.-5 p.m.

JACKSON
CASCADES FALLS PARK
1992 Warren Ave., Jackson, 517-788-4320; www.co.jackson.mi.us

This 465-acre park has fishing ponds, a pier, paddle-boat rentals, picnicking, a playground, 18-hole miniature golf, a driving range, a fitness and running trail, basketball, tennis and horseshoe courts, and a restaurant.

DAHLEM ENVIRONMENTAL EDUCATION CENTER
7117 S. Jackson Road, Jackson, 517-782-3453; www.dahlemcenter.org

This pretty nature center includes five miles of easy trails through forests, fields and marshes.

Admission: $3. Tuesday-Friday 9 a.m.-5 p.m., Saturday 10 a.m.-5 p.m., Sunday noon-5 p.m.

ELLA SHARP MUSEUM
3225 Fourth St., Jackson, 517-787-2320; www.ellasharp.org

This museum complex includes a Victorian farmhouse, a historic farm lane, a one-room schoolhouse, a log cabin, galleries with rotating art and historic exhibits, studios, a planetarium and a visitors center.

Admission: Galleries: adults $5, children 5-12 $3, children 4 and under free; House Tours: adults and children $3, children 4 and under free. Tuesday-Friday 10 a.m.-4 p.m., Saturday 11 a.m.-4 p.m.

ELLA SHARP PARK
3225 Fourth St., Jackson, 517-788-4040; www.ellasharppark.com

This park is made up of approximately 530 acres and includes an 18-hole golf course, tennis courts, ball fields, a swimming pool, miniature golf, picnic facilities and formal gardens.

Daily.

REPUBLICAN PARTY FOUNDING SITE
West Franklin and Second streets, Jackson

You can't miss this landmark—it's marked with a tablet dedicated by President William Howard Taft.

SPARKS ILLUMINATED CASCADES WATERFALLS
1992 Warren Ave., Jackson, 517-788-4320

About 500 feet of water cascades over 16 waterfalls and six fountains in continually changing patterns of light, color and music.

June-September, nightly.

KALAMAZOO
BITTERSWEET SKI AREA
600 River Road, Otsego, 269-694-2820; www.skibittersweet.com

This ski area has a quad, four triple chairlifts, a double chairlift, five rope tows, a school, rentals and 16 trails. The longest run is 2,300 feet with a vertical drop of 300 feet. There is also night skiing.

December-March, Monday-Thursday noon-10 p.m., Friday 10 a.m.-10:30 p.m., Saturday 9 a.m.-10:30 p.m., Sunday 9 a.m.-10 p.m.

BRONSON PARK
200 W. South St., Kalamazoo

A bronze tablet marks the spot where Abraham Lincoln made an antislavery speech in 1856.

ECHO VALLEY
8495 E. H Ave., Kalamazoo, 269-349-3291; www.echovalleyfun.com

Head to Echo Valley for tobogganing and ice skating. Rentals are available.

December-March, Friday-Sunday.

GILMORE CAR MUSEUM
6865 Hickory Road, Hickory Corners, 269-671-5089; www.gilmorecarmuseum.org

More than 120 antique cars tracing the significant technical developments in automotive transportation on 90 acres of landscaped grounds can be found at this interesting museum.

Admission: adults $10, seniors $9, students $8, children 6 and under free. May-October; Monday-Friday 9 a.m.-5 p.m., Saturday-Sunday 9 a.m.-6 p.m.

KALAMAZOO AIR ZOO
6151 Portage Road, Portage, 269-382-6555; www.airzoo.org

This is home to more than 70 beautiful historic and restored aircraft of the World War II period, many of which are still in flying condition. It also includes exhibits, video theater, a flight simulator and an observation deck.

Admission: free. Tours of Restoration Center: May-September. Flight of the Day: May-September, afternoons. Daily.

KALAMAZOO INSTITUTE OF ARTS
314 S. Park St., Kalamazoo, 269-349-7775; www.kiarts.org

The Kalamazoo Institute of Arts includes galleries, a school, a shop, a library and an auditorium. Stop here to see a collection of 20th-century American art

and touring exhibits like National Geographic's best portraits.
Admission: free. Tuesday-Saturday 10 a.m.-5 p.m., Sunday noon-5 p.m.

KALAMAZOO NATURE CENTER

7000 N. Westnedge Ave., Kalamazoo, 269-381-1574; www.naturecenter.org

This nature center includes a restored 1860s pioneer homestead—with tours available by appointment—a barnyard (May-September) and nature trails.
Admission: adults $6, seniors $5, children 4-13 $4, children 3 and under free. Monday-Saturday 9 a.m.-5 p.m., Sunday 1-5 p.m.

TIMBER RIDGE SKI AREA

7500 23 St., Gobles, 269-694-9449, 800-253-2928; www.timberridgeski.com

Timber Ridge offers four chairlifts, a Pomalift, three rope tows, a patrol, a school and snowmaking. The property has a total of 15 trails.
Late November-mid-March, Monday-Friday 11 a.m.-10 p.m., Saturday 9 a.m.-10 p.m., Sunday 9 a.m.-8 p.m.

WESTERN MICHIGAN UNIVERSITY

1903 W. Michigan Ave., Kalamazoo, 269-387-1000; www.wmich.edu

Contemporary plays, musical comedies, operas and melodramas are offered in the Shaw and York theaters. Touring professional shows, dance programs and entertainers can be found in Miller Auditorium, while dance and music performances are featured in the Irving S. Gilmore University Theatre Complex. Art exhibits are in Sangren Hall and East Hall.

LANSING

BRENKE RIVER SCULPTURE AND FISH LADDER

300 N. Grand Ave., Lansing

Located at North Lansing Dam on the Riverfront Park scenic walk, this sculpture encompasses the ladder designed by artist/sculptor Joseph E. Kinnebrew and landscape architect Robert O'Boyle.

FENNER NATURE CENTER

2020 E. Mount Hope Ave., Lansing, 517-483-4224; www.lansingmi.gov

In the park you'll find a bald eagle, two waterfowl ponds, a replica of a pioneer cabin and garden, and five miles of nature trails through a variety of habitats.
Nature center: Tuesday-Sunday. Trails: daily dawn-dusk.

IMPRESSION 5 SCIENCE CENTER

200 Museum Drive, Lansing, 517-485-8116; www.impression5.org

The center has more than 200 interactive, hands-on exhibits, including a computer lab and chemistry experiments. A restaurant is also on the premises.
Admission: adults and students $5, seniors $4.50, children 4 and under pay their age. Monday-Saturday 10 a.m.-5 p.m.

LEDGES

133 Fitzgerald Park Drive, Grand Ledge, 517-627-7351; www.grandledgemi.com

Edging the Grand River, the Ledges are 300-million-year-old quartz sandstone. They are a good place for experienced rock climbers to work it out.
Daily.

POTTER PARK ZOO

1301 S. Pennsylvania Ave., Lansing, 517-483-4222; www.potterparkzoo.org

This zoo on the Red Cedar River has more than 400 animals. You will also find educational programs, camel and pony rides, a playground and picnic facilities. *Admission: adults $10, seniors $8, children 3-16 $2, children 2 and under free. April-October, daily 9 a.m.-6 p.m.; November-March, daily 10 a.m.-4 p.m.*

R.E. OLDS TRANSPORTATION MUSEUM

240 Museum Drive, Lansing, 517-372-0529; www.reoldsmuseum.org

Named after Ransom Eli Olds, the museum houses Lansing-built vehicles, including Oldsmobile, REO, Star and Durant autos. Aside from older models, there is also a collection of newer concept cars from some of today's top manufacturers and car designers. *Admission: adults $5, seniors and students $3. Tuesday-Saturday 10 a.m.-5 p.m., Sunday noon-5 p.m.*

STATE CAPITOL

North Capital and West Michigan avenues, Lansing, 517-373-2353

Dedicated in 1879, this was one of the first state capitol buildings to emulate the dome and wings of the U.S. Capitol in Washington, D.C. Interior walls and ceilings reflect the work of many skilled artisans, muralists and portrait painters. Tours are offered daily and include a look at the House and Senate galleries along with the public areas of the Capitol. You'll learn about the history of the building and the legislative process. Reservations are required for groups of 10 or more. *Guided Tours: Monday-Friday 9 a.m.-4 p.m.*

WOLDUMAR NATURE CENTER

5739 Old Lansing Road, Lansing, 517-322-0030; www.woldumar.org

This 188-acre wildlife preserve has nature walks and trails for hiking and skiing. *Daily dawn-dusk.*

MOUNT PLEASANT
SOARING EAGLE CASINO

6800 Soaring Eagle Blvd., Mount Pleasant, 989-775-7777, 888-732-4537; www.soaringeaglecasino.com

This popular casino includes a 2,500-seat Bingo Hall, slot machines, blackjack, craps and roulette. There is also a spa onsite where you can squander your winnings in treatments. Entertainment acts range from Donny and Marie Osmond to T.I. and Ludacris. *Daily.*

MUSKEGON
HACKLEY AND HUME HISTORIC SITE

West Webster and Sixth streets, Muskegon, 231-722-7578; www.muskegonmuseum.org

These two restored Queen Anne/Victorian mansions were built by two wealthy lumbermen between 1888 and 1889. *Admission: $3. Tours mid-May-September, Wednesday, Saturday-Sunday; also some weekends in December.*

MICHIGAN'S ADVENTURE AMUSEMENT PARK
4750 Whitehall Road, Muskegon, 231-766-3377; www.miadventure.com

Hop on more than 50 attractions and amusement rides, including the Wolverine Wildcat, the largest wooden roller coaster in the state. Other thrill-inducing rides include a corkscrew roller coaster, a Mammoth River water slide and a log flume. In case you need something more low-key, the park offers games and an arcade. There is also a water park with a wave pool, a lazy river, body flumes, tube slides and family play areas.

Admission: adults $26, children 2 and under free. Mid-May-early September, daily.

MUSKEGON MUSEUM OF ART
296 W. Webster Ave., Muskegon, 231-720-2570; www.muskegonartmuseum.org

The permanent collection of this art museum includes American and European paintings, an extensive print collection, Tiffany and contemporary glass as well as paintings by heavyweights like Hopper, Inness, Whistler, Homer, Wyeth and others.

Admission: adults $5, children $5. Wednesday, Friday-Saturday 10 a.m.-4:30 p.m., Thursday 10 a.m.-8 p.m., Sunday noon-4:30 p.m.

MUSKEGON STATE PARK
3560 Memorial Drive, Muskegon, 231-744-3480, 800-447-2757; www.muskegonstatepark.com

This 1,165-acre area has a replica of a frontier blockhouse on one of the park's highest sand dunes. The park features swimming, beaches, bathhouse, water-skiing, fishing, boating (ramp, launch), as well as 12 miles of hiking trails, cross-country skiing, a skating rink, a luge run, picnicking, a playground and camping.

P.J. HOFFMASTER STATE PARK
6585 Lake Harbor Road, Muskegon, 231-798-3711, 800-447-2757; www.michigan.gov

The more than 1,000 acres here include forest-covered dunes along two miles of Lake Michigan shoreline. You will find a sandy beach and 10 miles of trails. There is also cross-country skiing (three miles of trails) in winter. The park has picnicking, concession and camping facilities. The visitors center has displays and exhibits on dune formation.

Daily.

USS SILVERSIDES AND THE GREAT LAKES NAVAL MEMORIAL AND MUSEUM
1346 Bluff St., Muskegon, 231-755-1230; www.silversides.org

Visit the famous World War II submarine that served with the Pacific Fleet along Japan's coasts. The Silversides' outstanding aggressive war record includes sinking 23 enemy ships, embarking on special mine-laying and recon-naissance missions, and rescuing two American aviators downed in air strikes over Japan.

Admission: Guided Tours: adults $15, seniors and students $12.50, children 5-11 $10.50, children 4 and under free. June-August, daily; April-May and September-October, Saturday-Sunday.

NEW BUFFALO

FOUR WINDS CASINO RESORT

11111 Wilson Road, New Buffalo, 866-494-6371; www.fourwindscasino.com

If you are looking to hit it big, bring your gambling bucks to Four Winds, which is the only casino in the area to have million-dollar jackpots and the only one in the Midwest to have a World Poker Tour poker room. But even those who don't like high-stakes games can have fun, since the casino offers penny slots.

RED ARROW HIGHWAY

Interstate 94 and Union Pier, New Buffalo

Many antiques stores, inns, galleries, shops and restaurants can be found along this road, which travels from Union Pier to Sawyer, between Lake Michigan and the Interstate.

NILES

FERNWOOD BOTANIC GARDENS

13988 Range Line Road, Niles, 269-695-6491; www.fernwoodbotanical.org

The scenic grounds at this botanical garden comprise more than 100 acres of woodland trails, spring-fed ponds, a tall grass prairie and nearly 20 gardens, including rock and fern gardens and a lovely Japanese garden. A nature center features interesting hands-on educational exhibits and panoramic bird observation windows.

Admission: adults $7, seniors $5, children 13-18 $4, children 6-12 $3, children 5 and under free. May-October, Tuesday-Saturday 10 a.m.-6 p.m., Sunday noon-6 p.m.; November-April Tuesday-Saturday 10 a.m.-5 p.m., Sunday noon-5 p.m.

FORT ST. JOSEPH MUSEUM

508 E. Main St., Niles, 269-683-4702; www.ci.niles.mi.us

This museum contains one of the top five Sioux art collections in the nation, including autobiographical pictographs by Sitting Bull and Rain-In-The-Face. Other collections have Fort St. Joseph and Potawatomi artifacts, local history memorabilia.

Admission: free. Wednesday-Friday 10 a.m.-4 p.m., Saturday 10 a.m.-3 p.m.

SAUGATUCK

KEEWATIN MARITIME MUSEUM

Harbour Village, 219 Union St., Douglas, 269-857-2464; www.keewatinmaritimemuseum.com

Go on a tour of a restored, turn-of-the-century passenger steamship of the Canadian Pacific Railroad, the S.S. Keewatin, maintained as an "in-service" ship. It features original, elegant furnishings, carved paneling and brass fixtures. The quadruple-expansion engine room also is open for viewing.

Admission: prices vary. June-September, daily 10 a.m.-4:30 p.m.

MASON STREET WAREHOUSE

Saugatuck Center for the Arts, 400 Culver St., Saugatuck, 269-857-4898; www.masonstreetwarehouse.org

This theater company stages summertime performances in downtown Saugatuck. It puts on everything from comedies to musicals and other light-hearted fare.

June-September, Tuesday-Sunday.

HIGHLIGHT

WHAT ARE SOME OF MICHIGAN'S BEST WINERIES?

Michigan is a real wine country with dozens of wineries scattered across the state. Here are some of Southwest Michigan's finest.

FENN VALLEY VINEYARDS AND WINE CELLAR

6130 122nd Ave., Fennville, 269-561-2396; www.fennvalley.com
This family-owned winery puts out a number of bottles, but the award-winning Riesling and ice wine warrant tastes. For something different, try the blueberry wine. Take a self-guided tour overlooking the wine cellar. An audiovisual program and wine tasting are part of the proceedings.
Daily.

ST. JULIAN WINE COMPANY

716 S. Kalamazoo St., Paw Paw, 269-657-5568; www.stjulian.com
The oldest and largest winery in the state offers wine tasting and tours, which begin every half hour.
Monday-Saturday 9 a.m.-6 p.m., Sunday noon-5 p.m.

TABOR HILL WINERY & RESTAURANT

185 Mount Tabor Road, Buchanan, 800-283-3363; www.taborhill.com
Take a tour of the popular Tabor Hill winery and vineyard and then make time for lunch or dinner in the restaurant. You can sample some of their award-winning wines in the comfortable tasting room, like the 2007 Lake Michigan Shore Riesling or the 2006 Lake Michigan Shore Cabernet Franc. The delicious restaurant has a large menu of seasonally-inspired dishes using ingredients from nearby farms. Afterward, enjoy a glass of wine on the terrace overlooking the vineyards. If you don't have time to head to the winery, stop by one of their tasting rooms: **Wine Port** *(214 Butler Street, Saugatuck, 269-857-4859)*; **Bridgman Champagne Cellar** *(10243 Red Arrow Highway, Bridgman, 269-465-6566)*; **Wine & Art Gallery** *(80 West Main Street, Benton Harbor, 269-925-6402).*
Tasting Bar: Monday-Tuesday 10 a.m.-5 p.m., Wednesday-Saturday 10 a.m.-9 p.m., Sunday noon-9 p.m. Guided walking tours: noon-4:30 p.m., every half-hour.

WARNER VINEYARDS

706 S. Kalamazoo St., Paw Paw, 269-657-3165, 800-756-5357; www.warnerwines.com
This family winery, which started up in 1938, produces wine and juices. Tour the grounds and end with a tasting.
Daily.

SPECIAL EVENT

NATIONAL CHERRY FESTIVAL

108 W. Grandview Parkway, Traverse City, 231-947-4230; www.cherryfestival.org
An annual event since 1926, this very popular festival features more than 150 events and activities, most of which are free. Enjoy events such as pageants, parades, concerts, a volleyball tournament and, of course, lots of cherry-related activities. There are cherry pie eating contests; a cherry farmer's market featuring jams, cherries, dried cherries, cherry barbecue sauce, and more; and culinary events. Children will love perks from being part of the Cherry Kids Club and adults will love the Global Wine Pavilion where they can enjoy wines from all over the world. They even host a Cherry Idol competition (like *American Idol*) where locals can compete in a singing competition.
Early July.

SAUGATUCK DUNE RIDES

6495 Washington Road, Saugatuck, 269-857-2253; www.saugatuckduneride.com
Go on buggy rides over the sand dunes near Lake Michigan.
Cash and travelers checks only. Late April-September, Monday-Saturday 10 a.m.-5:30 p.m., Sunday noon-5:30 p.m.; October, Saturday 10 a.m.-5:30 p.m., Sunday noon-5:30 p.m.

SOUTH HAVEN
MICHIGAN MARITIME MUSEUM

260 Dyckman Ave., South Haven, 269-637-8078, 800-747-3810;
www.michiganmaritimemuseum.org
At this museum, you'll see exhibits of Great Lakes maps, photographs, maritime artifacts and historic boats. It also has a boardwalk and park.
Admission: adults $5, seniors $4, children $3.50. Monday, Wednesday-Saturday 10 a.m.-5 p.m., Sunday noon-5 p.m.

VAN BUREN STATE PARK

23960 Ruggles Road, South Haven, 269-637-2788, 800-447-2757; www.michigan.org
The park's 326 acres include scenic wooded sand dunes. There's swimming, a bathhouse, hunting, picnicking, a playground and camping.

ST. JOSEPH
CURIOUS KIDS' MUSEUM

415 Lake Blvd., St. Joseph, 269-983-2543; www.curiouskidsmuseum.org
This interactive museum appeals to children with such exhibits as balloon flying and apple picking. Kids can even run their own TV station.
Admission: adults and children $6, children 2 and under free. Wednesday-Saturday 10 a.m.-5 p.m., Sunday noon-5 p.m.

DEER FOREST CHILDREN'S AMUSEMENT PARK

6800 Marquette Drive, Coloma, 269-468-4961, 800-752-3337; www.deerforest.com
Spanning approximately 30 acres, this park houses more than 500 animals and

birds. Little ones will jump at the chance to pet the llamas and alpacas.
Admission: $6.50. June-September, daily.

KRASL ART CENTER
707 Lake Blvd., St. Joseph, 269-983-0271; www.krasl.org

Three galleries at this center house contemporary and traditional works, fine and folk arts, local and major museum collections. There's also an art reference library, lectures, tours, films and a gift shop.

Admission: free. Monday-Wednesday, Friday-Saturday 10 a.m.-4 p.m.; Thursday 10 a.m.-9 p.m.; Sunday 1-4 p.m.

SARETT NATURE CENTER
2300 Benton Center Road, St. Joseph, 269-927-4832; www.sarett.com

The Michigan Audubon Society runs this bird sanctuary, which features 350 acres of habitats, including beaches, meadows, wooded trails, swamp forests and marshes.

Tuesday-Friday 9 a.m.-5 p.m., Saturday 10 a.m.-5 p.m., Sunday 1-5 p.m.

WARREN DUNES STATE PARK
12032 Red Arrow Highway, Sawyer, 269-426-4013; www.michigan.gov

Set on 1,499 acres on Lake Michigan, the park has swimming, a beach house, hiking, picnicking, a playground, camping and cabins. Warren Woods offers 200 acres of virgin forest.

TRAVERSE CITY
CLINCH PARK
181 E. Grandview Parkway, Traverse City, 231-922-4904

The park's zoo and aquarium houses animals native to Michigan (mid-April-November, daily). Con Foster Museum has exhibits on local history, Native American and pioneer life, and folklore (June-September, daily).

DENNOS ART CENTER
1701 E. Front St., Traverse City, 231-995-1055; www.dennosmuseum.org

This art center has three galleries and boasts one of the largest collections of Inuit art in the Midwest.

Admission: adults $6, children $4. Monday-Wednesday, Friday-Saturday 10 a.m.-5 p.m.; Thursday 10 a.m.-8 p.m.; Sunday 1-5 p.m.

SCHOONER MADELINE
322 Sixth St., Traverse City, 231-946-2647; www.maritimeheritagealliance.org

The schooner is a full-scale replica of 1850s Great Lakes sailing ship. The original Madeline served as the first schoolhouse in the Grand Traverse region.

Tours: early May-late September, Wednesday-Sunday afternoons.

WHITEHALL
WHITE RIVER LIGHT STATION MUSEUM
6199 Murray Road, Whitehall, 231-894-8265; www.whiteriverlightstation.org

This museum is in an 1875 lighthouse made of Michigan limestone and brick. Inside there's ship relics and artifacts on display, including a binnacle, a helm, a chronograph, compasses, a sextant, charts, models, photographs and paintings.

June-August, Tuesday-Friday 11 a.m.-5 p.m., Saturday-Sunday noon-6 p.m.; September-October, Tuesday-Friday 11 a.m.-4 p.m., Saturday-Sunday noon-5 p.m.; November-March by appointment.

WORLD'S LARGEST WEATHER VANE
Highway 31, Montague

If you love seeing kitschy Americana, make a stop at this working weather vane. This 48-foot-tall structure weighs 4,300 pounds and is topped with a model of the lumber schooner Ella Ellenwood that once traveled the Great Lakes.

WHERE TO STAY

BATTLE CREEK
★★★MCCAMLY PLAZA HOTEL
50 Capital Ave. S.W., Battle Creek, 269-963-7050, 888-622-2659; www.mccamlyplazahotel.com

This downtown Battle Creek hotel offers contemporary guest rooms and suites that have stainless-steel accents, granite vanity tops, upholstered headboards and drapes, and overstuffed chairs and ottomans. Amenities include a large indoor pool and whirlpool, an exercise room and a business center. When hunger hits, you have a choice between Porter's Steakhouse & Cigar Bar for an elegant dinner, or J.W. Barleycorn's for a casual meal.

239 rooms. Restaurant, bar. Complimentary breakfast. $61-150

GRAND RAPIDS
★★★AMWAY GRAND PLAZA
187 Monroe Ave. N.W., Grand Rapids, 616-774-2000, 800-253-3590; www.amwaygrand.com

Opened in 1913 as the Pantlind Hotel, this Michigan landmark quickly earned a reputation for providing a distinguished residence for out-of-towners. Fronting the Grand River, the hotel is conveniently located in Grand Rapids' business and entertainment district. The lobby sets the tone with a magnificent gold-leaf ceiling. The guest rooms are appointed in either classically elegant or modern décor, with the Tower Rooms featuring views of the river and city. The 1913 Room, with its fine continental cuisine, is the jewel in the crown. Done up in a Louis XVI style, the restaurant serves classic, French-inspired cuisine.

682 rooms. Restaurants, bar. Pool. Tennis. $151-250

KALAMAZOO
★★★BAY POINTE INN AND RESTAURANT
11456 Marsh Road, Shelbyville, 269-672-8111, 888-486-5253; www.baypointeinn.com

Overlooking Gun Lake, this modern inn is in a charming resort area 30 minutes from Grand Rapids and Kalamazoo. A lobby features a fireplace and a flat-screen TV. But you'll want to head outdoors to visit the nearby marina, beach and small shops. Children will enjoy the free popcorn and kiddie flicks that are screened in the inn's movie theater. Meanwhile, parents will find the Terrace Grille Restaurant to be a nice spot for dinner, especially the outdoor tables with a view of the lake.

38 rooms. Restaurant, bar. Complimentary breakfast. Beach. $151-250

LANSING

★★★MARRIOTT EAST LANSING AT UNIVERSITY PLACE

300 M.A.C. Ave., East Lansing, 517-337-4440, 800-228-9290; www.marriott.com

Located in the heart of downtown East Lansing, this hotel is within walking distance of shopping and dining as well as the campus of Michigan State University, which is convenient if you're there visiting a student or to watch the Spartans play. Guest rooms are spacious and feature comfortable beds and overstuffed chairs and ottomans.

180 rooms. Restaurant, bar. $151-250

MOUNT PLEASANT

★★★SOARING EAGLE CASINO & RESORT

6800 Soaring Eagle Blvd., Mount Pleasant, 989-775-7777, 877-232-4532; www.soaringeaglecasino.com

This popular resort and casino has an Native American theme, which carries into the guest rooms' décor. Rooms have terra cotta terrazzo flooring, custom wall coverings, stained-glass artwork and cherry woodwork hand-carved in New Mexico. They also have patios or balconies, and some deluxe rooms offer Jacuzzi tubs. The property has multiple dining and entertainment options onsite.

512 rooms. Restaurant, bar. Spa. Casino. $61-150

TRAVERSE CITY

★★★GRAND TRAVERSE RESORT AND SPA

100 Grand Traverse Village Blvd., Acme, 231-534-6000, 800-748-0303; www.grandtraverseresort.com

Approximately eight miles north of Traverse City, this resort sits on several acres of rolling hills, with a spectacular view of East Grand Traverse Bay. The hotel features a lobby with marble floors and fresh flowers throughout. Numerous activities abound— in the summer there's golf, tennis, jet skiing and boat rentals at its beach, while in winter there's cross-country skiing, sleigh rides, ice skating and snowmobiling. Shops and numerous food and beverage options are available onsite. The beauty of the area will leave you relaxed and invigorated.

660 rooms. Restaurant, bar. Children's activity center. Spa. Beach. $151-250

★★★GREAT WOLF LODGE

3575 N. Highway 31 S., Traverse City, 231-941-3600, 866-478-9653; www.greatwolflodge.com

This family-friendly property is at a central spot for

WHICH ARE THE BEST FAMILY-FRIENDLY HOTELS?

Bay Pointe Inn and Restaurant:
While the hotel's private beach offers plenty of opportunities for kids activities, the little ones will want to catch one of the children's films in the inn's own movie theater. Plus, they'll get free popcorn.

Great Wolf Lodge:
Children will spend hours getting soaked in the hotel's 51,000-square-foot water park, which includes a tree-house water fort, water slides and a lazy river. To dry off, they can play a round on the 18-hole miniature golf course.

shoppers; it's one mile from the Horizon Outlet Mall, within two miles of the Grand Traverse mall and within five miles of downtown Traverse City. Despite its proximity to mall culture, the all-suite hotel tries for a rustic vibe, with rooms decorated with pine log furniture. The theme carries throughout the interior and exterior of the hotel, and the lobby features a huge stone fireplace. The main draw is the 51,000-square-foot indoor water park, complete with slides, pools for all ages and a floating river. If you'd rather get some sun, head to the outside pool area, with basketball hoops and dunking pails that fill with water and splash guests.

300. Restaurant, bar. Pool. $151-250

RECOMMENDED

NEW BUFFALO
FOUR WINDS CASINO RESORT
11111 Wilson Road, New Buffalo, 866-494-6371; www.fourwindscasino.com

If you're looking for a weekend getaway or even just a night to relax, Four Winds Casino Resort offers everything you need to unwind, including luxurious and comfortable guest rooms, a casino, entertainment and fabulous restaurants. Guest rooms feature luxurious bedding, leather headboards, flat-screen TVs, granite counter tops in the bathrooms, and Kohler whirlpool tubs in the suites. If you really want to make an occasion special, book a Celebrity Suite, which include private waterfalls, 60-inch high-definition TVs with five speaker surround sound and deep-soaking tubs. For a juicy steak and a glass of wine from a lengthy wine list, head to Copper Rock Steakhouse, the resort's fine dining restaurant. Afterward, relax at one of four bars onsite. If you are looking to hit it big, bring your gambling bucks as this casino has million-dollar jackpots and is the only one in the Midwest to have a World Poker Tour poker room.

165 rooms. Restaurant, bar. Casino. $151-250

WHERE TO EAT

GRAND RAPIDS
★★★★1913 ROOM
Amway Grand Plaza, 187 Monroe Ave. N.W., Grand Rapids, 616774-2000, 800-253-3590; www.amwaygrand.com

This fine-dining restaurant is ideal for special occasions. The Louis XVI-style room is filled with white-linen-topped tables and overseen by a polished, confident staff. The menu, which features classic dishes with French influences, includes standouts like grilled beef filet, lobster terrine and seared Atlantic salmon with horseradish crust. A chef's tasting menu with accompanying wines is available for those who want to savor the talents of the creative kitchen staff.

Continental. Lunch, dinner. Reservations recommended. $36-85

★★★THE CHOP HOUSE
190 Monroe Ave. N.W., Grand Rapids, 616-451-6184, 888-456-3463; www.thechophouserestaurant.com

The Chop House is in downtown Grand Rapids across from the convention center and Amway Grand Plaza hotel. The centerpiece of the room is its beautiful black granite bar, accented with colorful floor-to-ceiling pillars and oil prints. The menu zeros in on the best in Midwestern, grain-fed meats and USDA Prime beef—look for Australian rib lamb chops, caviar and fresh lobster. A dessert and cigar lounge called La Dolce Vita, located on the lower level of the restaurant, is an intimate spot, and the wine cellar displays a variety of reds.

Steak. Dinner. Closed Sunday. Reservations recommended. Bar. $36-85

HOLLAND
★★★ALPENROSE

4 E. Eighth St., Holland, 616-393-2111; www.alpenroserestaurant.com

The space that houses this charming restaurant used to be the home of a run-of-the-mill discount store. Located in downtown Holland, it is now filled with hand-carved woodwork, stained-glass windows and chairs and tables from Austria and Germany—all contributing to the Alpine aesthetic the restaurant embraces. Locals come for the famous chicken shortcake, a mainstay on the changing menu. Dinner isn't the only popular meal here; the Sunday brunch and lunch buffet also draw crowds.

International. Lunch, dinner, Sunday brunch. Reservations recommended. Outdoor seating. Children's menu. $36-85

★★★PIPER

2225 S. Shore Drive, Macatawa, 616-335-5866; www.piperrestaurant.com

With its location overlooking Lake Macatawa, this casually elegant restaurant serves American cuisine with professional, friendly service. Try the shrimp nachos, artichoke ravioli or the chicken paella.

American. Dinner. Closed Sunday-Monday in winter. Children's menu. Bar. $36-85

KALAMAZOO
★★★BRAVO

5402 Portage Road, Kalamazoo, 269-344-7700; www.bravokalamazoo.com

The contemporary décor, fresh dishes and welcoming atmosphere make this Italian restaurant an excellent choice for lunch or dinner. It's an especially convenient choice for a pre-flight meal; Bravo is about one block from the airport and is easily accessible from Interstate 94. Its interior features a large wine display, open wood ovens, candlelit tables, natural wood and a fireplace in the main dining room. Expect dishes such as grilled stuffed pork chops filled with prosciutto and mozzarella with blue cheese mashed potatoes, or chicken gnocchi in mushrooms and cream served on crispy potato and spinach gnocchi.

American, Italian. Lunch, dinner, Sunday brunch. Children's menu. Bar. $16-35

★★★WEBSTER'S

100 W. Michigan Ave., Kalamazoo, 269-343-4444; www.webstersrestaurant.com

Located in the heart of downtown on the second floor of the Radisson Hotel, this contemporary, club-like restaurant features an elegant copper and brass display kitchen that turns out fresh seafood and grilled steaks as well as tableside Caesar salads and freshly prepared desserts. Live music entertains diners on Friday and Saturday nights.

American. Dinner. Closed Sunday. Bar. $36-85

MOUNT PLEASANT
★★★THE EMBERS
1217 S. Mission St., Mount Pleasant, 989-773-5007; www.theembersdine.com

The signature one-pound pork chop is the main attraction at this restaurant in Mount Pleasant. If that's not enough for you, come for the delicious smorgasbord held here the first and third Thursday of each month that's popular with locals and visitors. Tease, a more casual dining option, is also available within the building.

American. Dinner. Children's menu. Bar. $36-85

★★★WATER LILY
6800 Soaring Eagle Blvd., Mount Pleasant, 989-775-5496, 888-232-4532; www.soaringeaglecasino.com

Located inside of the Soaring Eagle Casino & Resort, Water Lily is an elegant dining destination that offers a menu of regional American cuisine for both breakfast and dinner. A number of egg dishes are featured at breakfast, including the market fresh omelet, with ham, sausage, mushrooms, bacon, spinach, cheddar, tomatoes and onions. Crustaceans dominate the menu at dinner, with choices such as seafood pasta, yellowfin tuna niçoise and crab Randolph, but a few beef and chicken entrées are also available.

American. Breakfast, dinner. Bar. $36-85

TRAVERSE CITY
★★★BOWERS HARBOR INN
13512 Peninsula Drive, Traverse City, 231-223-4222; www.bowersharborinn.net

This historic converted family mansion was built in the 1800s and overlooks West Grand Traverse Bay. It is approximately nine miles out on Old Mission Peninsula, a scenic and curvy drive along the bay. The restaurant's beautiful dark wood floors and wood trim provide a fine-dining atmosphere where you can sample favorites—such as fish in a bag, rack of lamb, lobster tails, steaks and seafood—accompanied by a selection from extensive wine list. An acoustic guitarist performs Wednesday through Saturday from May to October.

American. Dinner. Closed January-April, Sunday-Thursday. Reservations recommended. Children's menu. Bar. $36-85

DETROIT

Detroit, a city geared to the tempo of the production line, is the symbol throughout the world of America's automotive industry. It's the birthplace of mass production and the producer of nearly 25 percent of the nation's automobiles, trucks and tractors. This is the city of Ford, Chrysler, Dodge and the U.A.W. Detroit is also a major producer of space propulsion units, automation equipment, plane parts, hardware, rubber tires, office equipment, machine tools, fabricated metal, iron and steel forging and auto stampings and accessories.

Detroit was a quiet city before the automobile. The city rocketed out beyond its river-hugging confines, developing dozens of suburbs. Civic planning is now remodeling the face of the community, particularly downtown and along the riverfront. It's one of the few cities in the United States where you can look

BEST ATTRACTIONS

WHAT ARE DETROIT'S TOP SIGHTS?

DETROIT INSTITUTE OF ARTS

This art museum has one of the top collections in the country. Get an eyeful of amazing pieces like Diego Rivera's *Detroit Industry* murals, which the artist considered to be his most successful work, and Van Gogh's *Self-Portrait*.

GREEKTOWN

When you get hungry, bring your appetite to Greektown. The more than 100-year-old neighborhood has restaurants serving delicious souvlaki, moussaka, spinach pie and gyros.

HART PLAZA AND DODGE FOUNTAIN

In the middle of Hart Plaza, the 30-foot tall stainless-steel fountain is quite a sight with its 300 water jets and 300 lights. The plaza itself is a hot spot for summertime festivals, including the Detroit International Jazz Festival.

MGM GRAND DETROIT

Step into this casino and you might forget you're in the heartland. This outpost of the Vegas casino-hotel brings the Strip's razzle-dazzle to Detroit with gambling galore, celebrity-chef restaurants, and swinging clubs and lounges.

MOTOWN MUSEUM

For a sample of Detroit's musical legacy, visit this museum. There you'll find "Hitsville USA," the house where such legends as Stevie Wonder, Marvin Gaye, the Jackson 5 and the Temptations recorded their first songs.

due south into Canada. The city stretches out along the Detroit River between Lakes Erie and St. Clair, opposite the Canadian city of Windsor, Ontario. Detroit is 143 square miles and almost completely flat. The buildings of the Renaissance Center and Civic Center are grouped about the shoreline, and a network of major highways and expressways radiate from this point like the spokes of a wheel. The original city was laid out on the lines of the L'Enfant plan for Washington, D.C., with a few major streets radiating from a series of circles. As the city grew, a gridiron pattern was superimposed to handle the maze of subdivisions that had developed into Detroit's 200 neighborhoods.

WHAT TO SEE

BELLE ISLE

East Jefferson Avenue and East Grand Boulevard, Detroit, 313-852-4078

Between the U.S. and Canada, in sight of downtown Detroit, this 1,000-acre island park offers nine-hole golf, a nature center, guided nature walks, swimming and fishing (piers, docks). It also has picnicking, ball fields, tennis and lighted handball courts.

CHARLES H. WRIGHT MUSEUM OF AFRICAN AMERICAN HISTORY

315 E. Warren Ave., Detroit, 313-494-5800; www.maah-detroit.org

Exhibits here trace 400 years of history and achievements of African-Americans. The museum's major exhibit, "And Still We Rise," is an inspiring look at how African-American have endured throughout history, starting from prehistoric Africa to present-day Detroit.

Admission: adults and children $5, children 2 and under free. Sunday 1-5 p.m. Tuesday-Saturday, 9 a.m.-5 p.m.

CIVIC CENTER

Woodward and Jefferson avenues, Detroit

A dramatic group of buildings in a 95-acre downtown riverfront setting makes for a scenic spot in the city.

COBO CENTER

1 Washington Blvd., Detroit, 313-877-8111; www.cobocenter.com

Designed to be the world's finest convention, exposition and re-creation building, the Cobo Center features an 11,561-seat arena and 720,000 square feet of exhibit area and facilities.

Daily.

DETROIT CHILDREN'S MUSEUM

6134 Second Ave., Detroit, 313-873-8100; www.detroitsciencecenter.org

The Detroit Children's Museum, part of the Detroit Science Center, is the third-oldest museum for kids in the country. Exhibits at this fun museum look at Inuit culture, children's art, folk crafts, birds and mammals of Michigan. Kids can become mini-astronomers at the museum's planetarium demonstrations.

Admission: adults $13.95, seniors and children $11.95. Monday-Friday 9 a.m.-4 p.m.

DETROIT HISTORICAL MUSEUM

5401 Woodward Ave., Detroit, 313-833-1805; www.detroithistorical.org

The museum presents a walk-through history along reconstructed streets of Old Detroit, with period alcoves and costumes. Changing exhibits portray city life. The museum rotates exhibits that explore Detroit history, from automotive displays to Motown exhibitions.

Admission: adults $6, children $4. Tuesday-Friday 9:30 a.m.-5 p.m., Saturday 10 a.m.-5 p.m., Sunday 11 a.m.-5 p.m.

DETROIT INSTITUTE OF ARTS

5200 Woodward Ave., Detroit, 313-833-7900; www.dia.org

This respected art museum tells the history of humankind through artistic creations. Every significant art-producing culture is represented. Be sure to check out Diego Rivera's *The Detroit Industry* murals, Van Eyck's *St. Jerome,* Bruegel's *Wedding Dance* and Van Gogh's *Self-Portrait.* The museum also houses African-American, Indian, Dutch, French, Flemish and Italian collections; Medieval arms and armor; and an 18th-century American country house reconstructed with period furnishings.

Admission: adults $8, seniors $6, children 6-17 $4, children 5 and under free. Wednesday-Thursday 10 a.m.-4 p.m., Friday 10 a.m.-9 p.m., Saturday-Sunday 10 a.m.-5 p.m.

DETROIT LIONS (NFL)
Ford Field, 2000 Brush St., Detroit, 313-262-2003; www.detroitlions.com

The Lions are Detroit's professional football team. Their home base is the downtown Ford Field, which was the site of the 2006 Super Bowl.

DETROIT RED WINGS (NHL)
Joe Louis Arena, 600 Civic Center Drive, Detroit, 313-396-7444; www.detroitredwings.com

The Red Wings are the state's professional hockey team. Fans go nuts for the team, which boasts 11 Stanley Cup championship wins.

DETROIT SYMPHONY ORCHESTRA HALL
3711 Woodward Ave., Detroit, 313-576-5100; www.detroitsymphony.com

This restored public concert hall, originally made in 1919, features classical programs. Catch the Detroit Symphony Orchestra performing here.

DETROIT TIGERS (MLB)
Comerica Park, 2100 Woodward Ave., Detroit, 313-962-4000; www.tigers.com

Detroit's professional baseball team, the Tigers, slug it out at Comerica Park. Aside from offering games, the ballpark also entertains with a Ferris wheel, a carousel and water jets in center field.

DOSSIN GREAT LAKES MUSEUM
100 Strand Drive, Detroit, 313-833-5538; www.detroithistorical.org

See scale models of Great Lakes ships at this museum, which also houses a restored Gothic salon from Great Lakes liner, marine paintings, a reconstructed ship's bridge and a full-scale racing boat, Miss Pepsi.

Admission: free. Saturday-Sunday 11 a.m.-4 p.m.

EASTERN MARKET
2934 Russell St., Detroit, 313-833-9300; www.detroiteasternmarket.com

Built originally on the site of an early hay and wood market, this and the Chene-Ferry Market are the two remaining produce/wholesale markets in the city. Today this busy market encompasses produce and meat-packing houses, fish mongers and storefronts, offering everything from spices to paper. It is also recognized as the world's largest bedding flower market.

Saturday 5 a.m.-5 p.m.

FISHER BUILDING
3011 W. Grand Blvd., Detroit, 313-874-4444

Designed by architect Albert Kahn, this building was recognized in 1928 as the most beautiful commercial structure erected and given a silver medal by the Architectural League of New York. The building consists of a 28-story central tower and two 11-story wings. Housed here are the Fisher Theater, shops, restaurants, art galleries and offices. Underground pedestrian walkways and skywalk bridges connect to a parking deck and 11 separate structures, including General Motors World Headquarters and New Center One.

SPECIAL EVENT

DETROIT INTERNATIONAL JAZZ FESTIVAL

Hart Plaza and Campus Martius Park, Detroit, 313-447-1248; www.detroitjazzfest.com
More than 750,000 turn out to downtown Detroit for four days of free jazz concerts. Come to tap your foot to the 100 jazz acts performing on five stages in this Labor Day tradition. *Labor Day weekend.*

GREEKTOWN
Monroe Street, Detroit

For more than 100 years, this two-block area of Monroe Street has been known as Greektown. Local restaurants specialize in large portions of Greek specialties, including souvlaki, moussaka, lamb chops, spinach pie and gyros. Greektown bars are especially lively on Fridays and Saturdays, while local shops and groceries celebrate Greek culture every day of the week. To complete your tour of Greektown, visit the Annunciation Greek Orthodox Cathedral that anchors the neighborhood.

GREEKTOWN CASINO
555 E. Lafayette Ave., Detroit, 313-223-2999; www.greektowncasino.com

This buzzing casino is conveniently in the heart of Greektown and near Comerica Park (field of the Detroit Tigers), Ford Field (home of the Detroit Lions), Max M. Fisher Music Center and the Fox Theater. The casino includes more than 2,400 slot machines, plus a variety of table games, from craps and roulette to blackjack and seven-card stud.
Daily.

HART PLAZA AND DODGE FOUNTAIN
1 Hart Plaza, Detroit, 313-877-8077

This humongous stainless-steel structure may look like a spaceship. But it's a 30-foot-high fountain with a $2 million water display designed by sculptor Isamu Noguchi. The plaza hosts a number of summertime festivals, including the Detroit International Jazz Festival.

HAZEL PARK
1650 E. 10 Mile Road, Hazel Park, 248-398-1000; www.hazelparkraceway.com

Just north of Detroit, Hazel Park specializes in harness racing. It also has simulcasting, which allows you to watch and wager on all major harness and thoroughbred tracks across the country at the racetrack.
April-mid-October, Monday-Tuesday and Thursday-Saturday.

MARINERS' CHURCH
170 E. Jefferson Ave., Detroit, 313-259-2206

The oldest stone church in the city was completed in 1849 and was moved 800 feet to its present site as part of the Civic Center plan. Since that time it has been extensively restored and a bell tower with carillon has been added.
Tours by appointment.

MAX M. FISHER MUSIC CENTER
3711 Woodward Ave., Detroit, 313-576-5111; www.detroitsymphony.com

The home of the Detroit Symphony Orchestra, the Max M. Fisher Music Center was built around Orchestra Hall, which is reputed to have the best acoustics in the world. In addition, the Max complex includes the Music Box Theater, which is a smaller concert hall, a large rehearsal hall and an educational center.

Monday-Friday 10 a.m.-8 p.m., Saturday on performance days.

MGM GRAND CASINO
MGM Grand Detroit, 1777 Third St., Detroit, 877-888-2121; www.detroit.mgmgrand.com

This large, humming casino within the MGM Grand Detroit includes more than 2,000 slot machines, plus games like baccarat, blackjack, poker, roulette and more. It's also a great place for live entertainment and dining, particularly at Bourbon Steak, a Forbes Four Star restaurant.

Daily.

MOTORCITY CASINO
2901 Grand River Ave., Detroit, 877-777-0711; www.motorcitycasino.com

The MotorCity Casino offers more than 2,500 slot machines, plus blackjack, roulette, craps and many other games. A variety of cafés and restaurants can be found here as well. Onsite entertainment takes place all week.

Daily.

MOTOWN MUSEUM
2648 W. Grand Blvd., Detroit, 313-875-2264; www.motownmuseum.com

"Hitsville USA," the house where such legends as Diana Ross and the Supremes, Stevie Wonder, Marvin Gaye, the Jackson 5 and the Temptations recorded their first songs, is in this historical spot. The museum includes Motown's original Studio A, as well as artifacts, photographs, gold and platinum records and memorabilia. Guided tours are available.

Admission: adults $10, seniors and children $8. Tuesday-Saturday 10 a.m.-6 p.m.

NORTHVILLE DOWNS
301 S. Center St., Northville, 248-349-1000; www.northvilledowns.com

Like Hazel Park, Northville Downs offers live harness racing and year-round simulcast races. It also holds charity poker matches in the clubhouse every day. Children over 12 years only are allowed entry.

January and October-March, Monday-Tuesday, Thursday, Saturday.

RENAISSANCE CENTER
400 E. Jefferson Ave., Detroit, 313-568-5600

This seven-tower complex sits along the riverfront and includes a 73-story hotel, offices, restaurants, bars, movie theaters, retail shops and business services.

VETERANS' MEMORIAL BUILDING
151 W. Jefferson Ave., Detroit

This building rests on the site where Cadillac and the first French settlers landed in 1701. This $5.75 million monument to the Detroit-area war dead was the first unit of the $180 million Civic Center to be completed. The massive sculptured marble eagle on the front of the building is by Marshall Fredericks, who also sculpted *Spirit of Detroit* at the City-County Building.

WHITCOMB CONSERVATORY
East Jefferson Avenue and East Grand Boulevard, Detroit, 313-852-4064

The conservatory teems with ferns, cacti, palms and orchids. Special exhibits are also featured.

Admission: free. Monday-Saturday 10 a.m.-5 p.m.

NORTH AMERICAN INTERNATIONAL AUTO SHOW
Cobo Center, 1 Washington Blvd., Detroit, 248-643-0250; www.naias.com

This large auto show attracts executives, media and consumers from all over the world who come to see the most eagerly awaited new cars make their big debut. Of course, it's fitting that the show is held in Motor City.

January.

WOODWARD DREAM CRUISE
Woodward Avenue, Detroit, 800-338-7648; www.woodwarddreamcruise.com

Each year, more than 1.5 million people-watch or ride in 30,000 classic and vintage cars touring Woodward Avenue. The wildly popular event is billed as the world's largest one-day celebration of car culture. A parade-like atmosphere means you'll find plenty to eat and drink, vendors selling T-shirts and other items commemorating the event, and street entertainers providing music and more.

Third Saturday in August, 9 a.m.-9 p.m., with some events held the preceding Thursday and Friday.

WHERE TO STAY

★★★MARRIOTT DETROIT RENAISSANCE CENTER
Renaissance Center, Detroit, 313-568-8000, 800-352-0831; www.marriott.com

This Marriott hotel is in a 73-story building that also houses the world headquarters of General Motors, along with numerous shops and restaurants. Located along the RiverWalk in the heart of Detroit, the Marriott offers views of the Detroit River and Windsor, Ontario. More pluses include large guest rooms and closets, well-appointed facilities and an array of services and amenities for the business or leisure traveler.

1,328 rooms. Restaurant, bar. $151-250

★★★★MGM GRAND DETROIT
1777 Third St., Detroit, 877-888-2121; www.mgmgranddetroit.com

Feel like you're visiting Vegas without leaving Detroit. Located downtown, this mega-resort features non-stop action with a casino, five restaurants and five bars. You can get ready for a big night out at the full-service salon, then refresh and revitalize at the Immerse Spa the next morning. The rooms and suites are sophisticated and spacious, while unique amenities—such as 42-inch plasma TVs and oversized showers with dual rain showerheads—complete the luxurious experience. Enjoy a meal at Michael Mina's Bourbon Steak, a Forbes

Four Star restaurant, which offers a contemporary American steakhouse menu. Then head to one of the many clubs or bars here for some cocktails and dancing. To recover the next day, head back to the spa to make use of the private cabanas at the infinity pool.

400 rooms. Restaurant, bar. Fitness center. Pool. Spa. Casino. $251-350

★★★OMNI DETROIT RIVER PLACE

1000 River Place Drive, Detroit, 313-259-9500, 800-843-6664; www.omnihotels.com

This elegant hotel, which dates back to 1902, is in downtown Detroit on the historic waterfront. It was once the home of the Parke Davis Company, and Stroh's Brewery was also a previous occupant. Guest rooms boast views of the river and the Canadian border. The hotel has a championship croquet court, which is the only United States Croquet Association-sanctioned court in Michigan, so bring your mallet. Feel free to also bring Fido along for the trip—pets under 25 pounds are welcome, and the hotel offers treats and a walking service.

108 rooms. Restaurant, bar. Pets accepted. Tennis. $151-250

WHERE TO EAT

★★★★BOURBON STEAK

MGM Grand Detroit, 1777 S. Third St., Detroit, 313-465-1644; www.mgmgranddetroit.com

Celebrity chef Michael Mina turns the traditional steakhouse on its head with this super-slick version. The chic space, with sleek furnishings and contemporary design, is equal parts upscale sports club and sultry nightclub. It's a carnivore's delight, as well—offering a variety of cuts of Angus, American Kobe and Japanese Wagyu beef. But thanks to quirky takes on classics, such as lobster corn dog appetizers and side dishes including rosemary duck-fat fries and truffle mac and cheese, this isn't your typical steak house.

American, steak. Dinner. Closed Monday. $36-85

★★★CAUCUS CLUB

150 W. Congress St., Detroit, 313-965-4970; www.caucusclubdetroit.com

One of the city's culinary legends, this English-style dining room serves American cuisine with European accents. The jumbo Dover sole in lemon butter is a signature dish and the cozy, dimly lit bar is a popular after-work hangout.

American. Lunch, dinner. Closed Sunday. $16-35

★★★IRIDESCENCE RESTAURANT

MotorCity Casino Hotel, 2901 Grand River Ave., Detroit, 313-237-6732; www.motorcitycasino.com

With huge windows that frame pretty views of the twinkling city lights, you don't have to guess how this restaurant, located atop the MotorCity Casino Hotel, got its name. Everything from the interior design—including hanging light bulb globes—to the cutting-edge table settings defines urban sophistication. The artfully plated, creative cuisine, much of it organic and seasonal, perfectly complements the swanky atmosphere. Be sure to save room for one of the sugary works of art created by award-winning pastry chef Patricia Nash.

Contemporary American. Dinner. Closed Monday. Reservations recommended. Bar. $36-85

★★★OPUS ONE

565 E. Larned St., Detroit, 313-961-7766; www.opus-one.com

Owner Jim Kokas has overseen this dressy dining room for more than 10 years. Executive chef Tim Giznsky creates inventive, American cuisine that can be enjoyed for dinner, weekday power lunches or before heading out to local theater. Try the pan-seared Chilean sea bass with basmati rice, jumbo shrimp in phyllo pastry with potato gratin or rack of New Zealand lamb with potato-fennel gratin.

American. Lunch, dinner. Closed Sunday. Bar. $36-85

★★★RATTLESNAKE CLUB

300 River Place, Detroit, 313-567-4400; www.rattlesnakeclub.com

This Rivertown destination is where well-known James Beard Award-winning chef Jimmy Schmidt offers seasonal, worldly American cuisine. There's also a beautiful riverside dining room and a superior, well-priced wine list. The menu focuses on sustainably harvested and seasonal ingredients, such as wild Alaskan king salmon or tea-cured free-range duck breast.

American. Lunch, dinner. Closed Sunday. Outdoor seating. Bar. $36-85

★★★SALTWATER

MGM Grand Detroit, 1777 S. Third St., Detroit, 313-465-1646; www.mgmgranddetroit.com

If Bourbon Steak is Michael Mina's paean to the farm, Saltwater is his love letter to the sea. Entering the elegant dining room feels like stepping aboard a luxury ocean liner, while the seafood-driven menu highlights Mina's talent for turning the standards upside down. Entrées include lobster pot pie, zucchini-wrapped salmon and almond-crusted halibut, but don't miss the signature mussel soufflé or caviar parfait. During the week, the three-course pre-theater menu is a good way to sample the chef's talents.

Contemporary American, seafood. Dinner. Closed Sunday-Monday. Bar. No children under 21. $36-85

★★★THE WHITNEY

4421 Woodward Ave., Detroit, 313-832-5700; www.thewhitney.com

Housed in what was once the home of lumber baron David Whitney Jr., this mansion was built in 1894 out of South Dakota Jasper (a rare pink granite) and was designed in the Romanesque style of architecture. Inside, find Tiffany stained-glass windows and crystal chandeliers. The menu features fish, beef, seafood and lamb and includes dishes like blue cheese soufflé with pecans and apple vinaigrette or Great Lakes whitefish with melted tomato and crispy potato. Enjoy these updated versions of traditional favorites in a variety of rooms, including the Music Room, Library or Asian Room.

American. Lunch, dinner, Sunday brunch. Closed Monday. Bar. $36-85

★★★WOLFGANG PUCK GRILLE

MGM Grand Detroit, 1777 S. Third St., Detroit, 313-465-1648; www.mgmgranddetroit.com

Wolfgang Puck's name may be on everything from pans to frozen pizzas, but the quality is always top-notch. His eponymous restaurant in the MGM Grand is no exception. Whether you're enjoying breakfast, lunch or dinner in this casual spot, you'll find upscale comfort food cooked with the freshest ingredients and served by a smiling staff of knowledgeable servers. There's an open kitchen, so even if you can't stand the heat, you'll get a behind-the-scenes look.

American. Breakfast, lunch, dinner. Bar. $36-85

SPA

★★★★IMMERSE SPA

MGM Grand Detroit, 1777 S. Third St., Detroit, 313-465-1656; www.mgmgranddetroit.com

It may be inside the noisy MGM Grand, but there isn't a better place to unwind than at the serene Immerse Spa. The facility boasts a well-equipped fitness center, indoor pool and full-service salon, but the real beauty of this spa lies in its restorative treatments. From ancient bathing rituals to purifying sea foam facials, this spa uses marine-based products to detoxify and revitalize. Guided relaxation and Japanese tea ceremonies accompany Immerse's signature rituals, which include customized facials and hypnotic massage.

WHAT ARE DETROIT'S BEST OVERALL RESTAURANTS?

Bourbon Steak: Celebrity chef Michael Mina's sleek steakhouse is a carnivore's delight, but that doesn't mean the chef's famous signature items are not also on hand, including Mina's decadent lobster corn dog and truffle mac and cheese.

Iridescence Restaurant: From the iridescent atmosphere to the creative cuisine to the divine pastries, this restaurant spells urban sophistication.

Rattlesnake Club: Well-known chef Jimmy Schmidt offers his seasonal, worldly American cuisine, with a superior wine list to match, at this Rivertown destination.

SOUTHEAST MICHIGAN

Although Detroit is the major city in this region, many other great cities pepper the Southeast area. Arguably the coolest town in Michigan, Ann Arbor is the home of the University of Michigan, which mingles its campus buildings with city attractions. The university, one of the largest in the United States, brings cultural and artistic flavor to the area. Downtown offers exceptional shops and a variety of eateries.

Auburn Hills recently rebuilt its downtown with street lamps and charming shops. Home of the Chrysler Tech Center and dozens of other high-tech companies, the city is best known for Great Lakes Crossing, a mega mall with more than 200 stores that attracts hardcore shoppers. But sports fans also frequent the city to see the Pistons and Shock shoot hoops.

Not to be outdone in the shopping department, Birch Run is buoyed by the more than one million visitors who bring their credit cards to the Outlets at Birch Run. If you're less into discounted designer goods and more into antiques, Brooklyn is your town. Its Antique Alley is a mecca for shoppers on the hunt for vintage finds. In the summer, Brooklyn really heats up when race fans come out for Michigan International Speedway.

For more historical pursuits, head to Dearborn. Aside from being the home of the Ford Motor Company's Rouge Assembly Plant and Ford World Headquarters, Dearborn hosts a complex made up of the Henry Ford Museum, Greenfield Village and other historical attractions. Although Dearborn has a long and colorful history, its real claim to fame is due to Henry Ford, who was born here in 1863.

Kids will want to make a detour into Royal Oak for the Detroit Zoo, ranked among the best animal homes in the nation. It's also one of Michigan's trendiest cities, a place where stylish shops and chic restaurants line the downtown area, so there will be something for you parents to do as well.

WHAT TO SEE

ANN ARBOR
DELHI
3780 W. Delhi Road, Dexter, 734-426-8211, 800-477-3191; www.metroparks.com
This 53-acre site is home to the Delhi Rapids. If rapids don't float your boat, there's also fishing, canoeing (May-September, rentals available), hiking trails, cross-country skiing, picnicking and a playground.

DEXTER-HURON METROPARK
6535 Huron River Drive, Ann Arbor, 734-426-8211, 800-477-3191; www.metroparks.com
This metropark offers fishing, canoeing, hiking trails, cross-country skiing, picnicking and a playground.

GERALD R. FORD PRESIDENTIAL LIBRARY
1000 Beal Ave., Ann Arbor, 734-741-2218; www.ford.utexas.edu
This research library houses 25 million pages of Ford's presidential, vice-presidential and congressional documents.
Admission: free. Monday-Friday 8:45 a.m.-4:45 p.m.

HUDSON MILLS METROPARK
8801 N. Territorial Road, Dexter, 734-426-8211, 800-234-3191; www.metroparks.com
This more than 1,600-acre recreation area offers fishing, boating, canoe rental, hiking, bicycle trails (rentals), an 18-hole golf course, cross-country skiing (winter), picnicking, a playground, camping and an activity center.

HIGHLIGHT

WHAT ARE THE TOP THINGS TO DO?

VISIT THE DETROIT ZOO
More than one million visitors come to this excellent zoo each year to see the 1,500 animal inhabitants in exhibits like the "Australian Outback Adventure," "Great Apes of Harambee" and "Penguinarium."

SHOP AT GREAT LAKES CROSSING
Frugal fashionistas will be tripping all over their Louboutin-clad feet to visit Great Lakes Crossing, the state's top shopping destination. They can get steals on designer labels at Michael Kors Outlet and BCBGMaxAzria Factory Store.

EXPLORE GREENFIELD VILLAGE
Part of the sprawling Henry Ford complex, this village is made up of 83 authentic, historic structures, like the home where Noah Webster wrote the first American dictionary and Thomas Edison's lab.

VISIT THE HENRY FORD MUSEUM
This expansive museum, which sits on 12 acres, has several must-see exhibits. A standout is the bus where Rosa Parks refused to give up her seat and helped spark the civil-rights movement in the United States.

CHECK OUT MICHIGAN INTERNATIONAL SPEEDWAY
When the summertime hits, race fans get their motors running at the Michigan International Speedway. That's when the speedway opens for the season and hosts NASCAR races and more on its track.

KELSEY MUSEUM OF ARCHAEOLOGY
434 S. State St., Ann Arbor, 734-764-9304; www.lsa.umich.edu

The museum houses more than 100,000 objects from the civilizations of the Mediterranean.

Admission: free. Tuesday-Friday 9 a.m.-4 p.m., Saturday-Sunday 1-4 p.m.

KEMPF HOUSE CENTER FOR LOCAL HISTORY
312 S. Division, Ann Arbor, 734-994-4898; www.kempfhousemuseum.org

An unusual example of Greek Revival architecture, this restored structure built in 1853 is owned and maintained by the city of Ann Arbor and includes antique Victorian furnishings.

Admission: free. Tours: Sunday 1-4 p.m.; closed January and August.

LAW QUADRANGLE
S. State Street and S. University Avenue, Ann Arbor, 734-764-9322; www.law.umich.edu

This beautiful quadrangle at the University of Michigan includes four beautiful

Gothic-style buildings. The law library, with an underground addition, has one of the nation's most extensive collections of legal research resources. The reading room, in particular, offers a beautiful and tranquil place for students to study with 50-foot stained glass windows and a neogothic design.

MICHIGAN STADIUM

1 E. Stadium Blvd., Ann Arbor, 734-764-1817; www.umich.edu

There's nothing quite like a football Saturday inside "The Big House," the largest stadium in the United States, seating 109,000 and constantly expanding. Fans pack the place for every game day, especially when the Wolverines are playing intrastate rival, Michigan State, and when up against bitter rival Ohio State University. The last game of the season with Ohio State has often determined the Big Ten Championship—hence, the intense rivalry.

POWER CENTER FOR THE PERFORMING ARTS

121 S. Fletcher, Ann Arbor, 734-763-3333; www.music.umich.edu

This 1,414-seat theater houses performances of drama, opera, music and dance.

AUBURN HILLS

DETROIT PISTONS (NBA)

5 Championship Drive, Auburn Hills, 248-377-0100; www.nba.com

Detroit's professional basketball team shoots hoops at the Palace of Auburn Hills.

DETROIT SHOCK (WNBA)

5 Championship Drive, Auburn Hills, 248-377-0100; www.wnba.com

The Shock, Detroit's professional women's basketball team, calls the Palace of Auburn Hills its home court.

GREAT LAKES CROSSING

4000 Baldwin Road, Auburn Hills, 877-746-7452; www.shopgreatlakescrossing.com

With 1.4 million square feet of shops, Great Lakes Crossing is Michigan's top shopping destination. Get high-end bargain-basement steals at discounted shops like the Neiman Marcus Last Call Clearance Center, Michael Kors Outlet and BCBGMaxAzria Factory Store. The center also features a high-tech playland, movie theaters, cafés and restaurants.
Daily.

BAY CITY

BAY CITY STATE RECREATION AREA

3582 State Park Drive, Bay City, 989-667-0717; www.michigan.gov

This recreation area spans approximately 200 acres and includes beaches, boating docks, hiking trails, picnicking, concessions and camping facilities.

CITY HALL AND BELL TOWER

301 Washington Ave., Bay City, 989-893-1222; www.tourbaycitymi.org

This meticulously restored Romanesque structure is from 1895. The council chamber has 31-foot-long woven tapestry depicting the history of Bay City. View of the city and its waterway from bell tower.
Monday-Friday.

SPECIAL EVENT

STREET ART FAIR

Ann Arbor, 734-994-5260, 800-888-9487; www.artfair.org
Since it started in 1960, nearly 1,000 artists and craftspeople display and sell works at this popular juried art fair each summer. More than 500,000 people come out to browse and buy art, enjoy music and dance performances, watch artist demonstrations, and take part in art activities. A Townie Street Party for locals kicks off the fest at the beginning of the week.
Four days in mid-July.

BIRCH RUN
THE OUTLETS AT BIRCH RUN
12240 S. Beyer Road, Birch Run, 989-624-7467
This popular outlet mall includes more than 200 stores, including Coach, Nike, J. Crew, Eddie Bauer, Ann Taylor, Laura Ashley, Polo/Ralph Lauren, TJ Maxx, Aldo, Saks Off Fifth, Neiman Marcus Last Call, and a lot more. When you need to give your feet a break from walking, catch a flick at the movie theater or grab a bite in the large food court.
Daily.

BLOOMFIELD HILLS
CRANBROOK EDUCATIONAL COMMUNITY
39221 Woodward Ave., Bloomfield Hills, 248-645-3000, 877-462-7262; www.cranbrook.edu
This well-known campus is the site of the renowned center for the arts, education, science and culture. Located on more than 300 acres, Cranbrook is noted for its exceptional architecture, gardens and sculpture.

CRANBROOK GARDENS
380 Lone Pine Road, Bloomfield Hills, 248-645-3147; www.cranbrook.edu
The lovely gardens here include more than 40 acres of formal and informal gardens, trails, fountains and an outdoor Greek theater.
Admission: Tours: adults $6, seniors $5. May-August, daily; September, afternoons only; October, Saturday-Sunday afternoons.

CRANBROOK HOUSE
380 Lone Pine Road, Bloomfield Hills, 248-645-3147; www.cranbrook.edu
This Tudor-style structure was designed by Albert Kahn and built in 1908. It contains exceptional examples of decorative and fine art from the late 19th and early 20th centuries.
Admission: Tours (includes garden visit): adults $10, seniors and students $8.

CRANBROOK INSTITUTE OF SCIENCE
39221 Woodward Ave., Bloomfield Hills, 248-645-3200; www.cranbrook.edu
This natural history and science museum includes an observatory, a nature

center, a planetarium and laser demonstrations.

Admission: adults $9.50, seniors and children 2-12 $7.50, children 1 and under free; Friday 5-10 p.m.: adults $5.50, seniors and children 2-12 $4.50, children 1 and under free. Sunday-Thursday, Saturday 10 a.m.-5 p.m., Friday 10 a.m.-10 p.m.

BROOKLYN

ANTIQUE ALLEY

The 50-mile drive west from Saline to Somerset Center with a side trip up Highway 50 to Brooklyn is known locally as Antique Alley, and it makes for a great day of shopping. Go there to search for antiques, glassware and other collectibles.

BRICK WALKER TAVERN ANTIQUES

11705 Highway 12, Brooklyn, 517-467-6961

Brick Walker Tavern Antiques, set in an 1854 building constructed as a three-story inn along the Detroit-Chicago Pike, features collectible glassware, pottery and china.

IRISH HILLS ANTIQUES AND OUTDOOR MARKET

10600 Highway 12, Brooklyn, 517-467-4646

Irish Hills Antiques sells antique wood- and coal-burning parlor kitchen stoves, brass cash registers, porcelain signs and gasoline pumps, in case you're looking to redecorate your home.

MICHIGAN INTERNATIONAL SPEEDWAY

12626 Highway 12, Brooklyn, 517-592-6666, 800-354-1010; www.mispeedway.com

This racetrack is nestled among 1,400-plus acres in the lovely Irish Hills. But the scenic surroundings shouldn't detract from the hardcore racing that takes place on its tracks. NASCAR, ARCA, IROC and Indy car races burn rubber on the speedway's two-mile oval track.

Mid-June-mid-August.

DEARBORN

GREENFIELD VILLAGE

20900 Oakwood Blvd., Dearborn, 313-271-1620; www.hfmgv.org

This village comprises more than 80 18th- and 19th-century buildings. They've moved here from all over the country to form a community that brings history alive. Homes, shops, schools, mills, stores and laboratories that figured in the lives of such historic figures as Lincoln, McGuffey, Carver, the Wright brothers, Edison and Ford are on display. Among the most interesting buildings are the courthouse where Abraham Lincoln practiced law, the Wright brothers' cycle shop, Henry Ford's birthplace and Edison's Menlo Park laboratory.

Admission: adults $22, seniors $21, children 5-12 $16, children 4 and under free. Monday-Saturday 9:30 a.m.-5 p.m., Sunday noon-5 p.m. Interiors also closed January-mid-March.

HENRY FORD ESTATE-FAIR LANE

4901 Evergreen Road, Dearborn, 313-593-5590; www.henryfordestate.com

Built by automotive pioneer Henry Ford in 1915, the mansion cost more than $2 million and stands on 72 acres of property. Designed by William Van Tine, the manse reflects Ford's penchant for simplicity and functionalism. Its systems for heating, water, electricity and refrigeration were entirely self-sufficient at that time. The powerhouse, boathouse and gardens have been restored, and some original furniture and a children's playhouse have been returned to the premises. The estate now is a popular rental facility for weddings and other big events. The estate will be closing due to renovations sometime in 2011 and will reopen in phases in 2013; so call before you visit to check on the status.

Admission: Tours: adults $12, seniors and students $11, children 6-12 $8, children 5 and under free. Guided Tours: January-March, Tuesday-Sunday 1:30 p.m.; April-December, Tuesday-Sunday 10:30 a.m., 11:30 a.m., 12:30 p.m., 1:30 p.m., and 2:30 p.m.

HENRY FORD MUSEUM
20900 Oakwood Blvd., Dearborn, 313-271-1620; www.hfmgv.org

This interesting museum occupies 12 acres and includes major collections in transportation, power and machinery, agriculture, lighting, communications, household furnishings and appliances, ceramics, glass, silver and pewter. Make it a point to see the bus where Rosa Parks started a movement and the limo that carried President Kennedy when he was assassinated.

Admission: adults $15, seniors $14, children 5-12 $11, children 4 and under free. Monday-Saturday 9 a.m.-5 p.m., Sunday noon-5 p.m.

SUWANEE PARK
Dearborn

The park includes an early 20th-century amusement center with an antique merry-go-round, a steamboat, a train ride, a restaurant and a soda fountain (mid-May-September). In addition, you can take narrated rides in a horse-drawn carriage, on a steam train or on a riverboat. There's also 1931 Ford bus rides available (mid-May-September). Varied activities are scheduled throughout the year.

FLINT

CROSSROADS VILLAGE/HUCKLEBERRY RAILROAD
6140 Bray Road, Flint, 810-736-7100, 800-648-7275; www.geneseecountyparks.org

This restored living community of the 1860-1880 period is made up of 28 buildings and sites, including a railroad depot, a carousel, a Ferris wheel, a general store, a schoolhouse and several homes. There is also a working sawmill, gristmill, cidermill, blacksmith shop and an eight-mile steam train ride. Paddlewheel riverboat cruises are available and there are special events most weekends.

June-September, Tuesday-Sunday 10 a.m.-5 p.m.

FLINT INSTITUTE OF ARTS
1120 E. Kearsley St., Flint, 810-234-1695; www.flintarts.org

Permanent collections in this museum include Renaissance decorative arts, Asian art, 19th- and 20th-century paintings and sculpture, paperweights.

Admission: Permanent collection: free; Temporary exhibits: adults $7, seniors and students $5, children 12 and under free. Tuesday-Saturday 10 a.m.-5 p.m., Sunday 1-5 p.m.

SPECIAL EVENTS

BAVARIAN FESTIVAL

Heritage Park, 335 S. Main St., Frankenmuth, 989-652-8155, 800-386-3378;
www.bavarianfestival.com
Frankenmuth is a picture-perfect place and the Bavarian Fest is a great way to get a flavor
for this wonderful German hamlet. The festivities including music, dancing, parades and
lots of eating.
Four days in early June.

FRANKENMUTH OKTOBERFEST

635 S. Main St., Frankenmuth, 989-652-6106, 800-386-8696; www.frankenmuth.org
Experience Oktoberfest just as they do in Munich. It's as authentic as it gets in charming
Frankenmuth, where German food, music and entertainment are gamely celebrated.
Third weekend in September.

ROBERT T. LONGWAY PLANETARIUM
1310 E. Kearsley St., Flint, 810-237-3400; www.longwayplanetarium.com
The state's largest planetarium includes ultraviolet, fluorescent murals and a
Spitz projector. There are also laser light shows and frequent special events,
including a laser "spooktakular" for Halloween.
*Admission: Sky and laser shows: adults $5, seniors and children 3-11 $4, children 2 and under
free. Show times vary.*

SLOAN MUSEUM
1221 E. Kearsley St., Flint, 810-237-3450; www.sloanmuseum.com
See a collection of antique autos and carriages, most manufactured in Flint.
Exhibitions also look at Michigan history and health and science.
*Admission: adults $6, seniors $5, children 3-11 $4, children 2 and under free. Monday-Friday
10 a.m.-5 p.m., Saturday-Sunday noon-5 p.m.*

FRANKENMUTH
BRONNER'S CHRISTMAS WONDERLAND
25 Christmas Lane, Frankenmuth, 989-652-9931, 800-255-9327; www.bronners.com
Billing itself as the world's largest Christmas store, Bronner's stocks more than
50,000 trims and gifts from around the world. The store, open since 1945,
features a 20-minute multi-image presentation called "World of Bronner's,"
260 decorated Christmas trees in varying themes and an outdoor display of
100,000 festive lights along Christmas Lane (dusk-midnight).
Daily, hours vary by season.

FRANKENMUTH RIVERBOAT TOURS
445 S. Main St., Frankenmuth, 989-652-8844
Take a narrated tour along the Cass River.
May-October, daily (weather permitting).

GLOCKENSPIEL
713 S. Main St., Frankenmuth, 989-652-9941

This 35-bell carillon atop the Frankenmuth Bavarian Inn includes carved wooden figures moving on a track that act out the story of the Pied Piper of Hamelin.

MICHIGAN'S OWN MILITARY & SPACE MUSEUM
1250 S. Weiss St., Frankenmuth, 989-652-8005; www.michigansmilitarymuseum.com

This military and space museum pays respects to locals. It features uniforms, decorations and photos of men and women from Michigan who served the nation and displays about Medal of Honor recipients, astronauts and former governors.

Admission: adults $5, seniors $4, children $2. March-December, Monday-Saturday 10 a.m.-5 p.m., Sunday 11 a.m.-5 p.m.

HOLLY
DAVISBURG CANDLE FACTORY
634 Broadway, Davisburg, 248-634-4214, 800-748-9440; www.candlefactorymi.com

Located in a 125-year-old building, this factory produces unique and beautiful handcrafted candles.

Demonstrations by appointment (weekdays). Monday-Saturday 10 a.m.-5 p.m., Sunday noon-4 p.m.

DTE ENERGY MUSIC THEATRE
7774 Sashabaw Road, Clarkston, 248-377-0100; www.palacenet.com

This outdoor amphitheater features summer concerts by top performers. Seats are available close to the stage, but many concertgoers brace being alfresco and bring blankets for the much cheaper and more charming lawn area.

HISTORIC BATTLE ALLEY
110 Battle Alley, Holly, 248-634-5208

Once known for its taverns and brawls, Battle Alley is now a restored 19th-century street featuring antiques, boutiques, specialty shops and dining at the Historic Holly Hotel. On the Alley is a mosaic of the bicentennial logo made from 1,000 red, white and blue bricks.

Daily.

MOUNT HOLLY SKI AREA
13536 S. Dixie Highway, Holly, 248-634-8269, 800-582-7256; www.skimtholly.com

You'll find three quads, three triple, a double chairlift, six rope tows, a patrol, a school, rentals and snowmaking at Mount Holly. It has a run with a vertical drop of 350 feet, and night skiing is available.

December-March, daily.

PONTIAC
ALPINE VALLEY SKI RESORT
6775 E. Highland, White Lake, 248-887-4183; www.skialpinevalley.com

Alpine Valley offers 10 chairlifts, 10 rope tows, a patrol, a school, rentals and snowmaking. The longest run has a vertical drop of 320 feet.

November-March, daily.

HIGHLAND

3500 Wixon Road, Pontiac, 248-685-2433

On 5,524 wooded acres, Highland has swimming, a bathhouse, fishing, boating (launch), hiking, horseback riding, hunting in season, cross-country skiing, picnicking, a playground and camping.

PONTIAC LAKE

7800 Gale Road, Waterford

Pontiac Lake spans approximately 3,700 acres and offers swimming, water-skiing, fishing, boating (launch), horseback riding, a riding stable, seasonal hunting, archery and rifle ranges, winter sports, picnicking, a playground and camping.

PORT AUSTIN

ALBERT E. SLEEPER STATE PARK

6573 State Park Road, Caseville, 989-856-4411; www.michigan.gov

Spread across 723 acres, this park includes sandy beaches and offers plenty of recreational activities, like fishing, hunting, hiking, cross-country skiing, picnicking, a playground and camping.
Daily.

PORT HURON

HURON LIGHTSHIP MUSEUM

1115 Sixth St., Port Huron, 810-982-0891; www.phmuseum.org

Lightships were created as floating lighthouses, anchored in areas where lighthouse construction was not possible, using their powerful lights and fog horns to guide ships safely past points of danger. Built in 1920, the Huron was stationed at various shoals in Lake Michigan and Lake Huron until her retirement in 1971.

Admission: adults $7, seniors and students $5, children 4 and under free. Daily 11 a.m.-5 p.m.

LAKEPORT STATE PARK

7605 Lakeshore Road, Lakeport, 810-327-6765; www.michigan.gov

This park is made up of more than 600 acres on Lake Huron and includes a beach. There is waterskiing, fishing for perch, boating, hiking, picnicking, a playground and camping.
Daily.

PORT HURON MUSEUM

1115 Sixth St., Port Huron, 810-982-0891; www.phmuseum.org

The museum showcases historical and fine arts exhibits, a pioneer log home, Native American collections, Thomas Edison's boyhood home, marine lore, natural history displays and period furniture.

Admission: adults $7, seniors and students $5, children 4 and under free. Daily 11 a.m.-5 p.m.

ROCHESTER

MEADOW BROOK HALL

2200 N. Squirrel Road, Rochester, 248-370-3140; www.oakland.edu

This English Tudor mansion was built by lumber baron Alfred Wilson and his wife, Matilda Dodge. The spectacular structure has nearly all of its original furnishings and art. The library and Wilson's personal office have hand-carved paneling; the dining room has a sculptured ceiling and table that can seat several dozen guests; a two-story ballroom has elaborate stone and woodwork. Outside the mansion is Knole Cottage, Francis Wilson's playhouse featuring pint-sized luxury accommodations. The hall also serves as a cultural and conference center for the university.

Admission: adults $15, seniors $10, children free. Daily tours, times vary.

OAKLAND UNIVERSITY ART GALLERY
2200 N. Squirrel Road, Rochester, 248-370-3005; www.oakland.edu

The gallery features a series of contemporary, primitive and Asian art exhibitions, including a permanent collection of African art as well as an outdoor sculpture garden adjacent to music festival grounds.

Admission: free. October-May, Tuesday-Sunday.

ROYAL OAK
DETROIT ZOO
8450 W. 10 Mile Road, Royal Oak, 248-541-5717; www.detroitzoo.org

The Detroit Zoo is one of the world's outstanding zoos, with 40 exhibits featuring more than 1,500 animals in natural habitats. It includes chimpanzee, reptile, bear, butterfly, hummingbird and Arctic animal exhibits.

Admission: adults $11, seniors $9, children 2-14 $7, children 1 and under free. April-August, daily 9 a.m.-5 p.m.; September-October 10 a.m.-5 p.m.; November-March 10 a.m.-4 p.m.

SAGINAW
CASTLE MUSEUM OF SAGINAW COUNTY HISTORY
500 Federal, Saginaw, 989-759-2861; www.castlemuseum.org

Housed in a replica of a French chateau, this museum keeps collections pertaining to the history of the Saginaw Valley and central Michigan.

Admission: adults $1, children $.50. Tuesday-Saturday 10 a.m.-4:30 p.m., Sunday 1-4:30 p.m.

CHILDREN'S ZOO
1730 S. Washington Ave., Saginaw, 989-759-1408; www.saginawzoo.com

This zoo is home to small animals, including llamas, macaws, swans, snakes and porcupines. There's also a contact yard featuring goats and train and pony rides.

Admission: $7. May and September, Monday-Saturday 10 a.m.-5 p.m., Sunday noon-5 p.m.; June-August, Monday-Friday 10 a.m.-5 p.m., Saturday 10 a.m.-6 p.m., Sunday noon-5 p.m.; some weekends in October.

JAPANESE CULTURAL CENTER & TEA HOUSE
527 Ezra Rust Drive, Saginaw, 989-759-1648

This spot on Lake Linton, designed by Yataro Suzue, has a 3-acre garden of weeping cherry trees, stone lanterns and an Asian-inspired gazebo. After strolling the grounds, get a cup of tea at the tea house.

Admission: free. April-October, Tuesday-Sunday noon-4 p.m.

MARSHALL M. FREDERICKS SCULPTURE GALLERY
Saginaw Valley State University, 7400 Bay Road, University Center, 989-964-7125; www.svsu.edu

The gallery houses an extraordinary collection of more than 200 works by the

world-renowned sculptor.
Admission: free. Monday-Saturday noon-5 p.m.

SAGINAW ART MUSEUM
1126 N. Michigan Ave., Saginaw, 989-754-2491; www.saginawartmuseum.org

The art museum focuses on American and European art, with decorative arts, drawings, prints and sculpture among the offerings. You'll see paintings by Jean-Baptiste-Camille Corot and Jasper Cropsey, along with works on paper by masters such as Kandinsky and Picasso. There's also a children's gallery and a historic formal garden on the grounds.

Admission: adults $5, students $3, children 16 and under free. Thursday-Saturday 10 a.m.-5 p.m., Sunday 1-5 p.m.

WHERE TO STAY

ANN ARBOR
★★★WEBER'S INN
3050 Jackson Ave., Ann Arbor, 734-769-2500, 800-443-3050; www.webersinn.com

This full-service hotel is near the University of Michigan. In fact, the football players often stay here before a game. Opened in 1937, the rooms have balconies or easy access to the pool area, large work desks, safes, coffee makers and Gilchrist & Soames bath amenities. Head outside for the four-season pool, whirlpool, sundeck, café and teak chaise lounges—a perfect way to relax after a busy day or a long game. After spending time at the pool or in the fitness center, enjoy a relaxing dinner of prime rib, steak or seafood at Weber's restaurant.

158 rooms. Restaurant, bar. Complimentary breakfast. Fitness center. Pool. $61-150

AUBURN HILLS
★★★HILTON SUITES AUBURN HILLS
2300 Featherstone Road, Auburn Hills, 248-334-2222, 800-774-1500; www.auburnhillssuites.hilton.com

This all-suite hotel offers roomy spaces with separate sleeping areas, refrigerators and microwaves. The atrium-style lobby is warm and welcoming, and the hotel is situated near several Auburn Hills attractions, including Great Lakes Crossing Shopping Center. Be sure to visit the lobby before bedtime; the staff provides guests with complimentary cookies and milk by the lobby fireplace each night.

224 rooms. Restaurant, bar. Pets accepted. $61-150

BIRMINGHAM
★★★★THE TOWNSEND HOTEL
100 Townsend St., Birmingham, 248-642-7900, 800-548-4172; www.townsendhotel.com

Located in the quiet community of Birmingham, where tree-lined streets brim with boutiques and cafés, this hotel is conveniently less than an hour from Detroit. The guest rooms are handsomely furnished with jewel tones, four-poster beds and full kitchens in the suites and penthouses. The cherry wood paneling and the warm glow of the fireplace make Rugby Grille an inviting space. The Corner bar has appealing interiors that are a perfect match for its Asian-inspired appetizers and creative cocktails.

152 rooms. Restaurant, bar. Business center. Fitness center. Pets accepted. $351 and up

DEARBORN
★★★MARRIOTT DEARBORN INN
20301 Oakwood Blvd., Dearborn, 313-271-2700,
800-228-9290; www.marriott.com

This property looks more like a bed and breakfast than a hotel. Built in 1931 on the grounds of the Ford Motor Company, the historic spot rests on 23 beautifully landscaped acres with manicured gardens. The grounds consist of a Georgian-style inn built by Henry Ford, two Colonial-style lodges and five Colonial-style houses. Early American décor and furnishings are found throughout.

222 rooms. Restaurant, bar. $151-250

RECOMMENDED

THE HENRY
Fairlane Plaza, 300 Town Center Drive, Dearborn,
313-441-2000; www.marriott.com

Taking over for the Ritz-Carlton at this location, The Henry is one of the new additions to Marriot's Autograph Hotel Group. Located only 15 minutes from downtown Detroit, this hotel is part of a nearly 7-acre complex in historic Dearborn. The popular hotel was just given a multi-million dollar facelift and recently renovated guest rooms are a perfect match for demanding travelers, with state-of-the-art technology, oversized bathrooms and handsome appointments. An on-site restaurant as well as fitness center and indoor pool are just some of the amenities.

Restaurant, bar. Fitness center. Pool. $151-250

PONTIAC
★★★MARRIOTT PONTIAC AT CENTERPOINT
3600 Centerpoint Parkway, Pontiac, 248-253-9800,
800-228-9290; www.marriott.com

This Marriott hotel is a peaceful place to stay that is virtually in the middle of everything the Detroit area has to offer, including Somerset mall, Ford Field and Palace of Auburn Hills. Guest rooms are standard but spacious, with queen- or king-sized beds and ergonomic work areas. The outdoor pool is a welcome spot during warmer months.

295 rooms. Restaurant. Pool. $151-250

ROCHESTER
★★★ROYAL PARK HOTEL
600 E. University Drive, Rochester, 248-652-2600;
www.royalparkhotel.net

This luxurious boutique hotel, just 30 minutes from Detroit, is a modern homage to the English manor

---

WHICH ARE THE BEST BOUTIQUE HOTELS?

Royal Park Hotel:
This hotel is like a modern English manor. It even has a European-built glass conservatory. Rooms have similar Old World touches, like four-poster beds, but they also have oversized seven-foot beds, soaking tubs and heated bathroom floors.

The Townsend Hotel:
The Townsend is considered to be one of the top hotels in the area. It exudes European elegance with chandeliers and fresh flowers in the lobby. The rooms are more relaxed, with flat-screen TVs, marble bathrooms and terry robes and slippers.

style. Attention to detail is found throughout, from the glass conservatory to the four-poster beds in some rooms and suites. The onsite Brookshire Restaurant offers dishes like pappardelle with baby spinach, wild mushrooms and puttanesca, or cedar plank Arctic char with roma tomato gratin and asparagus.

143 rooms. Restaurant, bar. $251-350

WHERE TO EAT

ALLEN PARK

★★★MORO'S

6535 Allen Road, Allen Park, 313-382-7152; www.morosdining.com

Veal is on the star of the menu at this restaurant, with cuts coming straight from the onsite butcher. Many dishes are prepared tableside, and due to popular demand, the menu never changes. Since opening in 1980, this romantic spot has seen many marriage proposals. It is the perfect setting, after all—dim lighting, a small fireplace, dark wood, brick walls and a singing waiter who performs mid-week from September to May.

International. Lunch, dinner. Closed Sunday June-August. $16-35

ANN ARBOR

★★★BELLA CIAO

118 W. Liberty St., Ann Arbor, 734-995-2107; www.bellaciao.com

This quaint eatery radiates a romantic feeling. The inviting interior includes brick walls and colorful, intriguing art. The menu changes monthly and incorporates seasonal, fresh ingredients into dishes, such as pancetta-wrapped shrimp with lemon-sautéed spinach and grilled polenta or roasted Amish chicken with fresh artichokes and caramelized lemons.

Italian. Dinner. Reservations recommended. Outdoor seating. Bar. $36-85

★★★THE GANDY DANCER

401 Depot St., Ann Arbor, 734-769-0592; www.muer.com

Locals consider this one of the most romantic restaurants in the area. The grand yet intimate atmosphere owes its splendor to the Michigan Central Depot Station, from which it was converted in 1969. The building was originally constructed of granite in 1886 and has two massive stone arches, one of which is in the main entry. Seafood is the main focus, but appealing nonfish options are available, such as the Cajun chicken tortellini and London broil.

American, seafood. Lunch, dinner, Sunday brunch. Reservations recommended. Outdoor seating. Children's menu. Bar. $36-85

RECOMMENDED

ZINGERMAN'S DELI

422 Detroit St., Ann Arbor, 734-663-3354; www.zingermansdeli.com

Known by foodies all over, this Ann Arbor institution is the place to go to on game days—or any day—for the gigantic sandwiches and wonderful artisanal products. This is not your average deli. For one, in taste tests, top chefs including Mario Batali have given their vote to Zingerman's corned beef. The deli also makes wonderful fresh breads and has a fantastic array of farmhouse cheese. Of course, there are all kinds of other goodies, including the famous magic brownies, cakes, pies, cookies and rugelach. If you like something, you can sign up for one of their food on the month clubs.

Deli. Breakfast, lunch, dinner. $15 and under

BIRMINGHAM
★★★FORTÉ
201 S. Old Woodward Ave., Birmingham, 248-594-7300; www.forterestaurant.com

This see-and-be-seen restaurant is in the heart of upscale Birmingham and next to the Downtown Theatre. The tastefully decorated space features lavender ceilings, ocean-blue walls, distinctive light fixtures, rich upholstery accents and two giant framed mirrors in the main dining room. The open kitchen allows diners to watch executive chef Rich Travis create dishes such as butternut squash risotto, short ribs and soy-wasabi-marinated yellowfin tuna.

International. Lunch, dinner. Reservations recommended. Bar. $36-85

★★★RUGBY GRILLE
Townsend Hotel, 100 Townsend St., Birmingham, 248-642-5999; www.townsendhotel.com

Located in the European-style Townsend Hotel, this internationally inspired restaurant offers a dinner menu filled with fine steak and chops, fresh seafood and housemade pastas. Breakfast and lunch are also available. The elegant dining room is decorated with an abundance of fresh flowers, cherry wood walls and a cozy fireplace, making it the perfect choice for a special-occasion meal.

International. Breakfast, lunch, dinner. Reservations recommended. Children's menu. Bar. $36-85

BLOOMFIELD HILLS
★★★★THE LARK
6430 Farmington Road, West Bloomfield, 248-661-4466; www.thelark.com

Dining at the Lark is like escaping to a quiet European hideaway. The room—a beautiful space with Portuguese-style tile murals and a trellised terrace—is warm and welcoming. The ambitious menu features classics like lobster Thermidor, as well as hearty dishes like rack of lamb Genghis and Chinese oven-roasted duck with figs, dates, almonds and brandy. The world-class wine list fits the seasonal, modern French-influenced menu like a glove. The Lark is also known for its dessert trolley,

---

WHAT'S THE TOP CLASSIC RESTAURANT?

The Lark:
This longtime restaurant brightens up its dining room with lots of paintings and Portuguese-style tile murals. The food is classic all the way: Dishes like lobster Thermidor get whipped up by chef John Somerville, a cheftestant on *Top Chef* season seven.

loaded with every kind of cake, tart, cookie and pastry imaginable.

French. Dinner. Closed Sunday-Monday. Reservations recommended. Outdoor seating. Jacket required. Bar. $36-85

FARMINGTON HILLS
★★★TRIBUTE

31425 W. 12 Mile Road, Farmington Hills, 248-848-9393; www.tributerestaurant.com

This Asian-inspired, contemporary international restaurant attracts a moneyed suburban Detroit crowd. The industrial building and luxuriously whimsical dining room are the property of Lawrence Wisne, a Detroit automotive-industry millionaire whose lavish investment has put this interactive, guest-driven restaurant on the nation's culinary map. Although diners can order à la carte, there are several seven-course menus available and a 21-course menu for those with an adventurous palate. The extensive wine list of more than 2,200 labels gives you plenty of choices. For a romantic night out, make reservations for the chef's table in the kitchen.

International. Dinner. Closed Sunday-Monday. Reservations recommended. Bar. $36-85

WARREN
★★★ANDIAMO ITALIA

7096 E. 14 Mile Road, Warren, 586-268-3200; www.andiamoitalia.com

This family-owned, authentic Italian restaurant is very popular among locals (there are several other locations around the Detroit area), and it is usually a busy, lively place every night of the week. The main dining room's ceiling mural at this location creates an open, airy feeling, which makes for an ideal setting to enjoy the made-from-scratch fare that includes several good pasta dishes and fresh vegetables for sides. You can also choose a complementary wine from the extensive list. If you become a regular, you could get a personal cellar with an engraved nameplate.

Italian. Lunch, dinner. Reservations recommended. Bar. $16-35

UPPER PENINSULA

When you need to get away from it all, Michigan's Upper Peninsula can help. The remote U.P. offers a rustic, outdoorsy retreat, whether you go for a peaceful walk in one of the many forests or hit the mountains for some skiing.

Active types hit Houghton Lake. The area is best known for its fishing, including ice fishing in winter. It's also become popular among snowmobilers because of the heavy snowfall that accumulates in the middle portion of the Lower Peninsula.

Skiing is the basis of Ishpeming's recreation and tourism business. In 1887, three Norwegians formed a ski club in Ishpeming. That ski club eventually became the U.S. Ski Association, which hosts the National Ski Hall of Fame and Ski Museum, located here. The national ski jumping championships are held in Ishpeming annually.

Mackinac Island will ensure you're road rage-free because cars aren't allowed here—leaving horse-drawn carriages and bicycles as the chief modes of transportation. In view of the five-mile-long Mackinac Bridge, the largest expansion bridge in the world, it has been a famous resort area for the last century. Southern planters and their families summered here prior to the Civil War; wealthy Chicagoans took their place in the years following. Today, the island remains the home of the governor's summer mansion, where a long line of Michigan's top leaders have spent at least a portion of their vacations.

Located at the north end of the Mackinac Bridge, across the Straits of Mackinac from Mackinaw City, St. Ignace is the gateway to Michigan's Upper Peninsula, which offers beautiful scenery and vast opportunities for outdoor recreation.

Mackinaw City has the distinction of being the only place in America where one can see the sun rise on one Great Lake (Huron) and set on another (Michigan). It sits in the shadow of the five-mile-long Mackinac Bridge. But the area isn't only the gateway to the island, but a shopping destination.

The largest city in the Upper Peninsula, Marquette is the regional center for retailing, government, medicine and iron ore shipping. Miles of public beaches and picnic areas flank the dock areas on Lake Superior.

Located in the middle of the eastern Upper Peninsula, Newberry is centrally located to all of the U.P.'s attractions: Lake Superior, Tahquamenon Falls, Paradise and Whitefish Bay, Pictured Rocks and the Hiawatha National Forest. Enjoy hunting in the fall, a range of sports in winter and fishing and blueberry picking in summer.

Ontonagon is a beautiful, sleepy town on the shores of Lake Superior that is unspoiled by tourists. Its quaint drawbridge stops traffic every now and then, but the pace of this town is so slow, you'll hardly notice. The reason to visit is Porcupine Mountains, which have rugged hiking trails that reward you with breathtaking mountaintop views.

WHAT TO SEE

COPPER HARBOR

BROCKWAY MOUNTAIN DRIVE
Highways 41 and 26, Copper Harbor
Take this scenic drive and stop at the lookouts for views of Lake Superior and thick forests.

COPPER HARBOR LIGHTHOUSE TOUR
Copper Harbor Marina, 326 Shelden Ave., Houghton, 906-289-4966; www.copperharborlighthouse.com
Hop on a 20-minute boat ride to one of the oldest lighthouses on Lake Superior. The ticket includes a guided tour of lighthouse.
Admission: adults $16, children $11. June-mid-October, daily, weather permitting.

DELAWARE MINE TOUR
7804 Delaware Mine Road, Copper Harbor, 906-289-4688; www.copperharbor.org
This guided tour will take you through the underground copper mine dating back to the 1850s and teach you about the people who mined its ore.
June-August 10 a.m.-6 p.m., September-October 10 a.m.-5 p.m.

FERRY SERVICE TO ISLE ROYALE NATIONAL PARK
60 Fifth St., Houghton, 906-482-0984; www.nps.gov
Four ferries and a floatplane provide transportation to the park.
Admission: varies. June-September, daily; some trips in May.

HIGHLIGHT

WHAT ARE THE TOP THINGS TO DO IN THE UPPER PENINSULA?

SKI COOPER PEAK

If you want to take ski jumping to the extreme, lug your gear over to Cooper Peak for some ski flying. As the only ski flying facility in North America, it's a great spot to try the sport, which allows you to soar farther than 500 feet.

EXPLORE PORCUPINE MOUNTAINS WILDERNESS STATE PARK

At this mountainous state park, you might spot otters, bears, coyotes and bald eagles. But don't forget to stop and appreciate the beautiful surroundings, which include scenic overlooks and waterfalls.

SMELL THE ROSES AT DOW GARDENS

These lovely gardens have towering trees, tons of flowers, trickling streams and waterfalls spread amid the 110-acre grounds. In the Children's Garden, kids can hang out in a treehouse.

HIKE HIAWATHA NATIONAL FOREST

At the 893,000-acre forest, you have your choice of outdoorsy activities: camping, hiking, horseback riding, cross-country skiing, snowmobiling, fishing, swimming, sailing and canoeing. The list goes on and on.

VISIT MACKINAC ISLAND STATE PARK

This park makes up 80 percent of rural Mackinac Island. The peaceful escape also offers vistas of the straits of Mackinac, prehistoric geological formations and a number of trails.

FORT WILKINS STATE PARK

Highway 41, Copper Harbor, 906-289-4215; www.michigan.gov

The 200-acre park contains a historic army post completed in 1844 on Lake Fanny Hooe and one of the first lighthouses built on Lake Superior from 1866. The stockade has been restored and the buildings preserved to maintain the frontier post atmosphere. Costumed guides demonstrate the old army lifestyle. If that's not the life for you, try your hand at fishing, boating, cross-country skiing and camping. A museum on the grounds has relics of early mining days and various exhibits depicting army life in the 1870s.

Daily.

ISLE ROYALE QUEEN III EVENING CRUISES
Copper Harbor, 906-289-4437; www.isleroyale.com

See the sun set aboard this ship during a narrated one-hour cruise on Lake Superior. Reservations are recommended.

Admission: adults $20, seniors $18, children 5-14 $15, children 4 and under free. Early July-late August, Monday, Wednesday, Friday, Saturday, times vary.

SNOWMOBILING
326 Shelden Ave., Houghton, 906-482-2388

There is a series of interconnecting snowmobiling trails totaling several hundred miles; some overlook Lake Superior from high bluffs. There's also 17 miles of cross-country trails.

December-March.

ESCANABA
HIAWATHA NATIONAL FOREST
2727 N. Lincoln Road, Escanaba, 906-786-4062; www.fs.fed.us

This 893,000-acre forest offers scenic drives, hunting, camping, picnicking, hiking, horseback riding, cross-country skiing, snowmobiling, winter sports, lake and stream fishing, swimming, sailing, motorboating and canoeing. It has shoreline on three Great Lakes—Huron, Michigan and Superior. The eastern section of the forest is close to Sault Ste. Marie, St. Ignace and the northern foot of the Mackinac Bridge.

Daily.

HOUGHTON
A.E. SEAMAN MINERALOGICAL MUSEUM
Electrical Energy Resources Center, 1400 Townsend Drive, Houghton, 906-487-2572;
www.museum.mtu.edu

The museum exhibits one of the nation's best mineral collections.

Admission: free. Monday-Friday 9 a.m.-4:30 p.m., Saturday noon-4 p.m.

MONT RIPLEY SKI AREA
1400 Townsend Drive, Houghton, 906-487-2340; www.aux.mtu.edu

Mont Ripley has a double chairlift, a T-bar, a patrol, a school, rentals and snow-making.

Early December-late March, daily.

HOUGHTON LAKE
HIGGINS LAKE
Houghton Lake

One of the most beautiful in America, crystal-clear Higgins Lake covers 10,317 acres and has 25 miles of sandy shoreline.

HOUGHTON LAKE
Houghton Lake

This is the largest inland lake in Michigan and the source of the Muskegon River. This lake has a 32-mile shoreline and 22,000 acres of water, as well as 200 miles of groomed and marked snowmobile trails. A variety of resorts are in the area.

IRONWOOD

BIG POWDERHORN MOUNTAIN

Powderhorn Road, Bessemer, 906-932-4838, 800-501-7669; www.bigpowderhorn.net

Big Powderhorn has nine double chairlifts, a patrol, a school, rentals, three restaurants, a cafeteria, three bars and a nursery. Among its 25 runs, the longest is one mile with a vertical drop of 600 feet.

Thanksgiving-early April, daily 9 a.m.-4 p.m.

BLACKJACK

Blackjack Road, Bessemer, 906-229-5115, 800-848-1125; www.skiblackjack.com

Here, you'll find four double chairlifts, two rope tows, a patrol, a school and rentals. The longest run is a mile with a vertical drop of 465 feet.

November-March, daily.

COPPER PEAK SKI FLYING

Copper Peak Road, Ironwood, 906-932-3500; www.copperpeak.org

Copper Peak is the only ski-flying facility in North America and one of six in the world. Athletes test their skills in an event that requires more athletic ability than ski jumping. Skiers reach speeds of more than 60 miles per hour and fly farther than 500 feet. An international tournament is held every winter. In the summer, chairlift and elevator rides take you 240 feet above the crest of Copper Peak for a view of three states, Lake Superior and Canada.

Mid-June-Labor Day, daily; September-October, weekends.

HIAWATHA: WORLD'S TALLEST INDIAN

Houk Street, Ironwood

This statue of the famous Iroquois stands 52 feet high and looks north to the legendary "shining big-sea-water"—Gitchee Gumee, otherwise known as Lake Superior.

LITTLE GIRL'S POINT PARK

104 S. Lowell St., Ironwood, 906-932-1420; www.gogebic.org

This park is notable for the agate pebbles on its beaches. There are picnic tables, campsites and Native American burial grounds on the premises as well.

May-September.

MOUNT ZION

4946 Jackson Road, Ironwood, 906-932-3718

This is one of the highest points on the Gogebic Range, located 1,150 feet above Lake Superior. It has a double chairlift, two rope tows, a patrol, a school and rentals. The longest run has a vertical drop of 300 feet. There are also two miles of cross-country ski trails.

Mid-December-March, Tuesday-Sunday.

OTTAWA NATIONAL FOREST

2100 E. Cloverland Drive, Ironwood, 906-932-1330; www.fs.fed.us

This national forest includes wooded hills, picturesque lakes and streams, waterfalls, a nursery, harbor, scenic trails and more.

Daily.

ISHPEMING
NATIONAL SKI AND SNOWBOARD HALL OF FAME AND MUSEUM
610 Palms Ave., Ishpeming, 906-485-6323; www.skihall.com

Affiliated with the U.S. Ski Association, this museum houses national trophies and displays of old skis and ski equipment, and it includes a replica of the oldest-known ski and ski pole in the world. The Roland Palmedo National Ski Library maintains a collection of ski publications.

Admission: free. Monday-Saturday 10 a.m.-5 p.m.

SUICIDE BOWL
Ishpeming, 906-485-4242

If the name doesn't scare you off, bring your skis to the Suicide Bowl trails so that you can try your luck on five ski-jumping hills from a mini-hill to a 70-meter hill. There are also four cross-country trails; one is lighted for evening use.

VAN RIPER STATE PARK
851 County Road AKE, Champion, 906-339-4461; www.michigan.gov

Van Riper sits on approximately 1,000 acres along Lake Michigamme. It offers swimming, waterskiing, a bathhouse, fishing, boating, hunting, hiking, picnic grounds and camping.

Daily.

MACKINAC ISLAND
ARNOLD MACKINAC ISLAND FERRY
Mackinac Island, 906-847-3351, 800-542-8528; www.arnoldline.com

The company's large, fast ferries travel from Mackinaw City and St. Ignace to Mackinac Island.

May-December, daily.

FORT MACKINAC
7127 Huron Road, Mackinac Island, 906-847-3328; www.mackinacparks.com

High on a bluff overlooking the Straits of Mackinac, this 18th- and 19th-century British and American military outpost has massive limestone ramparts, a cannon, a guardhouse, blockhouses, barracks, costumed interpreters and reenactments.

Mid-May-mid-October, daily.

INDIAN DORMITORY
Mackinac Island

Built in 1838 as a place for Native Americans to live during annual visits to the Mackinac Island office of the U.S. Indian Agency, this dormitory includes interpretive displays, craft demonstrations and murals depicting scenes from Longfellow's *Hiawatha*.

Mid-June-Labor Day, daily.

MACKINAC ISLAND STATE PARK
300 S. Washington Square, Mackinac Island, 906-847-3328; www.mackinacparks.com

This park comprises approximately 80 percent of the island. Michigan's first state park has views of the straits of Mackinac; prehistoric geological formations, such as Arch Rock; and shoreline and inland trails. The visitors center at Huron Street has informative exhibits and guidebooks (mid-May-mid-October, daily). Be sure to check out Marquette Park *(401 E. Fair Ave.)* within the State Park. It features more than 60 varieties of lilacs.

SHEPLER'S MACKINAC ISLAND FERRY
556 E. Central Ave., Mackinaw City, 231-436-5023; www.sheplersferry.com

This ferry departs from 556 E. Central Ave., Mackinaw City, or from downtown St. Ignace.

Early May-early November.

STAR LINE FERRY
587 N. State St., St. Ignace, 906-643-7635, 800-638-9892; www.mackinacferry.com

This Mackinac Island ferry company provides Hydro Jet service from Mackinaw City and St. Ignace.

May-October.

MACKINAW CITY
COLONIAL MICHILIMACKINAC
102 E. Straits Ave., Mackinaw City, 231-436-5563; www.mackinacparks.com

At this reconstructed French and British outpost and fur-trading village, costumed interpreters provide music and military demonstrations, pioneer cooking and crafts, children's programs and reenactments.

MACKINAC BRIDGE
Mackinaw City

This imposing structure has reduced crossing time to the Upper Peninsula over the Straits of Mackinac to 10 minutes. It connects Michigan's upper and lower peninsulas between St. Ignace and Mackinaw City. The 8,344-foot distance between cable anchorages makes it one of the world's longest suspension bridges. The total length of the steel superstructure is 19,243 feet. The height above water at midspan is 199 feet and clearance for ships is 155 feet.

MILL CREEK
9001 S. Highway 23, Mackinaw City, 231-436-7301; www.mackinacparks.com

This scenic 625-acre park features working water-powered sawmill from 1790, nature trails, forest demonstration areas, a maple sugar shack, and more. Sawmill demonstrations take place between mid-June-Labor Day, Monday-Friday. Stop by the visitors center for information.

Mid-May-mid-October, daily.

WILDERNESS STATE PARK
903 E. Wilderness Park Drive, Carp Lake, 231-436-5381, 800-447-2757; www.wildernessstatepark.net

Set on approximately 8,200 acres, the park offers beaches, waterskiing, fishing, boating, seasonal hunting, snowmobiling, cross-country skiing, picnic areas and playgrounds. Trailside cabins and camping are also available.

MARQUETTE
MARQUETTE MOUNTAIN SKI AREA
4501 County Road, Marquette, 906-225-1155, 800-944-7669; www.marquettemountain.com

The ski area has three double chairlifts, a rope tow, a patrol, a school, rentals, snowmaking, night skiing, weekly NASTAR, a cafeteria, a bar and a nursery. The longest run is one mile with a vertical drop of 600 feet.

Late November-April, daily 9:30 a.m.-5 p.m. Cross-country trails (three miles) nearby.

PRESQUE ISLE PARK

Lakeshore Boulevard, Marquette, 906-228-0460

The park has picnic facilities, four picnic sites for the disabled, and swimming. A bog walk in Presque Isle Park features a 4,000-foot trail with plank walkways and observation decks

May-October, daily; rest of year, open only for winter sports.

SUGAR LOAF MOUNTAIN

County 550, Marquette

A 3,200-foot trail leads to the summit for a panoramic view of the Lake Superior coastline and forestland.

UPPER PENINSULA CHILDREN'S MUSEUM

123 W. Baraga Ave., Marquette, 906-226-3911, 888-590-8726; www.upcmkids.org

All exhibits at this museum are products of kids' imaginations; regional youth planned their conceptual development. Kids can pilot a plane and talk to air-traffic control in the "Over the Air" exhibit or check out an engine in "The Cloverland Car Garage."

Admission: adults and children $5, infants free. Monday-Wednesday 10 a.m.-6 p.m., Thursday 10 a.m.-7:30 p.m., Friday 10 a.m.-8 p.m., Saturday 10 a.m.-6 p.m., Sunday noon-5 p.m.

MENOMINEE

FIRST STREET HISTORIC DISTRICT

10th Avenue, Menominee

The historical district offers a variety of specialty shops in a setting of restored 19th-century buildings. There's also a marina, parks, restaurants and galleries.

HENES PARK

Henes Park Drive and Third Street, Menominee, 906-863-2656; www.cityofmenominee.org

This small zoo has deer yards, nature trails, a bathing beach and a picnic area.

Memorial Day-mid October, daily.

J.W. WELLS STATE PARK

N7670 Highway 35, Cedar River, 906-863-9747; www.michigan.gov

The park spans approximately 700 acres, including two miles along Green Bay and 1,400 feet along Big Cedar River. It has swimming, a bathhouse, water-skiing, fishing, boating (ramp), hunting, snowmobiling, cross-country skiing, picnicking, a playground, camping, cabins and shelters.

MENOMINEE MARINA

Doyle Drive, Menominee, 906-863-8498; www.menomineemarina.com

The marina is one of the best small-craft anchorages on the Great Lakes. There's a swimming beach and lifeguard on duty.

May-October, daily.

STEPHENSON ISLAND
Menominee

You can reach this island via a bridge that also carries traffic between the sister cities on Highway 41. On the island are picnic areas and the Marinette County Historical Museum.

MIDLAND
ARCHITECTURAL TOUR
315 Post St., Midland, 989-839-2744; www.abdow.org

Go on a self-guided driving tour of buildings designed by Alden B. Dow, son of Herbert H. Dow. The younger Dow studied under Frank Lloyd Wright at Taliesin. He designed more than 45 buildings in Midland, including the architect's house and studio, churches, Stein House (his Taliesin apprentice project) and Whitman House, for which he won the 1937 Grand Prix for residential architecture. Many buildings are privately owned and not open to the public.

CHIPPEWA NATURE CENTER
400 S. Badour Road, Midland, 989-631-0830; www.chippewanaturecenter.com

On more than 1,000 acres, the nature center has 14 miles of marked and mowed trails, a wildflower walkway and pond boardwalk, a reconstructed 1870s log cabin, a barn, a sugarhouse, a one-room schoolhouse, a visitors center, a museum depicting evolutionary natural history of the Saginaw Valley, an auditorium and a library.
Daily.

DOW GARDENS
1809 Eastman Ave., Midland, 989-631-2677, 800-362-4874; www.dowgardens.org

These gardens, originally the grounds of the residence of Herbert H. Dow, founder of the Midland-based Dow Chemical Company, include 110 acres of trees, flowers, streams and waterfalls, as well as a greenhouse and conservatory.
Admission: adults $5, children 6-17 $1. Tours by appointment. Daily 9 a.m.-dusk.

MIDLAND CENTER FOR THE ARTS
1801 W. St. Andrews, Midland, 989-631-5930; www.mcfta.org

This center houses the Alden B. Dow Museum of Science and Art, which features temporary exhibits and includes the "Hall of Ideas," a permanent interactive exhibit. It also hosts concerts and plays. The Dow architectural tour begins here.
Admission: adults $8, children 4-14 $5, children 3 and under free. Tuesday-Saturday 10 a.m.-6 p.m., Sunday noon-6 p.m.

NEWBERRY
LUCE COUNTY HISTORICAL MUSEUM
411 W. Harrie St., Newberry, 906-293-5946; www.exploringthenorth.com

This restored Queen Anne structure, completed in 1894, has stone on the lower portion that is Marquette or Jacobsville sandstone, some of the oldest rock in the country. Originally a sheriff's residence and jail, it was saved from razing and is now a museum. The stateroom fireplace is original; many of the rooms have been refurbished to hold records, books and other artifacts; jail cells are still intact.
Admission: free. Tuesday-Thursday 2-4 p.m.

SENEY NATIONAL WILDLIFE REFUGE
Highway 77, Seney, 906-586-9851; www.fws.gov

On 95,455 acres, this wildlife refuge is home to Canada geese, bald eagles, sandhill cranes, loons, deer, beavers, otters and several species of ducks. The visitors center has exhibits, films and information on wildlife observation. You can do some fishing, picnicking and limited hunting on the grounds.
Mid-May-September, daily.

ONTONAGON
PORCUPINE MOUNTAINS WILDERNESS STATE PARK
412 S. Boundry Road, Ontonagon, 906-885-5275; www.michigan.gov

This 63,000-acre forested, mountainous semi-wilderness area harbors otters, bears, coyotes, bald eagles and many other species. There are many streams and lakes with fishing for bass, perch and trout; boating (launch); hunting in season for grouse, deer and bear; downhill and cross-country skiing and snow-mobiling; hiking trails with overnight rustic cabins (reservations available) and shelters; and scenic overlooks, waterfalls and abandoned mine sites.
Daily.

SAULT STE. MARIE
THE HAUNTED DEPOT
317 W. Portage Ave., Sault Ste. Marie, 906-635-0093

Guided tours take you through the depot's many unusual chambers. You can "fall uphill" in the mystery bedroom, walk through a "storm" in the cemetery or "lose your heads" at the guillotine.
June-October, daily.

SOO LOCKS
119 Park Place, Sault Ste. Marie, 906-632-3311

The famous locks can be seen from both the upper and lower parks, which parallel them. The upper park has three observation towers. There is a scale model of the locks at the east end of the MacArthur Lock and a working lock model, photos and a movie in the visitor building in the upper park.
March-February, daily.

SOO LOCKS BOAT TOURS
515 and 1157 E. Portage Ave., Sault Ste. Marie, 906-632-6301; www.soolocks.com

Two-hour narrated excursions travel through the Soo Locks, focusing on their history. Sunset dinner cruises, which last about two hours, are available. Reservations are suggested.
Mid-May-mid-October, daily.

TOWER OF HISTORY
326 E. Portage Ave., Sault Ste. Marie, 906-632-3658, 888-744-7867; www.thevalleycamp.com

The 21-story observation tower has a 20-mile view of Canadian and various American cities. There's a show in the lobby as well as displays.
Admission: adults $6.50, children 6-17 $3.25. Mid-May-mid-October, daily 10 a.m.-6 p.m.

SPECIAL EVENTS

ARTS AND CRAFTS DOCKSIDE AND ST. IGNACE POWWOW

560 N. State St., St. Ignace, 906-643-8717; www.saintignace.org
A juried arts and crafts show is held each year in conjunction with the Bridge Walk. It features a traditional Native American powwow as part of the festivities.
Labor Day weekend.

MACKINAC BRIDGE WALK

1213 Center St., St. Ignace, 517-347-7891, 800-434-8642; www.michiganfitness.org
This is the only day of the year when walking across the bridge is permitted—don't worry, some lanes will be open to motor vehicles. Michigan's governor leads the walk, which begins in St. Ignace at 7 a.m., on the north side of the bridge, and ends in Mackinaw City, on the south side. Buses return you to your starting point.
Labor Day.

MACKINAW MUSH SLED DOG RACE

Mackinaw City, 231-436-5574; www.mackinawchamber.com
Dogs have been mushing at this sled race for more than 20 years. It's the biggest dog-sled competition in the contiguous United States.
First week in February.

TWIN SOO TOUR

315-317 W. Portage Ave., Sault Ste. Marie, 906-635-5241
Two- to four-hour guided tours lead you to both Canadian and American cities of Sault Ste. Marie and provides a view of Soo Locks. You may disembark in Canada.
June-October, daily.

SOO JUNCTION
TOONERVILLE TROLLEY AND RIVERBOAT TRIP TO TAHQUAMENON FALLS

Soo Junction Road, Soo Junction, 906-876-2311, 888-778-7246; www.superiorsights.com
Take a narrated six-hour, 53-mile round-trip jaunt through the Tahquamenon region on a narrow-gauge railroad and riverboat, with a one-hour stop at Upper Tahquamenon Falls. The trolley leaves Soo Junction (mid-June-early October, daily). There's also an hour-long train tour.
Admission: adults $45, seniors $42.50, children 9-15 $29, children 4-8 $20, children 3 and under free. July-August, Tuesday-Saturday.

ST. IGNACE

CASTLE ROCK

Castle Rock Road, St. Ignace, Mackinac Bridge, 906-643-8268; www.stignace.com

Climb the 170 steps to the top of this 200-foot-high rock to see excellent views of Mackinac Island and Lake Huron. At the foot of Castle Rock, you'll find statues of Paul Bunyan and Babe, the blue ox.

Daily.

FATHER MARQUETTE NATIONAL MEMORIAL

St. Ignace, adjacent to Mackinac Bridge Authority Plaza

This 52-acre memorial pays tribute to the life and work of the famed Jesuit explorer who came to area in the 1600s.

MARQUETTE MISSION PARK AND MUSEUM OF OJIBWA CULTURE

500 N. State St., St. Ignace, 906-643-9161

Here lies the gravesite of Father Marquette. There's also a museum that interprets 17th-century Native American life and the coming of the French.

Memorial Day-Labor Day, daily; after Labor Day-September, Tuesday-Saturday.

WAKEFIELD

INDIANHEAD MOUNTAIN-BEAR CREEK SKI RESORT

500 Indianhead Road, Wakefield, 906-229-5181, 800-346-3426; www.indianheadmtn.com

The resort has a quad, a triple, three double chairlifts, a Pomalift, two T-bars, a beginner's lift, a patrol, a school, rentals and snowmaking. The longest run is one mile with a vertical drop of 638 feet.

November-mid-April, daily.

WHERE TO STAY

MACKINAC ISLAND

★★★GRAND HOTEL

1 Grand Ave., Mackinac Island, 906-847-3331, 800-334-7263; www.grandhotel.com

The hotel, an island landmark built in 1887, sits regally on a bluff overlooking the Straits of Mackinac. Sit in one of the giant rocking chairs on the longest front porch in America and watch the Great Lake freighters glide by. Presidents Clinton, Bush, Ford, Kennedy and Truman have visited the hotel. The interior is traditionally decorated, but no two rooms are alike. You'll see lots of geraniums incorporated into the décor—the geranium is the official hotel flower, as it has grown on the front porch since the 1920s. The hotel offers a variety of shops, afternoon tea and carriage rentals.

385 rooms. Restaurant, bar. Golf. Tennis. Closed December-mid-May. $351 and up

★★★HOTEL IROQUOIS ON THE BEACH

298 Main St., Mackinac Island, 906-847-3321; www.iroquoishotel.com

This Victorian hotel was originally built in 1902 as a private residence. Run by the McIntire family since 1954, the hotel offers guest rooms and suites at a lakefront location on the Straits of Mackinac at the confluence of Lakes Michigan and Huron. Enjoy fine dining at the Carriage House or a drink at the Piano Bar.

46 rooms. Restaurant, bar. Beach. Closed November-April. $251-350

★★★ISLAND HOUSE

6966 Main St., Mackinac Island, 906-847-3347, 800-626-6304; www.theislandhouse.com

The Island House, built in 1852, is Mackinac Island's oldest operating hotel. After a short ferry ride to the island, guests are welcomed to the hotel with the aroma of fresh-baked cookies. Each guest room is decorated differently, but expect to see floral patterns and sunny pastels. The 1852 Grill Room offers delicious dining, in case you need something more than those check-in cookies to tide you over. The lovely front porch offers a quiet spot to take in the view.

93 rooms. Restaurant, bar. Complimentary breakfast. Closed mid-October-mid-May. $151-250

★★★MISSION POINT RESORT

1 Lakeshore Drive, Mackinac Island, 906-847-3312, 800-833-7711; www.missionpoint.com

This luxurious getaway looks and feels like a country inn, yet it operates with the amenities and services of a full-fledged resort. You are greeted at the ferry dock and taken via horse-drawn carriage to the resort. The guest rooms are decorated with nautical, lodge and northern Michigan themes and have garden, forest or Lake Huron views. Activities abound, from an 18-hole putting green to bicycle rentals to hayrides, bocce ball and lawn bowling. In summer, the turn-of-the-20th-century movie theater shows first-run and classic films on Monday evenings. The seven-story-high Tower Museum offers historical information on the resort, the island and the straits and Great Lakes ships. The resort's four restaurants attract diners with casual fare and friendly service.

242 rooms. Restaurant, bar. Pool. Closed November-late December. $251-350

WHERE TO EAT

RECOMMENDED
COPPER HARBOR

HARBOR HAUS

77 Brockway Ave., Copper Harbor, 906-289-4502; www.harborhaus.com

It's hard to get a bad seat in the Harbor Haus. The restaurant, set inside a bed and breakfast, has big picture windows that overlook Lake Superior. The menu changes daily, but you can count on appetizers like foie gras and grilled bison sausage and entrees like jager schnitzel with spätzle. If your server disappears around 6 or 6:30 p.m., look through those windows and you'll probably see him dancing on the restaurant's patio. It's a nightly tradition welcoming passengers aboard the Isle Royale Queen who are coming from Isle Royale National Park, so you'll get dinner and a show.

German. Lunch, dinner. $16-35

MACKINAC ISLAND

1852 GRILL ROOM

Island House, 6966 Main St., Mackinac Island, 906-847-3347, 800-626-6304; www.theislandhouse.com

You'll get a waterfront view with your prime rib at this restaurant, which is inside the Island House hotel. The menu is upscale, though you will find housemade potato chips with garlic sea salt and a warm blue cheese dipping sauce among the appetizers. But for the most part, it's meat options here, such as chicken

Mackinac with sautéed mushrooms and onions, double-smoked bacon and Gruyère and Swiss cheeses, or a Lake Michigan perch with dill tartar sauce.

American. Dinner. $16-35

MARQUETTE

SWEET WATER CAFÉ

517 N. Third St., Marquette, 906-226-7009; www.marquettedining.addr.com

Local artists' works adorn the walls of this light wood-filled dining room. Whether you begin or end your day here, you'll be guaranteed hearty fare. For breakfast, you can have smoked whitefish from Lake Superior on oatmeal-wheat bread. At dinner, try the steak sautéed in garlic butter, flamed in whiskey and finished with heavy cream.

American. Breakfast, lunch, dinner. $16-35

WELCOME TO MINNESOTA

ALTHOUGH KNOWN AS THE MOTHER OF the Mississippi, and dotted by more than 4,000 square miles of water surface, Minnesota is not the "Land of 10,000 Lakes" as it so widely advertises—a recount indicates that the figure is closer to 12,000. Minnesotans may tell you that the lakes were stamped out by the hooves of folk hero Paul Bunyan's giant blue ox, Babe; geologists maintain that retreating glaciers during the Ice Age are responsible. In any case, the lakes are certainly one of Minnesota's main draws.

Taking full advantage of all that water is easy: Fish in a lake, canoe in the Boundary Waters along the Canadian border, or search out the Northwest Angle (near Baudette), which is so isolated that until recently it could be reached only by boat or plane. In winter, ice fish, snowmobile or ski the hundreds of miles of downhill and cross-country areas. Meanwhile, Minneapolis and St. Paul—the Twin Cities—offer spectator sports, nightlife, shopping, music, theater and sightseeing.

Explored by Native Americans, fur traders and missionaries since the dawn of its known history, Minnesota surged ahead on the economic tides of lumber, grain and ore. Today, the state has 79,000 farms covering 28 million acres. Agricultural production ranks high in sugar beets, butter, turkeys, sweet corn, soybeans, sunflowers, spring wheat, hogs and peas. Manufacturing is important as well, and the state is a wholesale transportation hub and the financial and retailing center of the Upper Midwest. But you likely know it as a shopping hub; the Mall of America in Bloomington is the country's largest mall. Aside from the massive mall, dense forests, vast grain fields, rich pastures, wilderness parks, outstanding hospitals and universities, high-tech corporations and a thriving arts community make the state a well-rounded destination.

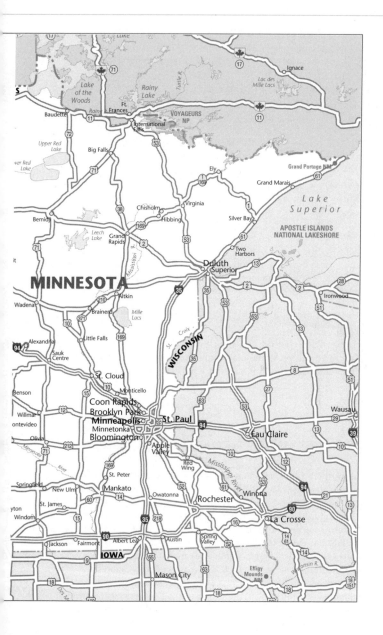

BEST ATTRACTIONS

MINNESOTA'S BEST ATTRACTIONS

BLOOMINGTON

Bloomington's biggest attraction is the massive Mall of America, the largest shopping center in the country. But it also has Valleyfair theme park, the Minnesota Zoo and a wildlife refuge.

DULUTH

When you want to spend time in the great outdoors, head to Duluth. Take in the scenery at Superior National Forest, with 2,000 lakes, rugged shorelines, picturesque islands and deep woods, and Boundary Waters Canoe Area, a great spot for a canoe ride.

MINNEAPOLIS

As the state's urban metropolis, Minneapolis teems with excellent museums, top-notch restaurants and more. Check out art in the Walker Art Center, go to a show in the Guthrie Theater or see the Minnesota Twins play at Target Field.

ST. PAUL

St. Paul rivals its Twin City, Minneapolis, when it comes to leisure pursuits. It has the excellent Minnesota Children's Museum, the Science Museum of Minnesota and Como Park, a zoo, park and conservatory all in one.

NORTHERN MINNESOTA

The northern region of Minnesota is an outdoorsman's playground. The area is home to the state's largest lakes and thick forests, which attract everyone from anglers to hikers. Located at the western tip of Lake Superior, Duluth offers everything from museums to brewpubs, but most visit for its setting. The great Minnesota northwoods begin almost at the city's boundaries, and from here the North Shore Drive follows Lake Superior into Canada. Plus, Superior National Forest and Boundary Waters Canoe Area are found here.

At the head of navigation on the Mississippi River, Grand Rapids was named for nearby waters. For years it served as a center for logging, but paper production and tourism are the principal industries today. The forested area surrounding the town includes more than a thousand lakes. Four of them—Crystal, Hale, Forest and McKinney—are within the city limits.

The tiny town of Kabetogama sits on the shores of deep-blue Kabetogama Lake, which offers more than 500 miles of shoreline and more than 200 small islands. Fishing here is solitary and peaceful, and the waters hold bass, crappies, perch, northern pike, sauger and walleye. In fall, the colors surrounding the lake are spectacular, making it a popular spot for canoeing and kayaking.

Lutsen, situated on Lake Superior and next to Lutsen Mountains, is an outdoors paradise. Visitors can downhill ski, cross-country ski, hike, mountain bike, canoe or kayak, play golf or see fall colors. At Lutsen Mountains' Sawtooth Mountain Park, there's even more to do: glide down an Alpine slide or go on an aerial tram.

Roseau is a snowmobiler's dream. Aside from having a number of snowmobile trails, the city's is the base for Polaris Industries, the first mass producer of snowmobiles. You can tour the leading snowmobile manufacturer's facility.

The region also is known for its animal residents. They get top billing at Thief River Falls, which sits at the confluence of the Thief and Red Lake rivers. The area's biggest attraction is the Agassiz National Wildlife Refuge, which teems with migratory birds and other wildlife. Come outside and see northern Minnesota.

WHAT TO SEE

AITKIN

RICE LAKE NATIONAL WILDLIFE REFUGE
36289 Highway 65, McGregor, 218-768-2402, 800-877-8339; www.fws.gov

An 18,127-acre refuge that includes 4,500-acre Rice Lake, this place has migration and nesting area for ducks and Canada geese along the Mississippi Flyway. Take in the wildlife by walking or driving along the trails. You also can do some fishing in Rice Lake.

Daily.

SAVANNA PORTAGE STATE PARK
55626 Lake Place, McGregor, 218-426-3271; www.dnr.state.mn.us

A 15,818-acre wilderness area built around a historic portage linking the Mississippi River and Lake Superior, the state park has swimming, fishing, boating, canoeing, hiking, cross-country skiing, snowmobiling, picnicking and camping.

DULUTH

AERIAL LIFT BRIDGE
525 Lake Ave. S., Foot of Lake Avenue, Duluth, 218-722-3119; www.duluthshippingnews.com

At 138 feet high, 336 feet long and 900 tons, this bridge connects the mainland with Minnesota Point, lifting 138 feet in less than a minute to let ships pass.

DEPOT, ST. LOUIS COUNTY HERITAGE AND ARTS CENTER
506 W. Michigan St., Duluth, 218-727-8025; www.duluthdepot.org

This building was originally Union Depot, but now houses three museums— including the Lake Superior Railroad Museum and the Duluth Children's Museum—a visual arts institute and four performing arts organizations.

Admission (includes entry to all exhibiting organizations): adults $12, children 3-13 $6, children 2 and under free. Memorial Day-Labor Day, daily 9:30 a.m.-6 p.m.; Labor Day-Memorial Day, daily 10 a.m.-5 p.m.

DULUTH CHILDREN'S MUSEUM

506 W. Michigan St., Duluth, 218-733-7543; www.duluthchildrensmuseum.org.

This museum covers natural, world and cultural history and features a giant walk-through tree in the habitat exhibit. Aspiring little rock stars also can create their own tunes in "Music Alley" or become Bob the Builder by playing with pulleys and conveyer belts in "Little Builders."

Admission (includes entry to all of the Depot's exhibiting organizations): adults $12, children 3-13 $6, children 2 and under free. Memorial Day-Labor Day, daily 9:30 a.m.-6 p.m.; Labor Day-Memorial Day, daily 10 a.m.-5 p.m.

DULUTH LAKEWALK

600 E. Superior St., Duluth, 800-438-5884; www.visitduluth.com

Walk along Lake Superior to the Aerial Lift Bridge and see statues, kiosks and horse and buggy rides along the way.

DULUTH-SUPERIOR EXCURSIONS

323 Harbor Drive, Duluth, 218-722-6218; www.vistafleet.com

This two-hour tour of Duluth-Superior Harbor and Lake Superior takes place on the Vista King and Star.

Mid-May-mid-October, daily.

FITGER'S BREWERY COMPLEX

600 E. Superior St., Duluth, 218-722-8826, 888-348-4377; www.fitgers.com

This historic renovated brewery was transformed into more than 25 specialty shops and restaurants on the shore of Lake Superior. Stores in residence include clothing chain United Colors of Benetton and hip urban footwear shop Shoe Fly. There's also a museum that honors the complex's beer-making past. But for a real taste of its history, order some suds at Fitger's Brewhouse Brewery and Grille.

Monday-Saturday 10 a.m.-9 p.m., Sunday 11 a.m.-5 p.m.

GLENSHEEN

3300 London Road, Duluth, 218-726-8910, 888-454-4536; www.d.umn.edu

This historic 22-acre Great Lake estate on the west shore of Lake Superior is owned by the University of Minnesota. You can tour the 39-room mansion to see the original furnishings as well as the formal gardens, which also stay true to the early design.

Admission for tours: adults $13, seniors and students $12, children 6-12 $7, children 5 and under free. May-October, daily 9:30 a.m.-4 p.m.; November-April, Saturday-Sunday 11 a.m.-2 p.m.

LAKE SUPERIOR MARITIME VISITORS CENTER

600 Lake Ave. S., Duluth, 218-727-2497; www.lsmma.com

At the center, look for ship models, relics of shipwrecks, reconstructed ship cabins and exhibits related to the maritime history of Lake Superior and Duluth Harbor and the Corps of Engineers. Vessel schedules and close-up views of passing ship traffic are also offered.

March 25-late December, daily.

HIGHLIGHT

WHAT ARE THE TOP THINGS TO DO?

ROW YOUR BOAT GENTLY DOWN BOUNDARY WATERS CANOE AREA WILDERNESS

Part of Superior National Forest, Boundary Waters offers more than 1,200 miles of canoe routes. The waterways, which are near the international border, provide a beautiful backdrop to any canoe trip.

GO ON RIDES AT SAWTOOTH MOUNTAIN PARK

This isn't your typical Minnesota park. Sawtooth adds an amusement park element to the rustic setting by offering you the chance to glide down an Alpine slide and take an aerial tram ride above Lake Superior.

SEE WHERE THE WILD THINGS ARE AT AGASSIZ NATIONAL WILDLIFE REFUGE

The 61,500 acres of forest, water and marshland at this wildlife refuge are home to 280 species of migratory birds, wolves, moose and waterfowl. More than 20,000 people visit Agassiz each year.

LAKE SUPERIOR ZOO

72nd Avenue West and Grand Avenue, Duluth, 218-730-4900; www.lszoo.org

This 12-acre zoo has more than 80 exhibits and picnicking. A pack of grey wolves are some of the newest animals to join the zoo. Stop by the popular "Polar Shores" exhibit to play ball with Berlin the polar bear.

Admission: adults $9, children 3-12 $4, children 2 and under free. Late May-August, daily 10 a.m.-5 p.m.; September-late May, daily 10 a.m.-4 p.m.

S.S. WILLIAM A. IRVIN

301 Harbor Drive, Duluth, 218-722-5573; www.williamairvin.com

Enjoy guided tours of the former flagship of the United States Steel's Great Lakes fleet that sailed inland waters from 1938 to 1978. Explore the decks and compartments of the restored 610-foot ore carrier, including the engine room, elaborate guest staterooms, the galley, the pilothouse, the observation lounge and the elegant dining room.

Admission: adults $10, seniors and students $8, children 10 and under free with adult ticket. Daily.

SPIRIT MOUNTAIN SKI AREA

9500 Spirit Mountain Place, Duluth, 218-628-2891, 800-642-6377; www.spiritmt.com

The ski area includes double chairlifts, a ski patrol, a school, rentals and

snowmaking, plus a bar, cafeteria and children's center.
November-March, daily.

SUPERIOR NATIONAL FOREST
8901 Grand Ave Place, Duluth; www.fs.fed.us

With more than 2,000 beautiful clear lakes, rugged shorelines, picturesque islands and deep woods, this park covers a magnificent portion of Minnesota's famous northern area. Inside the forest, you'll find Boundary Waters Canoe Area Wilderness, whose scenic water routes near the international border offer opportunities for adventure. It's a great place to paddle; the BWCAW provides more than 1,200 miles of canoe routes. The 1.3 million-acre spot also has 11 hiking trails and 2,000 campsites. If you want to visit, be sure to apply for a permit beforehand; it's required for entry.

GRAND PORTAGE

FERRY SERVICE TO ISLE ROYALE NATIONAL PARK
White Bear Lake, Grand Portage, 715-392-2100, 888-746-2305; www.grand-isle-royale.com

From Grand Portage, there is passenger ferry service to Isle Royale National Park within Michigan state waters. Rates vary.

GRAND PORTAGE NATIONAL MONUMENT
315 S. Broadway, Grand Portage, 218-387-2788; www.nps.gov

This area was once a rendezvous point and central supply depot for fur traders operating between Montreal and Lake Athabasca. The partially reconstructed summer headquarters of the North West Company includes a stockade, great hall, kitchen and warehouse. The Grand Portage begins at the stockade and runs eight miles northwest from Lake Superior to the Pigeon River. Primitive camping is available at Fort Charlotte (accessible only by hiking the Grand Portage or by canoe).
Mid-May-mid-October, Daily.

GRAND RAPIDS

CHIPPEWA NATIONAL FOREST
200 Ash Ave. N.W., Cass Lake, 218-335-8600; www.fs.fed.us

The forest has 661,400 acres of timbered land and 1,321 lakes, with 699 larger than 10 acres. The vast land and water makes it a good spot for swimming, boating, canoeing, hiking, hunting, fishing, picnicking, camping and winter sports.

FOREST HISTORY CENTER
2609 County Road 76, Grand Rapids, 218-327-4482; www.mnhs.org

The center includes a museum building, re-created 1900 logging camp and log drive wanigan—a floating cook shack—all of which are maintained by the Minnesota Historical Society.
June-Labor Day, Monday-Saturday 10 a.m.-5 p.m., Sunday noon-5 p.m.; October-May, Monday-Friday 8 a.m.-4:30 p.m.

JUDY GARLAND BIRTHPLACE AND MUSEUM
2727 Highway 169 S., Grand Rapids, 218-327-9276, 800-664-5839; www.judygarlandmuseum.com

As Dorothy said, there's no place like home. You can see the childhood home of Judy Garland, along with a 1-acre memorial garden with 50 Judy Garland rose bushes.

Daily 10 a.m.-5 p.m.

KABETOGAMA
ELLSWORTH ROCK GARDENS
Voyageurs National Park, Kabetogama, 218-283-9821; www.ncptt.nps.gov

Located within Voyageurs National Park, the Ellsworth Rock Gardens were created over a span of 20 years by Jack E. Ellsworth, a retired Chicago building contractor. With Kabetogama Lake as a background, large stones and granite mix with flowers, trees and other plantings to create a rich and stunning setting.

KABETOGAMA LAKE
Highway 53, Kabetogama, 800-524-9085; www.kabetogama.com

This lake is 22 miles long and six miles wide with hundreds of miles of rugged shoreline, numerous islands and secluded bays. Come here for fishing, sand beaches, woodland trails, snowmobiling and cross-country skiing.

LUTSEN
SAWTOOTH MOUNTAIN PARK
467 Ski Hill Road, Lutsen, 218-663-7281; www.lutsen.com

Nestled in the Lutsen Mountains is Sawtooth Mountain Park. The park's offerings go beyond hiking—though there's plenty of that, too. You can whiz down the mountain's half-mile track on an Alpine slide, take an aerial tram ride 1,000 feet above Lake Superior—with a stop at a chalet for refueling—or go on a canoe tour in hopes of spotting deer, otters, waterfowl, moose, bears and timber wolves. It's like a rustic amusement park.

Admission: Rides are priced individually; packages are available. Days and times vary.

ROSEAU
HAYES LAKE STATE PARK
48990 County Road 4, Roseau, 218-425-7504; www.dnr.state.mn.us

The 2,950-acre park offers swimming, fishing, hiking, cross-country skiing, snowmobiling, picnicking and camping.

PIONEER FARM AND VILLAGE
Highway 11, Roseau, 218-463-3052; www.roseaupioneerfarm.com

This pioneer village's restored buildings include a log barn, museum, church, parish hall, printery, log house, school, store, blacksmith shop and post office.

Mid-May-mid-September, schedule varies.

POLARIS EXPERIENCE CENTER
205 Fifth Ave. S.W., Roseau, 218-463-4999; www.polarisindustries.com

In essence a snowmobile museum, the center mixes exhibits of snowmobile designs throughout history with photographs and videos, all of which are featured on the self-guided tour. The main Polaris manufacturing plant is also open for tours daily at 4 p.m.

Monday-Saturday noon-8 p.m., Sunday noon-6 p.m.

ROSEAU RIVER WILDLIFE MANAGEMENT AREA
27952 400th St., Roseau, 218-463-1557

More than 2,000 ducks are raised here annually on 65,000 acres. There's also a bird-watching area, canoeing on the river and hunting during season.

THIEF RIVER FALLS
AGASSIZ NATIONAL WILDLIFE REFUGE
Marshall County Road 7 E., Middle River Falls, 218-449-4115; www.fws.gov

This wildlife refuge is made up of approximately 61,500 acres of forest, water and marshland. It is a haven for 280 species of migratory and upland game birds and includes 41 species of resident mammals.

Refuge headquarters Monday-Friday; auto tour route daily, except winter.

PEDER ENGELSTAD PIONEER VILLAGE
Highway 32 South and Oakland Park Boulevard, Thief River Falls, 218-681-5767; www.exploreminnesota.com

A reconstructed village features 19 turn-of-the-century buildings, including a one-room schoolhouse, general store, candy shop, blacksmith shop, barber shop and church, along with two railroad depots and several homes and cabins. The museum houses historic vehicles and farm equipment as well as Norwegian and Native American artifacts, reflecting the town's history.

Admission: adults $5, children free. Memorial Day-Labor Day, daily 1-5 p.m.

VIRGINIA
MINE VIEW IN THE SKY
403 First St. N., Virginia, 218-741-2717

This observation building (and visitors information center) gives a view of a Mesabi Range open-pit mine 650 feet below.

May-September, daily.

WORLD'S LARGEST FLOATING LOON
1409 N. Broadway, Virginia, 218-748-7500

You'll do a double take when you see this large bird floating in the water. Listed in the Guinness World Records, this 20-foot-long, 10-foot-high, 7-foot-wide fiberglass loon swims on Silver Lake, which is in the heart of the city, during the summer months.

WALKER
LEECH LAKE
Walker

The third-largest lake in the state stretches across 111,000 acres with more than 600 miles of shoreline. It's a prime spot for fishing and swimming.

WHERE TO STAY

RECOMMENDED
DULUTH
THE INN ON LAKE SUPERIOR
350 Canal Park Drive, Duluth, 218-726-1111, 888-668-4352; www.theinnonlakesuperior.com

The front of the inn has an unassuming brick exterior, but out back you'll see its greatest amenity—it has a prime spot overlooking Lake Superior and a patio where you can sit and enjoy the view. There are nightly bonfires with s'mores and barbecue cookouts, a rooftop pool and deck that are heated year-round, as well as bicycle and wagons that you can borrow and ride along the lakefront. Kids get bedtime stories and in the morning, everyone receives a hot breakfast with dishes like Belgian waffles. Rooms come with microwaves, refrigerators and free WiFi, and many have private patios or balconies.

175 rooms. Complimentary breakfast. Business center. Fitness center. Pool. Pets accepted. $151-250

WALKER
CHASE ON THE LAKE
502 Cleveland Blvd., Walker, 218-547-7777; www.chaseonthelake.com

Sitting along Leech Lake, Chase offers a slew of outdoorsy activities for all seasons, including biking, skiing, jet skiing, canoeing and snowmobiling. But there's plenty inside of the resort to keep you busy, with indoor pools, a Nintendo Wii game room and even a two-lane bowling alley. When you tire yourself out, retreat to your room, which is decked out in neutral shades and dark wood furniture. All rooms come with a microwave, mini-fridge and flat-panel television. Or head to the onsite Copper Door, an Aveda spa, where you can get reenergized with a deep-tissue chakra massage.

118 rooms. Restaurant, bar. Fitness center. Pool. Spa. Beach. $151-250

WHERE TO EAT

DULUTH
★★★BELLISIO'S
405 Lake Ave. S., Duluth, 218-727-4921; www.grandmasrestaurants.com

This restaurant features floor-to-ceiling wine racks and white tablecloths with full table settings to help guests enjoy a true Italian experience. Of course, the true Italian experience is in dishes like handmade gnocchi stuffed with spinach, ricotta and Parmigiano-Reggiano or pasta alla arrabbiata with fennel sausage doused in a hot and spicy tomato sauce. To complete the meal, choose from among the more than 4,000 bottles of wine.

Italian. Lunch, dinner. Reservations recommended. Outdoor seating. Bar. $16-35

RECOMMENDED

MARSHALL
LANDMARK BISTRO
100 W College Drive, Marshall, 507-337-6600; www.landmarkbistro.com

Step inside this warm wood-filled restaurant and its adjacent lounge, with its stone fireplace, and you'll feel at home. The menu is similarly comforting, with dishes such as house-smoked barbecue pork porterhouse. For more casual fare, try the wood-fired pizza, such as the buffalo chicken with spicy sauce, ranch dressing, celery, bacon, mozzarella and blue cheese. To up the comfort factor, cap it off with mini cheesecakes or the stout cake with buttercream frosting.

American, steak. Lunch (Tuesday-Friday), dinner. Closed Sunday. Outdoor seating. Children's menu. Bar. $16-35

RECOMMENDED

WALKER
RECOMMENDED

THE 502
502 Cleveland Blvd., Walker, 218-547-7777; www.chaseonthelake.com

Try to grab a table on the patio at the casual 502, where you can gaze at lovely Leech Lake while sipping a Very Berry Lemonade (with 99 blackberry schnapps and raspberry syrup) and noshing on jalapeño cheese curds. For dinner, you can get typical pub grub, such as burgers, but there's also almond-fried walleye and local free-range duck on the menu. On Fridays and Saturdays, the restaurant provides live entertainment.

Contemporary American. Breakfast, lunch, dinner, Sunday brunch. Outdoor seating. Bar. $16-35

CENTRAL MINNESOTA

The landscape of Central Minnesota varies from rural folk hero territory to urban jungle. Brainerd calls itself the hometown of Paul Bunyan and is the center of lore and legend about the giant folk hero lumberjack and his blue ox, Babe. Today it retains that rustic vibe; there are 465 pine-studded, sandy-bottomed lakes within a 25-mile radius.

A vacation and resort community, Ely is also the gateway to one of the finest canoeing areas—the Boundary Waters Canoe Area Wilderness—and is in the heart of the Superior National Forest. From the Laurentian Divide, south of here, all waters flow north to the Arctic.

For more than 100 years, visitors have sought out Lake Elmo for the excellent fishing opportunities in its five lakes: Horseshoe Lake and Lakes Demontreville, Elmo, Jane and Olson. Anglers catch bluegill, crappie, largemouth bass, northern pike, panfish, sunfish and walleye. In winter, snowmobiling and ice fishing are popular, and summer brings golfing on the four local courses.

Travelers in search of a less countrified and more suburban destination visit places like Bloomington, located south of Minneapolis. Its Mall of America, the largest shopping center in the United States, draws an astounding 2.5 million visitors each year, more than Walt Disney World, the Grand Canyon and Graceland combined. But Bloomington has more than stores. A 10,000-acre wildlife refuge offers opportunities to view bald eagles and other wildlife, hike, cycle and horseback ride, while the city's zoo is considered one of the finest in the nation.

The urban area in the region is St. Paul. At the bend of the Mississippi and tangential to the point where the waters of the Mississippi and Minnesota rivers meet, St. Paul and its twin city, Minneapolis, form a northern metropolis. A terraced city of diversified industry and lovely homes, St. Paul boasts 30 lakes within a 30-minute drive, as well as more than 90 parks. It's also home to 3M and other major corporations. Tourists come to visit the park, zoo and conservatory grounds of Como Park, explore the Science Museum of Minnesota or catch the Minnesota Wilds hit the ice at Xcel Energy Center. So whether you want Paul Bunyan country, suburban super malls or city museums, central Minnesota has a destination for you.

WHAT TO SEE

BEMIDJI

BEMIDJI TOURIST INFORMATION CENTER
300 Bemidji Ave., Bemidji, 800-458-2223; www.visitbemidji.com

The center houses a collection of Paul Bunyan tools and artifacts with amusing descriptions. Fireplace of the States has stones from every state (except Alaska and Hawaii) and most Canadian provinces.

Memorial Day-Labor Day, daily; October-April, Monday-Saturday.

LAKE BEMIDJI STATE PARK
3401 State Park Road N.E., Bemidji, 218-308-2300; www.dnr.state.mn.us

This 1,688-acre park offers swimming, picnicking, fishing and hiking in a virgin pine forest. Boating, cross-country skiing, camping and biking are also available as well as naturalist programs and a visitors center.

BLOOMINGTON

MALL OF AMERICA
60 E. Broadway, Bloomington, 952-883-8800; www.mallofamerica.com

This complex houses more than 600 stores and restaurants. The mall also features plenty of non-shopping activities for kids, such as Knott's Camp Snoopy, the LEGO Imagination Center; Golf Mountain miniature golf course; a movie complex; and Underwater World, a walk-through aquarium.

Monday-Saturday 10 a.m.-9:30 p.m., Sunday 11 a.m.-7 p.m.

MINNESOTA VALLEY NATIONAL WILDLIFE REFUGE
3815 American Blvd., Bloomington, 952-854-5900; www.fws.gov

One of the only urban wildlife refuges in the nation, this 34-mile corridor of marsh and forest is home to coyotes, badgers and bald eagles and offers miles of trails for hiking, biking, horseback riding and skiing.

Daily; visitors center: Tuesday-Sunday 9 a.m.-5 p.m.

MINNESOTA ZOO
13000 Zoo Blvd., Apple Valley, 952-431-9200, 877-660-4629; www.mnzoo.com

Simulated natural habitats here house 504 species of animals, including Chinese takin, wolverines, Atlantic bottlenose dolphins, Mexican wolves and gibbons. Catch daily presentations like the Coral Reef Dive Show, where you can watch aquarium staff members scuba dive with sharks and fish.

Admission: adults $23, seniors and children 3-12 $16, children 2 and under free. Daily, times vary.

VALLEYFAIR
1 Valleyfair Drive, Shakopee, 952-445-6500; www.valleyfair.com

A 68-acre family amusement park bordering the Minnesota River has more than 75 rides and attractions, including four roller coasters, an antique carousel and special rides for children. Admission also gets you entry into Soak City, a 7-acre water park with a wave pool, water slides, whitewater tube ride and more. Entertainment includes an IMAX theater and musical shows.

Admission: $27. Memorial Day-Labor Day, daily; May and September, some weekends.

BEST ATTRACTIONS

WHAT ARE THE BEST PLACES FOR FAMILY FUN?

MALL OF AMERICA

This behemoth may be the largest mall in the country, but forget the stores. Kids will want to visit the Nickelodeon Universe theme park, the LEGO Imagination Center, the Golf Mountain mini-golf course and Underwater World, an aquarium.

VALLEYFAIR

The whole family will have a ball at this 68-acre amusement park. It has more than 75 rides and attractions, not to mention Soak City, a water park within Valleyfair complete with a wave pool, water rides and more.

COMO PARK

Como Park will keep parents and their kids busy. The grounds of the 448-acre park contain a conservatory, an amusement area and a zoo. When you visit the zoo, be sure to check out the new "Polar Bear Odyssey."

MINNESOTA CHILDREN'S MUSEUM

This top-notch interactive museum caters to kids of all ages. Toddlers can crawl around in the "Habitots" exhibit to learn about the environment while older children can do the same in "Earth World."

BRAINERD

CROW WING COUNTY HISTORICAL SOCIETY MUSEUM

320 Laurel St., Brainerd, 218-829-3268

This restored sheriff's residence and remodeled jail features exhibits on domestic life, logging, mining and the railroad.

Admission: $3. Memorial Day-Labor Day, Monday-Friday 10 a.m.-4 p.m.; rest of the year, Tuesday-Friday 1-5 p.m., Saturday 10 a.m.-3 p.m., closed first week in August.

PAUL BUNYAN STATE TRAIL

Highway 371 and Excelsior Road, Brainerd; www.paulbunyantrail.com

This 100-mile recreational trail is for joggers, walkers, bikers, hikers and snowmobilers (rentals are available). The trail passes by six communities, nine rivers and 21 lakes.

DETROIT LAKES
TAMARAC NATIONAL WILDLIFE REFUGE
35704 County Highway 26, Rochert, 218-847-2641

On 43,000 acres, this refuge has 21 lakes, abundant wild rice, picnicking and fishing, plus trumpeter swans, grouse, beavers, deer, and a flyway sanctuary for thousands of songbirds, ducks and geese.

Visitors center: Memorial Day-Labor Day, daily; rest of year, Monday-Friday.

ELY
DOROTHY MOLTER MUSEUM
2002 E. Sheridan St., Ely, 218-365-4451; www.canoecountry.com

Dorothy Molter was the last living resident of the Boundary Waters Canoe Area Wilderness—she died in December 1986. She lived in the woods for 56 years. The museum features two of her furnished cabins as they were in the wilderness.

Tours: adults $6, seniors $5, children 6-17 $4, children 5 and under free. Memorial Day-Labor Day, Monday-Saturday 10 a.m.-5:30 p.m., Sunday noon-5:30 p.m.; May, September, Saturday-Sunday.

INTERNATIONAL WOLF CENTER
1396 Highway 169, Ely, 800-359-9653; www.wolf.org

You can see a wolf pack safely behind the observation windows of this center. The center also offers exhibits like "Wolves and Human," which explores the conflicts that threaten wolves' survival. Look for animal tracking, hikes and tours of abandoned wolf dens and wolf communication mini-classes.

Admission: adults $8.50, seniors $7.50, children 3-12 $4.50, children 2 and under free. May 15-June 4, daily 10 a.m.-5 p.m.; June 15-August 14, daily 10 a.m.-7 p.m.; August 15-September 30, daily 10 a.m.-5 p.m.; October 1-May 14, Saturday-Sunday 10 a.m.-5 p.m.

HASTINGS
AFTON ALPS
6600 Peller Ave. S., Hastings, 651-436-5245, 800-328-1328; www.aftonalps.com

Find 15 double chairlifts, two rope tows, a patrol, a school and rentals here. The longest run is 3,000 feet with a vertical drop of 330 feet.

November-March, Daily.

ALEXIS BAILLY VINEYARD
18200 Kirby Ave., Hastings, 651-437-1413; www.abvwines.com

This is the first vineyard to make wine with one hundred percent Minnesota-grown grapes.

Wine tastings: May-Thanksgiving, Friday-Sunday 11 a.m.-5:30 p.m. Group tours by appointment.

CARPENTER ST. CROIX VALLEY NATURE CENTER
12805 St. Croix Trail, Hastings, 651-437-4359; www.carpenternaturecenter.org

This environmental education center has more than 15 miles of hiking trails and one mile of shoreline on the St. Croix River. There are various seasonal programs and activities as well.

Daily 8 a.m.-4:30 p.m.

TREASURE ISLAND RESORT AND CASINO
5734 Sturgeon Lake Road, Welch, 800-222-7077; www.treasureislandcasino.com

Treasure Island began as a one-room bingo hall and grew into a 24-hour casino that offers blackjack, slots, bingo, pull-tabs and national and local entertainment. *Daily.*

HINCKLEY

ST. CROIX STATE PARK
30065 St. Croix Road, Hinckley, 320-384-6591; www.dnr.state.mn.us

A 34,037-acre space, this park features lake swimming, fishing and canoeing plus hiking, riding trails, cross-country skiing, snowmobiling, picnicking, a six-mile blacktop bike trail and camping.

LAKE ELMO

LAKE ELMO PARK RESERVE
1515 Keat Ave. N., Lake Elmo, 651-430-8370; www.co.washington.mn.us

The reserve offers a range of outdoor activities, including archery, canoeing, fishing and swimming. You'll also find trails for cross-country skiing, hiking, horseback riding and mountain biking. The park also offers several orienteering courses, ranging from easy to difficult, plus playground, picnicking and a boat launch. *Daily.*

LITTLE FALLS

CHARLES A. LINDBERGH HOUSE AND HISTORY CENTER
1620 Lindbergh Drive S., Little Falls, 320-616-5421; www.mnhs.org

Home of C.A. Lindbergh, former U.S. congressman, and Charles A. Lindbergh, famous aviator, this homestead has been restored to its former appearance with original furniture. Check out the visitors center for additional exhibits.
Admission: adults $7, seniors $6, children 6-17 $5, children 4 and under free. Memorial Day-Labor Day, Tuesday-Saturday 10 a.m.-5 p.m., Sunday noon-5 p.m.; September-October, Saturday 10 a.m.-4 p.m., Sunday noon-4 p.m.

CHARLES A. LINDBERGH STATE PARK
1615 Lindbergh Drive S., Little Falls, 320-616-2525; www.dnr.state.mn.us

The 436 acres here provide hiking, cross-country skiing, picnicking and camping.

MINNESOTA MILITARY MUSEUM
15000 Highway 115, Little Falls, 320-632-7374; www.dma.state.mn.us

Located in a former regimental headquarters, this museum documents U.S. military history as it was experienced by Minnesotans, from frontier garrisons to the Persian Gulf. Look for exhibits, military decorations, tanks and aircraft.
Admission: free. September-May, Thursday-Friday 9 a.m.-4 p.m.; June-August, daily 10 a.m.-5 p.m.

ST. CLOUD

CLEMENS GARDENS & MUNSINGER GARDENS
13th Street and Kilian Boulevard, St. Cloud, 320-258-0389, 800-264-2940; www.munsingerclemens.com

Clemens modeled its White Garden after the lovely White Garden at

Sissinghurst Garden in Kent, England. Munsinger Gardens is surrounded by pine and hemlock trees.

Admission: free. Memorial Day-Labor Day 7 a.m.-10 p.m.

MINNESOTA AMATEUR BASEBALL HALL OF FAME

St. Cloud Civic Center, 541 Brook Lane, St. Cloud, 320-255-7272; www.mnamateurbaseballhof.com

Amateur and Minnesota-born professional baseball players get their due at this Hall of Fame. Even high school and college ballplayers are featured here. See uniforms, caps, bats, balls, gloves and photos at the museum, which is on the second floor of the civic center.

Admission: Free. Monday-Friday.

POWDER RIDGE SKI AREA

15015 93rd Ave., Kimball, 320-398-7200, 800-348-7734; www.powderridge.com

Powder Ridge has a quad, two double chairlifts, a J-bar, a rope tow, a patrol, a school, rentals, snowmaking, a bar and a cafeteria. There are 15 runs at the ski area.

Mid-November-March, daily.

STEARNS HISTORY MUSEUM

235 S. 33rd Ave., St. Cloud, 320-253-8424; www.stearns-museum.org

Located in a 100-acre park, the center showcases cultural and historical aspects of past and present life in central Minnesota. It contains a replica of a working granite quarry, agricultural and automobile displays and a research center and archives. Kids will keep busy in the hands-on activity center.

Admission: adults $5, children $2. Monday-Saturday 10 am-5 p.m., Sunday noon-5 p.m.

ST. PAUL

ALEXANDER RAMSEY HOUSE

265 S. Exchange St., St. Paul, 651-296-8760; www.mnhs.org

This was the home of Minnesota's first territorial governor and his wife, Anne. The house, built in 1872, is full of original Victorian furnishings and features carved walnut woodwork, marble fireplaces and crystal chandeliers. Guided tours show visitors what life was like in the 1870s; reservations are suggested.

Friday-Saturday 10 a.m.-3 p.m.

CAPITAL CITY TROLLEY

525 Farwell Ave., St. Paul, 651-223-5600; www.capitalcitytrolleys.com

This hour-long narrated tour takes visitors through the downtown area and along the Mississippi riverfront, stopping at historical sites such as the mansion of railroad magnate James J. Hill on Summit Avenue.

May-October, Thursday. Reservations are required.

CATHEDRAL OF ST. PAUL

239 Selby Ave., St. Paul, 651-228-1766; www.cathedralsaintpaul.org

The dome of this Classical Renaissance-style Roman Catholic cathedral, in which services began in 1915, is 175 feet high. The central rose window is a dominant feature.

Daily.

CITY HALL AND COURTHOUSE
15 W. Kellogg Blvd., St. Paul

This 1932 building, listed on the National Register of Historic Places, is a prominent example of Art Deco. Carl Milles's 60-ton, 36-foot-tall onyx "Vision of Peace" statue graces the lobby.

COMO PARK
Midway and Lexington parkways, St. Paul, 651-266-6400; www.comozooconservatory.org

You'll find a park, zoo and conservatory at Como Park. The 448-acre park has a 70-acre lake. The glass-domed conservatory houses an authentic Japanese garden (May-September) and the Enchanted Garden and Frog Pond. Opened in 1897, the Como Zoo includes bison, lions and other big cats and Galapagos tortoises. The zoo opened the new "Polar Bear Odyssey," where the animals frolic in a 13,140-square-foot outdoor habitat, in 2010. The complex also has an amusement area (Memorial Day-Labor Day) with a carousel and other children's rides and a miniature golf course.

Admission: free. October-March, daily 10 a.m.-4 p.m.; April-September, daily 10 a.m.-6 p.m.

FORT SNELLING STATE PARK
1 Post Road, St. Paul, 612-725-2389; www.dnr.state.mn.us

This 4,000-acre park is at the confluence of the Minnesota and Mississippi rivers. Go there for swimming, fishing, boating, hiking, biking, cross-country skiing and picnicking. The grounds include historic Fort Snelling, a stone frontier fortress restored to its 1820's appearance. There are daily drills and cannon firings as well as craft demonstrations.

Daily 8 a.m.-4 p.m.

GREAT AMERICAN HISTORY THEATRE
30 10th St. E., St. Paul, 651-292-4323; www.historytheatre.com

The theater company puts on original plays and musicals with American and Midwestern themes.

Thursday-Sunday.

INDIAN MOUNDS PARK
Earl Street and Mounds Boulevard, St. Paul, 651-266-6400; www.nps.gov

This park, one of the oldest in the region, is made up of more than 25 acres and contains prehistoric Native American burial mounds built 1,500 to 2,000 years ago. Eighteen mounds existed on this site in 1856, but only six remain. The park also has picnic facilities, paved trails and outstanding views of the Mississippi River and the city skyline.

Daily, half an hour before sunrise-half an hour after sunset.

JAMES J. HILL HOUSE
240 Summit Ave., St. Paul, 651-297-2555; www.mnhs.org

This 1891 house, made of red sandstone, was the showplace of the city when it was built for the famous railroad magnate. Reservations are recommended for the guided tours, which depart every 30 minutes.

Tours: adults $8, seniors and students $6, children 6-17 $5, children 5 and under free. Wednesday-Saturday 10 a.m.-3:30 p.m., Sunday 1-3:30 p.m.

LANDMARK CENTER

75 W. Fifth St., St. Paul, 651-292-3233; www.landmarkcenter.org

This restored Federal Courts Building was constructed in 1902. It is the center for cultural programs and gangster history tours. It houses four courtrooms and a four-story indoor courtyard (the Musser Cortile).

Visitors can take 45-minute guided tours Thursday and Sunday; also by appointment. Daily.

MINNESOTA CHILDREN'S MUSEUM

10 W. Seventh St., St. Paul, 651-225-6000; www.mcm.org

This museum features hands-on learning exhibits for children and their adult companions. The museum store is stocked with unique puzzles, maps, toys, games and books. Toddlers can crawl around the padded "Habitot" to learn about prairies, caves, pond sand forests, while older kids can explore Minnesota's habitats in "Earth World." In the summer, kids can head to the "Rooftop ArtPark," where they can splash their hands around in a streambed, play in the sand cove or climb into the 12-foot tree fort.

Admission: $8.95. Monday-Thursday, Saturday-Sunday 9 a.m.-5 p.m.; Friday 9 a.m.-8 p.m.

MINNESOTA HISTORICAL SOCIETY CENTER

345 Kellogg Blvd. W., St. Paul, 651-296-6126, 800-657-3773; www.mnhs.org

Home to the historical society, the center houses a museum with interactive exhibits and an extensive genealogical and research library, as well as special events, two museum shops and a café.

Museum: Memorial Day-Labor Day, daily; rest of the year, Tuesday-Sunday. Library: Tuesday-Saturday.

MINNESOTA WILD (NHL)

Xcel Energy Center, 175 W. Kellogg Blvd., St. Paul, 651-222-9453; www.wild.com

See the Minnesota Wild, the state's professional hockey team, hit the ice at its home base in the Xcel Energy Center.

SCIENCE MUSEUM OF MINNESOTA

120 W. Kellogg Blvd., St. Paul, 651-221-9444; www.smm.org

This 8-acre museum showcases technology, anthropology, paleontology, geography and biology exhibits and a 3-D cinema. Kids can examine fossils in the Paleontology Lab or look at your cheek cells in a microscope in the Cell Lab. The William L. McKnight 3M Omnitheater shows IMAX films, and there's a new Mississippi River Visitor Center.

Admission: adults $11, seniors and children $8.50. Daily 9:30 a.m.-9:30 p.m.

SIBLEY HISTORIC SITE

1357 Sibley Memorial Highway, Mendota, 651-452-1596; www.mnhs.org

On this site sits the 1838 home of Gen. Henry Sibley, Minnesota's first governor, now preserved as a museum. Also on the grounds are three other restored limestone buildings, including the Faribault House Museum and the home of pioneer fur trader Jean-Baptiste Faribault, now a museum.

Admission: adults $6, seniors and students $5, children 6-17 $4, children 5 and under free. May-October, Tuesday-Sunday.

STILLWATER

ST. CROIX SCENIC HIGHWAY

Highway 95, Stillwater; www.stcroixscenicbyway.org

Coast along Highway 95 for a scenic ride. The highway runs 50 miles from Afton to Taylors Falls along the "Rhine of America," the St. Croix River. The 124-mile byway was established in 1855 and offers a range of activities along the way.

WASHINGTON COUNTY HISTORICAL MUSEUM

602 Main St. N., Stillwater, 651-439-5956; www.wchsmn.org

A former warden's house at an old prison site contains mementos of lumbering days, including a pioneer kitchen and furniture.

Admission: adults $5, children $1. May-October, Thursday-Sunday; also by appointment.

WILLIAM O'BRIEN STATE PARK

16 miles north on Highway 95, Stillwater, 651-433-0500; www.dnr.state.mn.us

You have your choice of swimming, fishing, boating (ramp); hiking, cross-country skiing, picnicking or camping at this 1,273-acre park.

TAYLORS FALLS

ST. CROIX AND LOWER ST. CROIX NATIONAL SCENIC RIVERWAY

Taylors Falls, 715-483-3284; www.nps.gov

From its origins in northern Wisconsin, the St. Croix flows southward to form part of the Minnesota-Wisconsin border before joining the Mississippi near Point Douglas. Two segments of the river totaling more than 250 miles have been designated National Scenic Riverways and are administered by the National Park Service.

TAYLORS FALLS SCENIC BOAT TOUR

37350 Wild Mountain Road, Taylors Falls, 612-465-6315, 800-447-4958; www.taylorsfallsboat.com

Jump aboard for trips through St. Croix Dalles. You can take a one-hour, seven-mile ride on Taylors' Falls Queen or Princess. There are scenic, brunch, luncheon and dinner cruises, as well as seasonal fall color cruises. For more of a workout, try Taylors Falls' one-way canoe rentals to Osceola or Williams O'Brien State Park.

May-mid-October, daily.

W.H.C. FOLSOM HOUSE

120 Government Road, Taylors Falls, 612-465-3125; www.mnhs.org

This Federal/Greek Revival mansion, built in 1855, reflects the New England heritage of early settlers and includes many original furnishings.

Admission: adults $5, children 6-12 $1. Memorial Day weekend-mid-October, daily.

WILD MOUNTAIN SKI AREA

County Road 16, Taylors Falls, 651-257-3550, 800-447-4958; www.wildmountain.com

There are four quad chairlifts, two rope tows, a patrol, a school, rentals, snow-making and a cafeteria at Wild Mountain. It also has 23 runs, the longest being 5,000 feet with a vertical drop of 300 feet.

November-March, daily.

WHERE TO STAY

BLOOMINGTON
★★★MINNEAPOLIS AIRPORT MARRIOTT
2020 E. American Blvd., Bloomington, 952-854-7441,
800-228-9290; www.marriott.com

Shoppers will want to check into the Marriott purely for its location. Just five minutes from the airport, this hotel is across the street from the famous Mall of America, the largest shopping center in the country. So feel free to pile up your purchases, since you won't have to lug all of those shopping bags very far. After a long day hitting the stores, relax in your warm red, beige and yellow room or in the indoor pool.

472 rooms. Restaurant, bar. Business center. Fitness center. Pool. $151-250

RECOMMENDED

SOFITEL MINNEAPOLIS
5601 W. 78th St., Bloomington, 952-835-1900; www.sofitel.com

About seven miles from the Mall of America, the Sofitel offers a respite from the hordes of tourist the moment you enter the atrium lobby. Hide from the crowds in the contemporary rooms done up in cozy deep reds and blues. They come with amenities like rain showers and plasma televisions. When hunger strikes, visit the onsite Chez Colette, a Parisian brasserie.

282 rooms. Restaurant, bar. Business center. Fitness center. $151-250

ST. PAUL
★★★THE SAINT PAUL HOTEL
350 Market St., St. Paul, 651-292-9292, 800-292-9292;
www.stpaulhotel.com

A historic hotel of America, this beautifully restored property was founded in 1910 by wealthy business-man Lucius P. Ordway (the hotel is within walking distance of the Ordway Center for the Performing Arts) and still maintains an old, European charm. Connected to the downtown skyway system, the hotel has hosted presidents Herbert Hoover, Woodrow Wilson and George W. Bush. The elegant guest rooms have splendid views of downtown, Rice Park or the St. Paul Cathedral, and feature dark wood furniture and upscale linens. The St. Paul Grill is known for steaks.

254 rooms. Restaurant, bar. $151-250

WHICH HOTELS HAVE THE BEST VIEWS?

The Saint Paul Hotel:
Peek out of the windows in the rooms at this historic downtown St. Paul hotel, and you'll see vistas of Rice Park, Cathedral Hill and the Capitol. For an even better perch to see the city, head up to the rooftop fitness center.

Water Street Inn:
Nestled on the banks of the St. Croix River, the Victorian-style inn offers guests a waterfront patio where they can linger and drink in the setting. But many of the rooms also have river views and balconies, where you can admire the scenery on your own.

WHERE TO EAT

BAYPORT
★★★BAYPORT COOKERY
328 Fifth Ave. N., Bayport, 651-430-1066; www.bayportcookery.com

The restaurant has only one nightly seating, but diners can expect an adventure of innovative cuisine at this St. Croix River Valley destination. Even city dwellers travel to experience the food, which features artistic presentations of local ingredients such as New York strip steak with cauliflower, sunchokes and Guinness sauce, or Alaskan halibut with miso, corn coulis and pioppini mushrooms.

American. Dinner. Closed Monday. Reservations recommended. Outdoor seating. $36-85

BLOOMINGTON
★★★KINCAID'S
8400 Normandale Lake Blvd., Bloomington, 952-921-2255; www.kincaids.com

Touted as a fish, chop and steak house, this restaurant delivers with a menu of well-portioned dishes, such as rock salt-roasted prime rib or étouffée with scallops, black tiger prawns, mussels, clams and andouille sausage. The décor is reminiscent of a turn-of-the-century saloon, and the service continues this relaxed social-center style.

American, steak. Lunch, dinner, Sunday brunch. $36-85

LAKE ELMO
★★★LAKE ELMO INN
3442 Lake Elmo Ave., Lake Elmo, 651-777-8495; www.lakeelmoinn.com

Enjoy the hearty portions of rich, creative cuisine at this statewide favorite housed in a restored 1881 inn. House specialties include "Sunnies," potato-crusted filets with a lemon vinaigrette, and Dijon-crusted rack of lamb. The charming outdoor seating is a perfect way to enjoy the stellar Sunday brunch, which comes with bottomless glasses of champagne.

American. Lunch, dinner, Sunday brunch. Outdoor seating. Children's menu. Bar. $16-35

LITTLE FALLS
★★★KOZLAK'S ROYAL OAK
4785 Hodgson Road, Shoreview, 651-484-8484; www.kozlaks.com

Diners receive the royal treatment here, beginning with personalized note pads or matchbooks left on the table. Next, get treated to dishes like African lobster tails or beef medallions atop garlic toast smothered in béarnaise. Of course, end with a dessert fit for a king or queen, such as the four-layer carrot cake or the Baileys tiramisu, with Kahlúa-soaked cookies and a Baileys-mascarpone filling. Take advantage of the scenic garden seating.

American. Lunch, dinner, Sunday brunch. Outdoor seating. Children's menu. Bar. $16-35

★★★OLD LAKE LODGE
3746 Sunset Drive, Spring Park, 952-471-8513; www.lordfletchers.com

This popular nautical respite about 14 miles west of Minnetonka resembles an old lodge, with cozy fireplaces for cooler days. Local ingredients and unusual flavors come together in the kitchen's inventive dishes. Test out appetizers like calamari curly fries with smoked garlic tartar sauce or tuna tartare nachos with wonton chips and walu and ahi tuna. For the main course, try lobster espagnole, with spinach tagliatelle, Maine lobster, spinach, chorizo, sweet corn and roasted tomatoes, or tournedos doused in béarnaise and bordelaise.

American, international. Lunch, dinner, Sunday brunch. Outdoor seating. Bar. $16-35

ST. PAUL

★★★FOREPAUGH'S

276 S. Exchange St., St. Paul, 651-224-5606; www.forepaughs.com

Some say the ghost of the former owner, St. Paul pioneer Joseph Lybrandt Forepaugh, haunts this romantic Victorian three-story 1879 house. That doesn't stop diners from visiting to get their fill of the restaurant's French-inspired dishes. Try shrimp scampi Marseillaise, entrecôte au poivre vert—New York sirloin with a peppercorn sauce—or grilled brochette of lamb. If you need to catch a show after your meal, the restaurant conveniently offers shuttle service to nearby theaters.

French. Lunch, dinner, Sunday brunch. Outdoor seating. Children's menu. Bar. $16-35

★★★W. A. FROST AND COMPANY

374 Selby Ave., St. Paul, 651-224-5715; www.wafrost.com

Located in the historic Dakotah Building, the four dining rooms of this restaurant are decorated with Victorian-style wallpaper, furnishings and oil paintings. The menu changes seasonally, but you can expect flavorful dishes like grilled togarashi-spiced ahi tuna or black angus filet mignon. If you're not hungry enough for a full meal, order some wine—the wine cellar has more than 1,100 pours—and a couple of selections from the vast artisan cheese list.

American. Lunch, dinner, late-night, Sunday brunch. Outdoor seating. Children's menu. Bar. $36-85

RECOMMENDED

MUFFULETTA IN THE PARK

2260 Como Ave., St. Paul, 651-644-9116; www.muffuletta.com

This cozy, candle-lit restaurant is named after a New Orleans sandwich, and you can find the hero-style muffuletta—piled high with ham, capicolla, pistachio mortadella, Genoa salami and provolone—among the offerings. But the bistro's menu also takes cues from other places with

WHERE ARE THE BEST PLACES FOR BRUNCH?

Lake Elmo Inn: This standout brunch is a favorite with locals. The meal starts off well: You get all the champagne you can drink and fresh caramel rolls. Then move onto the buffet spread, which includes everything from shrimp cocktail to eggs Benedict.

Kozlak's Royal Oak: Live jazz kicks the Sunday brunch at Kozlak's up a notch. The buffet does the same thing, with flavorful New Orleans dishes like eggs Sardou, jambalaya and Cajun ribs. Hit the dessert and sundae bar so you can linger and listen to the band.

W. A. Frost and Company: The restaurant's use of meats and cheeses from local farms elevates the brunch menu and gives you a true taste of the region. Foodies can opt for the four-course chef's brunch tasting menu for a fun culinary experience.

French-inspired dishes like the duck confit gnocchi and steak frites, and the Spanish-inspired bone-in chicken breast with chorizo and salsa romesco.

International. Lunch, dinner, Sunday brunch. Outdoor seating. Children's menu. $16-35

THE ST. PAUL GRILL

St. Paul Hotel, 350 Market St., St. Paul, 651-224-7455; www.stpaulhotel.com

This white-tablecloth eatery inside the St. Paul Hotel may be a steak house, but start off your meal with a seafood appetizer, like hot pepper shrimp or the tender crab cake. For the main event, order the meat. Try the bone-in ribeye or the bourbon pork chop. Save room for the decadent chocolate lust cake, which has layers of devil's food, chocolate cheesecake and chocolate truffle cake and slathered with fudge icing and cookie crumbles.

American, steak. Lunch, dinner, late-night, Sunday brunch. Bar. $15 and under

MINNEAPOLIS

Minneapolis is fast becoming the epicenter of all things cool. In 2010, Bicycling Magazine named it the best city for two-wheeling, thanks, in part, to a bicycle-sharing program and the pristine chain of lakes and trails that connect the vibrant, art-focused city of grand ideals and even grander architecture. In fact, Minneapolis is an architecture hot spot, with unique buildings that dot the city like gleaming trophies, such as the Herzog and de Meuron-designed Walker Art Center; the Frank Gehry-designed Weisman Art Museum; the magnificent Guthrie Theater that overlooks the dancing Mississippi River; and the downtown library whose glass walls offer a large-screen view of the thriving city streets.

While Minneapolis prospers on progressive concepts of mass transit and environmentalism, it doesn't mean the city is leaving its charmingly Midwestern past behind. Instead, the city is embracing its farming and grain-mill-fueled history, turning old grain mills into things like the Mill City Museum, which not only hosts a bustling farmers' market dedicated to regional goods but also an education center focused on agriculture and life on the Mississippi.

And at the end of summer, in an annual celebration of all things 'Sotan, is when Minneapolitans really embrace their past, descending onto the Minnesota State Fairgrounds for a 10-day festival filled with pigs, cows, rides, cheese curds—basically everything you can shake a stick at on a stick—and overflowing local pride.

It's a city that loves its past, present and future, and it has plenty of parks, luxury hotels, boutique shops and excellent restaurants to prove it.

WHAT TO SEE

AMERICAN SWEDISH INSTITUTE

2600 Park Ave., Minneapolis, 612-871-4907; www.americanswedishinst.org

This museum is housed in a turn-of-the-century, 33-room mansion and features hand-carved woodwork, porcelain tile stoves and sculpted ceilings.

Admission: adults $6, seniors $5, children 6-18 $4, children 5 and under free. Tuesday, Thursday-Saturday noon-4 p.m., Wednesday noon-8 p.m., Sunday 1-5 p.m.

BEST ATTRACTIONS

WHAT ARE THE TOP THINGS TO DO?

VISIT THE GUTHRIE THEATER

Big dramas like *A Streetcar Named Desire* shine at the Guthrie, but the theater is no secondary character. Sitting on the Mississippi, it offers a beautiful view of the city and has one of the largest cantilevers in the world.

TAKE IN THE FINE ART AT THE MINNEAPOLIS INSTITUTE OF ARTS

Art aficionados will want to spend the afternoon perusing the free museum's collection of fine art. To see some local talent, stop by the new wing dedicated to Minnesota artists and contemporary work.

CATCH A GAME AT TARGET FIELD

Take yourself out to the ballgame to see the Minnesota Twins swing into action. Target Field, a new LEED-certified ballpark in the Warehouse District, is the Twins' home base.

SEE GREAT CONTEMPORARY WORKS AT THE WALKER ART CENTER

This innovative contemporary art museum is called the "Pompidou of the United States." See works by noted artists such as Jasper Johns and Robert Motherwell, then walk across the street to see more art in the Minneapolis Sculpture Garden.

BELL MUSEUM OF NATURAL HISTORY

University and 17th avenues, Minneapolis, 612-624-7083; www.umn.edu

The natural history museum features dioramas showing Minnesota birds and mammals in natural settings. Exhibits on art, photography and natural history research change frequently. The Touch and See Room encourages hands-on exploration and comparison of natural objects.

Admission: adults $5, seniors and children $3, children 2 and under free. Tuesday-Friday 9 a.m.-5 p.m., Saturday 10 a.m.-5 p.m., Sunday noon-5 p.m.

BUCK HILL SKI AREA

15400 Buck Hill Road, Burnsville, 952-435-7174; www.buckhill.com

Buck Hill has a quad, three double chairlifts, a J-bar, three rope tows, snowmaking, a patrol, a school and rentals. During the spring and summer, you can go BMX racing, mountain biking and mountain boarding.

Late November-March, daily.

ELOISE BUTLER WILDFLOWER GARDEN AND BIRD SANCTUARY

Theodore Wirth Parkway and Glenwood Avenue, Minneapolis, 612-370-4903;
www.minneapolisparks.org

This horseshoe-shape glen contains a natural bog, swamp and habitat for
prairie and woodland flowers and birds. Guided tours are available.

Early April-mid-October, daily 7:30 a.m.-30 minutes before dusk.

FREDERICK R. WEISMAN ART MUSEUM

333 E. River Road, Minneapolis, 612-625-9494; www.weisman.umn.edu

The striking, stainless-steel exterior of this museum was designed by Frank
Gehry. Collections of early 20th-century and contemporary American art,
Asian ceramics and Native American Mimbres pottery are inside.

*Admission: free. Tuesday-Wednesday, Friday 10 a.m.-5 p.m., Thursday 10 a.m.-8 p.m.,
Saturday-Sunday 11 a.m.-5 p.m.*

GUTHRIE THEATER

818 S. Second St., Minneapolis, 612-377-2224; www.guthrietheater.org

This building on the Mississippi River is as stellar as the stage performances
it hosts. You can see everything from large-scale productions like *M. Butterfly*
on the main stage to more intimate theater and musical productions on the
two smaller stages. The building is a theatrical production itself, boasting an
exceptional and unique view of the city and an "endless bridge"—one of the
largest cantilevers in the world—that overlooks the Mississippi.

Nightly Tuesday-Sunday; matinees Wednesday, Saturday-Sunday.

HENNEPIN HISTORY MUSEUM

2303 Third Ave. S., Minneapolis, 612-870-1329; www.hhmuseum.org

This museum features permanent and temporary exhibits on the history of
Minneapolis and Hennepin County, including collections of textiles, costumes,
toys and material unique to central Minnesota.

Sunday, Wednesday, Friday-Saturday 10 a.m.-5 p.m., Tuesday 10 a.m.-2 p.m., Thursday 1-8 p.m.

HUBERT H. HUMPHREY METRODOME

900 S. Fifth St., Minneapolis, 612-332-0386; www.msfc.com

Home of the Minnesota Twins baseball team, the Minnesota Vikings football
team and University of Minnesota football, this stadium seats up to 63,000.

Monday-Friday.

IDS TOWER

80 S. Eighth St., Minneapolis

At 775 feet and 57 stories, this is one of the tallest buildings between Chicago
and the West Coast.

JAMES SEWELL BALLET

528 Hennepin Ave., Minneapolis, 612-672-0480; www.jsballet.org

The James Sewell Ballet performs beautiful and uniquely choreographed
ballets with a small ensemble of eight dancers. Two ballets are created each
year by critically acclaimed choreographer Sewell, and many of the company's
performances have a contemporary, creative and bold bent.

Mid-August-mid-May.

LAKEWOOD CEMETERY MEMORIAL CHAPEL

3600 Hennepin Ave., Minneapolis, 612-822-2171; www.lakewoodcemetery.com

A cemetery is rarely the first stop on a vacation, but the chapel at Lakewood Cemetery is an architectural wonder worth visiting. Stained-glass windows reflect brilliant light off the more than 10 million half-inch tiles that line the walls. (If the door is locked, stop by the cemetery administration building.) The cemetery grounds are also lovely.

Daily.

LYNDALE PARK GARDENS

1500 E. Lake Harriet Parkway, Minneapolis, 612-230-6400; www.minneapolisparks.org

These four distinctive gardens—one for roses, two for perennials and the Peace Garden—are a treasure. Look for displays of roses, bulbs and other annuals and perennials, exotic and native trees, rock gardens, two decorative fountains, and the adjacent bird sanctuary. April to September is the best time to visit.

Daily 7:30 a.m.-10 p.m.

METROCONNECTIONS

1219 Marquette Ave., Minneapolis, 612-333-8687, 800-747-8687; www.metroconnections.com

Hop aboard these motor coaches for tours like Twin Cities highlights (January-November); Stillwater, a historic river town (June-October); and Lake Minnetonka (June-August).

MINNEAPOLIS CITY HALL

350 S. Fifth St., Minneapolis, 612-673-2491; www.municipalbuildingcommission.org

Built in 1891, City Hall's "Father of Waters" statue in the rotunda is carved out of the largest single block of marble produced from quarries of Carrara, Italy. Take a self-guided tour or join a guided tour on the first Wednesday of the month.

Monday-Friday.

MINNEAPOLIS INSTITUTE OF ARTS

2400 Third Ave. S., Minneapolis, 612-870-3131, 888-642-2787; www.artsmia.org

Showcasing masterpieces from around the world and from every era, this breathtaking 126-year-old museum is a must-stop for any art lover. More than 80,000 works—from ancient to modern—make up the museum, which includes a newly designed wing dedicated to Minnesota artists and contemporary pieces.

Admission: free. Tuesday-Wednesday, Friday-Saturday 10 a.m.-5 p.m.; Thursday 10 a.m.-9 p.m.; Sunday 11 a.m.-5 p.m.

MINNEAPOLIS SCULPTURE GARDEN

Vineland Place and Lyndale Avenue South, Minneapolis, 612-375-7577

This 10-acre urban garden features more than 40 sculptures by leading American and international artists. Check out Claes Oldenburg and Coosje van Bruggen's *Spoonbridge and Cherry*, a ginormous spoon holding a bright red cherry.

Daily 6 a.m.-midnight.

MINNESOTA LYNX (WNBA)
Target Center, 600 First Ave. N., Minneapolis, 612-673-1600; www.wnba.com

The Lynx, Minnesota's professional women's basketball team, shoots hoops at the Target Center.

MINNESOTA TIMBERWOLVES (NBA)
Target Center, 600 First Ave. N., Minneapolis, 612-673-1600; www.nba.com

The Target Center is the official home of the Timberwolves, Minnesota's professional men's basketball team.

MINNESOTA TWINS (MLB)
Metrodome, 900 S. Fifth Ave., Minneapolis, 612-375-1366; www.twins.mlb.com

The Twins, the state's professional baseball team, play ball in the Metrodome.

MINNESOTA VIKINGS (NFL)
Metrodome, 900 S. Fifth Ave., Minneapolis, 612-338-4537; www.vikings.com

The Vikings, Minnesota's pro football team, uses the Metrodome as its home base.

MINNESOTA ORCHESTRA
Orchestra Hall, 1111 Nicollet Mall, Minneapolis, 612-371-5656; www.minnesotaorchestra.org

A highly regarded ensemble, the Minnesota Orchestra invariably presents a repertoire of top-notch classical music, as well as special guests of other genres. *Mid-September-June.*

RIVER CITY TROLLEY
Minneapolis Convention Center, 1301 Second Ave. S., Minneapolis, 612-378-7833; www.rivercitytrolley.com

See the city aboard one of these trolleys. The trolleys make a 40-minute loop that traverses the core of the downtown area, passing through the Mississippi Mile, St. Anthony Falls, the Warehouse District and other points of interest. A Chain of Lakes tour is also available. The tours, which have on-board narration, run approximately every 20 minutes. *May-October, daily, also Friday-Saturday evenings.*

ST. ANTHONY FALLS
Main Street Southeast and Central Avenue, Minneapolis

At the head of the navigable Mississippi River, the falls is the site of the village of St. Anthony. A public vantage point at the upper locks and dam provides a view of the falls and of the operation of the locks. The site also includes a renovated warehouse with shops, a movie theater and restaurants.

TARGET FIELD
1 Twins Way, Minneapolis; minnesota.twins.mlb.com

Home to the Minnesota Twins, this new, LEED-certified ballpark is setting standards for both baseball fields and green buildings. It's received more accolades than Twins power hitter Joe Mauer. The twinkling skyscrapers surrounding the outdoor ballpark are filled with people hoping to get a good view of the game.

WALKER ART CENTER

A visit to the Twin Cities wouldn't be complete without a visit stop to at this world-renowned contemporary art museum. Hailed by some as the "Pompidou of the United States," the Walker Art Center hosts a stellar 11,000-piece collection of contemporary works by acclaimed artists such as Jasper Johns, Robert Motherwell, Josephy Beuys, Matthew Barney and more, as well as and features revolving exhibitions of visual art, dance, film and stage performances every week.

Admission: adults $10, seniors $8, students $6, children free. Tuesday-Wednesday, Friday-Saturday 10 a.m.-5 p.m., Thursday 10 a.m.-9 p.m., Sunday 11 a.m.-5 p.m.

WHERE TO STAY

★★★CROWNE PLAZA NORTHSTAR DOWNTOWN

618 Second Ave. S., Minneapolis, 612-338-2288, 800-556-7827; www.cpminneapolis.com

Those looking for easy and chilly-free access to the best of Minneapolis, look no further than the Crowne Plaza. Aside from being near the Metrodome, the hotel is within the city's skyway, a heated, indoor network that connects visitors and residents to area shops, businesses, restaurants and more. You won't have any problems resting in your room, since it comes with a sleeping mask, soothing lavender spray and earplugs. But the earplugs aren't entirely necessary, as the hotel remains quiet despite its central location. If you still can't sleep, tire yourself out at the 24-hour fitness center.

222 rooms. Restaurant, bar. Business center. Fitness center. $151-250

★★★DEPOT HOTEL, A RENAISSANCE HOTEL

225 S. Third Ave., Minneapolis, 612-375-1700, 800-321-2211; www.thedepotminneapolis.com

A portion of this downtown Minneapolis hotel was once a 19th-century train depot for the city. The actual depot section is now a meeting space, and in the winter, an indoor skating rink. The attractive guest rooms nod to the building's rich past, featuring overstuffed leather chairs and ottomans, decorative mirrors and many historic framed photos. Modern amenities include flat-panel HDTVs and desks with ergonomic chairs. You can soothe sore muscles in the indoor pool and whirlpool or work them out in the well-appointed fitness room. The Metrodome, University of Minnesota, Guthrie Theater, Target Center and Minneapolis Convention Center are all nearby, making this property convenient for business and leisure travelers.

225 rooms. Restaurant, bar. Business center. Pool. $151-250

★★★GRAND HOTEL

615 Second Ave. S., Minneapolis, 612-288-8888, 866-843-4726;
www.grandhotelminneapolis.com

Eschewing contemporary chic for classic and cozy, this charming Old World hotel oozes charm. In the lobby, dark, rich woods and fireplaces greet you like old friends. And in the rooms, Aveda products, four-poster cherrywood beds, Tuscan furniture and curtains that tickle the floor make this downtown business-district hotel feel like an elegant B&B getaway in a bustling urban setting. Beds include fluffy down comforters and Egyptian linens of the highest thread count. Guests also receive complimentary access to the 58,000-square-foot

LifeTime Fitness facility, which has an indoor pool, racquetball and squash courts, and an aerobics studio, in addition to the usual cardiovascular and weight-training equipment.

140 rooms. Restaurant, bar. Fitness center. Spa. $129-499

★★★GRAVES 601

601 First Ave. N., Minneapolis, 612-677-1100, 866-523-1100; www.graves601hotel.com

This ultra-fashionable 22-story hotel rests in the center of downtown Minneapolis, just steps away from Target Center, Target Field and the State and the Orpheum theaters. The rooms offer refined, upscale luxury—each one is decorated in the minimalist style of a hip downtown loft and includes such high-scale accoutrements as a plasma TV and Hermès bath products. And the hotel restaurant, the Bradstreet Craftshouse, serves up some of the finest cocktails in town, including the Juliet & Romeo—Plymouth gin, lime, mint, cucumber and rose water—all handcrafted with all-natural ingredients by the bar's master mixologists. Cosmos Restaurant is a great choice for breakfast, lunch or dinner.

255 rooms. Restaurant, bar. Fitness center. $129-399

★★★★HOTEL IVY

201 11th St. S., Minneapolis, 612-746-4600; www.starwoodhotels.com

Located next to the convention center, Orchestra Hall and Nicollet Mall, this chic and pristine hotel is a favorite among the business-class visitors. It offers a sophisticated twist on classic charm: Italian linens, cushy robes and cozy slippers await in your skyline-view room, while the hotel restaurant, Porter and Frye, beckons with the scent of sizzling steaks. The 6,000-square-foot ultra-elegant restaurant, Porter & Frye boasts some of the city's top food talent. The hotel, located inside the historic Ivy Tower, also features the indulgent Ivy Spa, which attracts visitors and locals in search of pure escapist bliss.

157 rooms. Restaurant, bar. Business center. Fitness center. Spa. $251-350

★★★MINNEAPOLIS HYATT

1300 Nicollet Mall, Minneapolis, 612-370-1234, 800-233-1234; www.minneapolis.hyatt.com

Located on the historic Nicollet Mall and a few short blocks from the convention center, this downtown hotel features deluxe amenities including Egyptian linens, pillow-top beds and cozy duvets. If you need to relax or prep for an event (or just don't have the time when you're home), there's a brand-new health spa and a hair and nail salon. The fitness center offers group classes and a personal trainer, for those who want to work it out during an extended stay. The hotel is also steps away from the city's expansive skyway system and top restaurants like Vincent and Manny's.

533 rooms. Restaurant, bar. Business center. Fitness center. Pool. $151-250

★★★LE MERIDIEN CHAMBERS

901 Hennepin Ave. S., Minneapolis, 612-767-6900; www.chambersminneapolis.com

This hip, chic sister to New York's Chambers Hotel has the appropriately named Rock Star Suite. Offering floor-to-ceiling windows, an exceptional view of the city, a private 580-square-foot terrace and ultra-swanky contemporary art and furniture, this 1,000-square-foot suite is all about luxury and indulgence, much like the art hotel itself. Contemporary works by artists such as Damien Hirst and Tracy Emin decorate the gallery-like lobby and stylish guest rooms, which all offer fashionable décor and state-of-the-art gadgets like flat-panel televisions and iPod docking stations.

60 rooms. Restaurant, bar. $251-350

★★★MARRIOTT MINNEAPOLIS CITY CENTER

30 S. Seventh St., Minneapolis, 612-349-4000, 800-228-9290; www.minneapolismarriott.com

Located in City Center, an expansive shopping and business destination, the Marriott greets guests with nice views of downtown and cozy rooms with down comforters and feather pillows, as well as upscale granite and marble bathrooms. The hotel boasts a breathtaking atrium, numerous meeting rooms, boardrooms and "pre-meeting" areas, making it the perfect spot for conventions and business travelers, who will also appreciate the hotel's large work desks. Another perk is that the hotel is within walking distance of Target Center and Target Field.

583 rooms. Restaurant, bar. Business center. Fitness center. Pets accepted. $151-250

★★★THE MARQUETTE HOTEL

710 Marquette Ave., Minneapolis, 612-333-4545; www.marquettehotel.com

Nestled among the downtown skyscrapers and connected to the beautiful 57-story IDS Tower, the Marquette provides large, affordable rooms with amenities like Egyptian cotton linens and Posturepedic beds. Rooms measure more than 400 square feet, making them feel positively giant compared to some big-city hotel rooms. For a lovely dinner, head to Basil's, the in-house restaurant, which overlooks the IDS building's Crystal Court and offers dishes such as creamy wild rice chowder with almonds or nori-seared sushi-grade tuna.

281 rooms. Restaurant, bar. Pets accepted. $151-250

★★★W HOTEL—THE FOSHAY

821 Marquette Ave., Minneapolis, 612-215-3700; www.starwoodhotels.com

Located in the newly renovated 80-year-old Foshay Tower, the W Hotel mixes the Roaring '20s with the new millennium, boasting artful touches like bubble lights, neon-light-trimmed front desks and glass globes in the lobby, and flapper-era décor in its high-rise bar, Prohibition. The rooms also nod to both the modern world and the building's original charm, featuring contemporary, Japanese-inspired designs like bamboo wallpaper and Art Deco flavors such as patterned rugs, sleek furniture and round minibars the color of ruby lipstick. On the weekends, this hip hotel buzzes with a young crowd that flocks to the two lively bars, while guests retreat to their quiet rooms filled with art and amenities such as a down duvet, rainforest shower, flat-screen TV and DVD player.

229 rooms. Restaurant, bar. Business center. Spa. Pets accepted. $251-350

RECOMMENDED

ALOFT MINNEAPOLIS
900 Washington Ave. S., Minneapolis, 612-455-8400; www.starwoodhotels.com
Aloft doesn't sacrifice design to give travelers a more affordable hotel option. The flip side of the wooden headboard wall offers storage space, a magazine-filled rack and a drinks station. The compact bathroom has a frosted-glass shower stocked with Bliss toiletries. There are tech perks, too: Each room has complimentary WiFi, a 42-inch wall-mounted TV and a connectivity station that recharges your gadgets and links to the television. When you've had enough playing with the gizmos, head to the re:mix(SM) lounge for a game of pool or to buy a new flash drive.

155 rooms. Bar. Business center. Fitness center. $61-150

THE HOTEL MINNEAPOLIS
215 Fourth St. S., Minneapolis, 612-340-2000; www.thehotelminneapolis.com
Part of the new Autograph hotel collection from Marriott, the Hotel Minneapolis brings a chic modern boutique hotel to the city. Connected to the skyway, guests can easily walk to the Convention Center, Metrodome, City Hall and other attractions, making it a perfect choice for both business and leisure travelers. Guest rooms feature MP3 docking stations, flat-screen TVs, rainfall showers in the bathrooms and contemporary décor. The hotel's Restaurant Max offers seasonal local cuisine in a hip environment and a fun bar where locals love to grab cocktails. Check out The LB (Lobby Bar) for the breakfast buffet or happy hour, which takes place Monday-Friday from 5-7 p.m. and offers discounted drinks and appetizers.

222 rooms. Restaurant, bar. Business center. Fitness center. $61-150

WHERE TO EAT

★★★112 EATERY
112 N. Third St., Minneapolis, 612-343-7696; www.112eatery.com
Located in the historic Amsterdam building in Minneapolis' Warehouse District, this restaurant beckons funky foodies with its eclectic menu and convivial spirit. The menu is a veritable melting pot of Italian, Asian and down-home American flavors. Hard-to-resist items include the brick-pressed chicken, lamb scottadito with goat's milk yogurt, and the tagliatelle with foie gras meatballs. Side dishes such as cauliflower fritters and creamed corn will leave you sated, and the wine list is well-rounded.

Contemporary American. Dinner, late-night. Bar. $36-85

★★★B.A.N.K.

The Westin, 88 S. Sixth St., Minneapolis, 612-656-3255; www.bankmpls.com

Past and present come together beautifully at B.A.N.K. This restaurant, located in the former Farmers and Mechanics Bank, is right on the money with its seductive retro styling and fine food. From salmon tartare to mac and cheese, there's a mix of highbrow and comfy classics. It's all about tasting and sharing here, where you can even shake and stir your own signature cocktail. Grab a seat at the former teller counter and watch the chefs in action.

Contemporary American. Breakfast, lunch, dinner. Bar. $36-85

★★★BAR LA GRASSA

800 N. Washington Ave., Minneapolis, 612-333-3837; www.barlagrassa.com

Set in the hip and burgeoning North Loop, this expansive bar and restaurant received "best of" accolades from nearly every outlet in town after it opened its doors in 2009. Featuring an extensive wine list and artisan small plates—from citrus-infused gnocchi to marinated pork shoulder bruschetta—Bar La Grassa is the perfect place for foodies looking to nibble on unusual Italian-inspired dishes that span the globe. For folks with a heartier appetite, the small plates come in entrée-size portions. If you go that route, try one of the pasta specialties, like the linguini that comes with an entire pound of lobster and sprinkled with chili and mint.

Italian, international. Dinner. Bar. $36-85

★★★★LA BELLE VIE

510 Groveland Ave., Minneapolis, 612-874-6440; www.labellevie.us

This French restaurant, tucked inside a grand 1920s building abutting the Walker Art Center and Loring Park, is one of the finest in the Midwest. La Belle Vie is all about high design and architecture, whether it be the multicourse prix-fixe menu, decadent à la carte creations or the elegant, chandelier-lit lounge. Even the first plates are like mini sculptures, topped with a spectacular mousse or emulsion. But these sculptures—like grilled beef tenderloin with morel mushrooms, English peas, carrots and smoked bacon—are meant to be eaten. Executive chef Tim McKee is hands down one of the best chefs in the Midwest and his attention to detail shows in every plate, wine pairing and chef-created cocktail, including the fit-for-a-queen Mogwai Are the Stars, with top-shelf Scotch and a hint of salted habanero butterscotch.

French, Mediterranean. Dinner. Reservations recommended. $86 and up

★★★LUCIA'S

1432 W. 31st St., Minneapolis, 612-825-1572; www.lucias.com

This quaint, 11-table restaurant is a charming Uptown spot dedicated to local food and good wine. Lauded chef Lucia Watson uses fresh, seasonal ingredients along with local products to create elegant dishes like lamb shank with saffron spaetzle and handcrafted pasta with local spinach. The adjacent wine bar allows diners to choose from an ever-evolving wine list, with many options by the glass. The brunch is a weekend favorite.

French, contemporary American. Lunch (Tuesday-Friday), dinner, Saturday-Sunday brunch. Closed Monday. $36-85

★★★MANNY'S STEAKHOUSE

825 Marquette Ave., Minneapolis, 612-339-9900; www.mannyssteakhouse.com

For serious steaks, Minneapolitans and its many visitors head to Manny's, a local steak house that's found new roots in the renovated Foshay Tower. Everything at this steak joint would make the Rat Pack proud—and salivate—from the double porterhouse steak to the oysters Rockefeller to the oniony hash-brown side dishes. And though it's decidedly meat-and-potatoes old-school, the upscale Manny's has recently added healthier fare to its menu, including tuna and pan-roasted chicken. This is about as original and indulgent as it gets.

American. Breakfast, lunch, dinner. Reservations recommended. $36-85

★★★PORTER & FRYE

Hotel Ivy, 1115 Second Ave. S., Minneapolis, 612-353-3500; www.porterandfrye.com

It may be inside the historic Hotel Ivy, but Porter & Frye isn't your typical hotel restaurant. This all-day dining spot's fashionable setting, downtown location and haute heartland cooking make it a favorite of tourists and city dwellers alike. The names may sound familiar, but the gourmet takes on standards like the Reuben and grilled cheese sandwich are like nothing you've ever tasted. Dinner selections, such as tenderloin with dolce Gorgonzola, cater to an epicurean crowd.

Contemporary American. Breakfast, lunch, dinner, late-night. Reservations recommended. Bar. $36-85

★★★RESTAURANT ALMA

528 University Ave. S.E., Minneapolis, 612-379-4909; www.restaurantalma.com

The unique menu, fresh ingredients and exceptional attention to detail have garnered much praise for chef-owner Alex Roberts' eponymous restaurant. From farm-fresh produce to grass-fed beef, everything at Alma is focused on quality and sustainability. The blond-wood tables, exposed brick and concrete floors add a laid-back, casual vibe, though the food is anything but. Instead, a carefully selected tasting menu, featuring such delights as ricotta and rabbit agnolotti and sautéed halibut, is dedicated to Minnesota farms and a hard-to-please palate.

Contemporary American. Dinner. Reservations recommended. $36-85

★★★SOLERA

900 Hennepin Ave., Minneapolis, 612-338-0062; www.solera-restaurant.com

Sample the sunny cuisine of Spain at the upbeat Solera. This place knows how to entertain, especially on its rooftop, where live DJs spin tunes on the weekends and movies are played on Sundays and Mondays. There's even a late-night happy hour and menu offered until 2 a.m. (weekends only). Traditional tapas let diners taste a variety of items and many selections change with the seasons.

Spanish, tapas. Dinner, late-night. $16-35

RECOMMENED

VINCENT—A RESTAURANT

1110 Nicollet Mall, Minneapolis, 612-630-1189; www.vincentrestaurant.com

This downtown French bistro features a decadent happy hour even a food snob can love, with champagne drinks, artisan martinis, cheap appetizers and small plates, such as the restaurant's famous gourmet burger for around $7. That's right, along with its delectable menu featuring such delights as crêpes, pan-seared salmon and black truffle potatoes, this popular restaurant also serves up one of the best burgers in town, packed with ground beef, braised short ribs and a molten Gouda cheese center.

French. Lunch (Monday-Friday), dinner, late-night. Closed Monday. $36-85

WHERE TO SHOP

CORAZON

204 Washington Ave. N., Minneapolis, 612-333-1662

Decked out with cards, gifts, jewelry, kids' toys, housewares and a couple of racks of high-fashion clothing, Corazon is dedicated to all things boutique, fashionable and local. The shop is small but exceptionally organized, show-casing some of the best artisans in the Twin Cities. If you're looking for the perfect gift for a friend or for yourself, you're bound to find it here, whether it's a necklace, T-shirt, vase or letterpress card made by a local artist. There's even a revolving sale rack featuring some great deals on adorable clothes, handbags and more.

Monday-Saturday 10 a.m.-8 p.m., Sunday 11 a.m.-5 p.m.

I LIKE YOU

501 First Ave. N.E., Minneapolis, 612-827-9605

Peddling handmade clothing, accessories, pillows, purses and nearly every-thing two crafty hands can create, this Northeast gift shop celebrates all things local. One-of-a-kind hats, scarves, onesies, bibs, soaps, jewelry and more can be found at this shop, where more than 50 local designers showcase their whimsical wares. It's like a real-world Etsy.com. But here you get to try on and try out these gifts.

Tuesday-Friday 11 a.m.-7 p.m., Saturday 10 a.m.-6 p.m., Sunday 11 a.m.-5p.m.

MALL OF AMERICA

60 E. Broadway, Bloomington; www.mallofamerica.com

While it isn't in the city proper, the Mall of America is only 15 minutes from downtown and is the state's biggest shopping attraction. With more than 520 specialty stores, four department stores, an amusement park, an underwater world, a gigantic food court and 20 sit-down restaurants, the MOA is like a city in itself. The MOA is so massively gigantic that 258 Statues of Liberty could fit inside the always temperate, four-floored building. The MOA is the perfect tourist destination for shoppers and gawkers alike, with high-end shops like Betsey Johnson, Nordstrom, Coach, Burberry, Bloomingdale's and Francesca's Collections, as well as MOA-themed gift shops, discount retailers and chains, and weird one-off stores dedicated to things like University of Minnesota mascot Goldy Gopher. A view of the roller coaster, which snakes across the mall's center, is worth the visit alone. And as a bonus, this is where the TLC reality show *Mall Cops* is filmed, meaning you just might glimpse the quasi-celebrities watching over the racks.

Monday-Friday 10 a.m-9:30 p.m., Saturday 9:30 a.m.-9:30 p.m., Sunday 11 a.m.-7 p.m.

OPITZ OUTLET STORE
4320 Excelsior Blvd., St. Louis Park, 612-922-2435; www.opitzoutlet.com

Just a short drive from downtown, this St. Louis Park outlet store is nothing fancy. But it doesn't have to be, because here is where you can find designer goods—like a Marc Jacobs dress or Prada shoes—for as much as 70 percent off the retail value. While it's well-organized (everything is arranged by size and color), you might have to dig to find the best deals. But the store is stacked to the gills with name brands. The store receives new shipments on Tuesday, so try to plan a visit then, since the good stuff often is gone in a flash.

Monday-Wednesday noon-8 p.m., Thursday-Saturday 10 a.m.-8 p.m., Sunday noon-6 p.m.

SOUTHERN MINNESOTA

You'll find lots of different scenery in the southern half of Minnesota. In the region's central and western areas, there are prairies, rivers and lakes. And to the east is the great Mississippi River.

In a wooded valley where the Minnesota and Blue Earth rivers join, Mankato (Native American for "blue earth") takes its name from the blue clay that lines the riverbanks. You can see beautiful falls and a gorge at the city's Minneopa State Park.

Pipestone often hosts visitors en route to Pipestone National Monument. Travelers come to see the red Sioux quartzite from the quarries that are still used by Native American tribes today to make prayer pipes. The city is also home to Split Rock Creek State Park.

Legend has it that the city of Owatonna was named after a beautiful but frail Native American princess named Owatonna. It is said that her father, Chief Wabena, had heard about the healing water called "Minnewaucan." When the waters' curing powers restored his daughter's health, he moved his entire village to the site now known as Mineral Springs Park. A statue of Princess Owatonna stands in the park and watches over the springs that still provide cold, fresh mineral water.

The world-famous Mayo Clinic has transformed what was once a crossroads campground for immigrant wagon trains into a city of doctors, hospitals and lodging places. Each year thousands of people come to Rochester for medical treatment. It's has turned into a busy city with shopping malls, top restaurants and more.

New Englanders and Germans came to a site on the west bank of the Mississippi and built the industrial city of Winona. Now the city has its own vineyard, museums and parks that all sit along the Mississippi.

Whether you want to visit small prairie towns or thriving spots along the Mississippi River, you will find beautiful scenery everywhere.

WHAT TO SEE

MANKATO
HUBBARD HOUSE
415 Cherry St., Mankato, 507-345-4154; www.bechshistory.com

This 1871 historic Victorian home has cherry woodwork, three marble

BEST ATTRACTIONS

WHAT ARE THE TOP THINGS TO DO?

GET A BEER AT SCHELL GARDEN AND DEER PARK
These gardens have deer and peacocks, but the big reason to visit is for the onsite brewery. The more than 150-year-old Schnell's Brewing Co. sits on the garden grounds. Tour the brewery and pick up a six-pack as a souvenir.

SEE THE RARE ROCKS AT PIPESTONE NATIONAL MONUMENT
Native Americans quarried these ancient pipestones and carved them into pipes used for prayer. Although this is a national monument, the remaining red stone is available to all Native American tribes to carry out the tradition.

TAKE IN THE VISTA AT GARVIN HEIGHTS PARK
Bring your camera along and head to top of the 575-foot bluff in this park for an amazing view of Winona and the Mississippi River Valley. Snap some shots of the beautiful scenery below.

VISIT THE UPPER MISSISSIPPI RIVER NATIONAL WILDLIFE AND FISH REFUGE
At 261 miles, this is the longest river refuge in the continental United States. Grab an oar and canoe down the river to explore the marshes and backwoods. You probably will spot tundra swans and canvasback ducks in the spring and fall.

fireplaces, silk wall coverings, a carriage house and Victorian gardens.
Admission: adults $5, children 5-17 $2, children 4 and under free.

MINNEOPA STATE PARK
54497 Gadwall Road, Mankato, 507-389-5464; www.dnr.state.mn.us
This 1,145-acre park has scenic falls and a gorge, a historic mill site, fishing, hiking and camping.

NEW ULM

BROWN COUNTY HISTORICAL MUSEUM
2 N. Broadway St., New Ulm, 507-354-2016
This former post office houses historical exhibits on Native Americans and pioneers, and artwork, plus a research library with 5,000 family files.
Monday-Friday, also Saturday-Sunday afternoons.

FLANDRAU STATE PARK

1300 Summit Ave., New Ulm, 507-233-9800; www.dnr.state.mn.us

Composed of 801 acres on the Cottonwood River, the park has swimming, cross-country skiing (rentals), camping and hiking.

FORT RIDGELY

New Ulm, 507-426-7840; www.dnr.state.mn.us

This 584-acre park is home to the partially restored fort and interpretive center (May-Labor Day, daily). Also look for the nine-hole golf course, cross-country skiing, camping, hiking and an annual historical festival.

GLOCKENSPIEL

Fourth North and Minnesota streets, New Ulm, 507-354-4217

A 45-foot-high musical clock tower comes with performing animated figures and a carillon with 37 bells.

Performances daily, noon, 3 p.m. and 5 p.m.

HARKIN STORE

2 N. Broadway St., New Ulm, 507-354-8666; www.mnhs.org

This general store built by Alexander Harkin in 1870 was in the small town of West Newton, which died when it was bypassed by the railroad. It stayed open as a convenience shop until 1901, when rural free delivery closed the post office. The store has been restored to its original appearance and still has many original items on the shelves.

Admission: adults $3, seniors and children 6-17 $2, children 5 and under free. Memorial Day-Labor Day, Tuesday-Sunday 10 a.m. to 5 p.m.; May, September-October 15, Saturday-Sunday 10 a.m.-5 p.m.

HERMANN'S MONUMENT

Hermann Heights Park, Center and Monument streets, New Ulm, 507-354-4217; www.hermannmonument.com

Erected by a fraternal order, this monument recalls Hermann the Cheruscan, a German hero of A.D. 9. Towering more than 100 feet tall, the monument has a winding stairway that leads to a platform with views of the city and the Minnesota Valley.

June-Labor Day, daily.

SCHELL GARDEN AND DEER PARK

Schells Park, New Ulm, 507-354-5528

You'll spot deer and peacocks year-round at these gardens. But even better, on the grounds you'll find Schnell's Brewing Company. Tour the more than 150-year-old brewery, and if you get thirsty, pick up some suds in the gift shop.

Tours: adults $3, children free. Memorial Day-Labor Day, daily; rest of the year, Saturday.

NORTHFIELD

NERSTRAND-BIG WOODS STATE PARK

9700 170th St. E., Nerstrand, 507-333-4840; www.dnr.state.mn.us

At more than 1,280 acres, this heavily wooded park has hiking, cross-country skiing, snowmobiling, picnicking and camping.

NORTHFIELD ARTS GUILD
304 Division St. S., Northfield, 507-645-8877; www.northfieldartsguild.org
Check out exhibits of local and regional fine arts in a historic 1885 YMCA Building, as well as juried handcrafted items.
Monday-Saturday.

OWATONNA
MINNESOTA STATE PUBLIC SCHOOL ORPHANAGE MUSEUM
540 West Hills Circle, Owatonna, 507-451-7970, 800-423-6466;
www.orphanagemuseum.com
This museum is on the site of a former orphanage that housed nearly 13,000 children from 1886 to 1945. The main building is on the National Register of Historic Places.
Admission: free. Daily.

NORWEST BANK OWATONNA, NA BUILDING
101 N. Cedar Ave., Owatonna, 507-451-7970
Completed in 1908 as the National Farmers Bank, this nationally acclaimed architectural treasure was designed by one of America's outstanding architects, Louis H. Sullivan. The cubelike exterior, with huge arched stained-glass windows by Louis Millet, quickly earned widespread recognition.

OWATONNA ARTS CENTER
West Hills Complex, 435 Garden View Lane, Owatonna, 507-451-0533; www.oacarts.org
Housed in a historic Romanesque structure, this arts center's permanent collection includes a 100-piece collection of garments from around the world, and 14-foot stained-glass panels adorn the Performing Arts Hall. An outdoor sculpture garden includes works by Minnesota artists such as John Rood, Richard and Donald Hammel, Paul Grandlund and Charles Gagnon. There are changing gallery shows every month.
Tuesday-Sunday 1-5 p.m.

VILLAGE OF YESTERYEAR
1448 Austin Road, Owatonna, 507-451-1420; www.steelecohistoricalsociety.org
The 11 restored mid-1800s pioneer buildings here include a church, two log cabins, a schoolhouse, a large family home, an old fire department and a country store, plus a depot, a farm machinery building, a blacksmith shop and a museum. You can see period furnishings, memorabilia and a 1905 C-52 locomotive caboose.
Tours: adults $5, children 7-16 $3, children 6 and under free. May-September, Tuesday-Sunday afternoons.

PIPESTONE
PIPESTONE NATIONAL MONUMENT
36 N. Reservation Ave., Pipestone, 507-825-5464
The ancient pipestone in the quarries of this 283-acre area is found in few other places. The Native Americans quarried this reddish stone and carved it into ceremonial pipes. The Pipestone deposits—named catlinite for George Catlin, who first described the stone—run about a foot thick (most usable sections are about two inches thick). Principal features of the monument are Winnewissa

Falls, which flow over quartzite outcroppings; Three Maidens, a group of glacial boulders near quarries; Leaping Rock, used by Native Americans as a test of strength of young men; and Nicollet Marker, an inscription on a boulder that recalls the 1838 visit of Joseph Nicollet's exploring party. He carved his name and the initials of members of his party, including Lt. John C. Fremont. Established as a national monument in 1937, Pipestone protects the remaining red stone and preserves it for use by Native Americans of all tribes.
Daily.

SPLIT ROCK CREEK STATE PARK
Pipestone, 507-348-7908, 800-766-6000; www.pipestoneminnesota.com
Covering more than 1,300 acres, this park offers swimming, fishing, boating, hiking, cross-country skiing, picnicking and camping.

RED WING

CANNON VALLEY TRAIL
Highway 19, 825 Cannon River Ave., Cannon Falls, 507-263-0508; www.cannonvalleytrail.com
This 20-mile cross-country skiing trail connects Cannon Falls, Welch and Red Wing.

GOODHUE COUNTY HISTORICAL MUSEUM
1166 Oak St., Red Wing, 651-388-6024; www.goodhuehistory.mus.mn.us
This is one of the state's most comprehensive museums. Permanent exhibits explore local and regional history from the glacial age to present, and an extensive collection of Red Wing pottery and artifacts from the Prairie Island Native American community is also on display.
Admission: adults $5, seniors $3, children free. Tuesday-Friday 10 a.m.-5 p.m., Saturday-Sunday 1-5 p.m.

HIKING
Red Wing
A one-mile hiking trail to the top of Mount LaGrange (Barn Bluff) offers a scenic overlook of the Mississippi River. The Cannon Valley Trail provides 25 miles of improved trail following Cannon Bottom River to Cannon Falls.

RED WING STONEWARE
4909 Moundview Drive, Red Wing, 651-388-4610; www.redwingstoneware.com
This popular stoneware facility allows visitors to watch artisans create various types of pottery.

SHELDON THEATRE
443 W. Third St., Red Wing, 651-388-8700; www.sheldontheatre.org
Opened in 1904, this is the first municipal theater in the United States. Aside from the new multi-image screening facility, the theater has been restored to its early design. Performances are staged regularly, and pieces from regional artists are on display. Group tours are available.

SOLDIERS' MEMORIAL PARK/EAST END RECREATION AREA
Skyline Drive, Red Wing

On a plateau overlooking the city and the river, these 476 acres include five miles of hiking trails.

WELCH VILLAGE
26685 County Seven Blvd., Welch, 651-258-4567; www.welchvillage.com

Here you'll find three quads, five double and triple chairlifts. Plus there's a patrol, rentals, snowmaking and a cafeteria. The longest run is 4,000 feet with a vertical drop of 350 feet.

November-March, daily.

REDWOOD FALLS
LOWER SIOUX AGENCY AND HISTORIC SITE
32469 Redwood County Highway 2, Morton, 507-697-6321; www.mnhs.org

Exhibits, a trail system and a restored 1861 warehouse trace the history of the Dakota tribe in Minnesota from the mid-17th century through the present.

Admission: adults $6, seniors $5, children 6-17 $4, children 5 and under free. May-September, daily; rest of year, by appointment.

RAMSEY PARK
Redwood Falls; www.redwoodfalls.org

A 200-acre park of rugged woodland is carved by the Redwood River and Ramsey Creek. Spend the day picnicking, trail riding, cross-country skiing, hiking, or playing golf here. There is also a small zoo, a playground shelter and a 30-foot waterfall.

ROCHESTER
MAYO CLINIC
200 First St. S.W., Rochester, 507-284-2511; www.mayo.edu

More than 30 buildings now accommodate the famous group practice of medicine that grew from the work of Dr. William Worrall Mayo and his sons, Drs. William James Mayo and Charles Horace Mayo. There are now 1,041 doctors at the clinic as well as 935 residents in training in virtually every medical and surgical specialty. The 14-story Plummer Building includes a medical library and historical exhibit. The Conrad N. Hilton and Guggenheim buildings house clinical and research laboratories. The 19-story Mayo Building covers an entire block and houses facilities for diagnosis and treatment.

Clinic tours Monday-Friday.

MAYOWOOD
1195 W. Circle Drive S.W., Rochester, 507-282-9447

Home of Doctors C.H. and C.W. Mayo, this historic 38-room country mansion sits on 15 acres and is full of period antiques and works of art.

Tours: adults $5, children $5.

PLUMMER HOUSE OF THE ARTS
1091 Plummer Lane S.W., Rochester, 507-328-2525; www.rochestercvb.org

This is the former estate of Dr. Henry S. Plummer, a 35-year member of the Mayo Clinic. Today, 11 acres remain, with formal gardens, a quarry and a water tower. The five-story, circa 1920 house is an English Tudor mansion with 49 rooms, original furnishings and a slate roof.

Admission: $5. Tours June-August, Wednesday afternoons, also first and third Sunday afternoons.

WHITEWATER STATE PARK

19041 Highway 74, Altura, 507-932-3007; www.dnr.state.mn.us

A 1,822-acre park contains limestone formations in a hardwood forest and offers swimming, fishing, hiking, cross-country skiing, picnicking and primitive camping.

WINONA

GARVIN HEIGHTS PARK

Huff Street and Garvin Heights Road, Winona

The park's 575-foot bluff offers majestic views of the Mississippi River Valley. After you're done "oohing" and "ahhing," head to the picnic area for some lunch.

Dawn-dusk.

GARVIN HEIGHTS VINEYARDS

2255 Garvin Heights Road, Winona, 507-474-9463; www.ghvwine.com

Sitting atop a bluff overlooking Winona, this winery uses cold-climate grapes to make its own wines. Go see the vineyard and do some wine tasting. But pick up a bottle of the popular red raspberry wine for later. The winery purchases some grapes from Wisconsin, so look for bottles labeled "Minnesota Grown," to make sure you're getting the local stuff.

Tuesday-Sunday 10 a.m.-6 p.m.

MINNESOTA MARINE ART MUSEUM

800 Riverview Drive, Winona, 507-474-6626, 866-940-6626; www.minnesotamarineart.org

Its location along the banks of the Mississippi River is the perfect setting for this museum, which puts the spotlight on water-inspired art. The permanent collection features maritime paintings, ship models and navigational instruments. Check out the painted wooded sculptures by artistic husband-and-wife team Leo and Marilyn Smith. Their colorful folk art is a nod to small-town life and river lore. Afterward, go to the source of inspiration for all of this work; take a stroll along the riverwalk.

Admission: adults $6, children and students 5-21 $3, children 4 and under free. Tuesday-Saturday 10 a.m.-5 p.m., Sunday 11 a.m.-5 p.m.

UPPER MISSISSIPPI RIVER NATIONAL WILDLIFE AND FISH REFUGE

51 E. Fourth St., Winona, 507-452-4232

From Wabasha, Minn., extending 261 miles to Rock Island, Ill., the refuge encompasses 200,000 acres of wooded islands, marshes, sloughs and backwaters. Twenty percent of the refuge is closed for hunting and trapping until after duck hunting season. A boat is required for access to most parts of the refuge.

Daily.

WHERE TO STAY

ROCHESTER

★★★KAHLER GRAND

20 Second Ave. S.W., Rochester, 507-280-6200, 800-533-1655; www.thekahlerhotel.com

This original English Tudor structure has vaulted ceilings and paneling. Across from the Mayo Clinic in the downtown area, it is connected to the renowned hospital's campus through a climate-controlled skyway and subway. The subway also links the hotel to the Grand Shops, a mall with 65 stores. Inside the hotel, you'll find charming rooms and an indoor pool underneath a glass dome.

688 rooms. Restaurant, bar. Business center. Fitness center. Pets accepted. Pool. $61-150

★★★MARRIOTT ROCHESTER MAYO CLINIC

101 First Ave. S.W., Rochester, 507-280-6000, 877-623-7775; www.rochestermarriott.com

Shoppers will appreciate the Marriott's location. It's near the Galleria Mall and Miracle Mile Shopping Complex and is connected to the Grand Shops via subway. If you dig sports, there are tennis facilities and many golf courses nearby as well. After a day of hitting the stores or golfing, relax in your comfy maroon and gold room, which comes with an LCD television and a minifridge. Or unwind with a glass of pinot and a cheese flight at Vino, the hotel's wine bar and restaurant.

203 rooms. Restaurant, bar. Business center. Fitness center. Pool. Pets accepted. $151-250

WHERE TO EAT

RECOMMENDED
ROCHESTER

300 FIRST

300 First Ave. N.W., Rochester, 507-281-2451; www.cccrmg.com

Walk into the restaurant's dining room, and on one side you'll see the full display kitchen and on the other people in raised booths sipping one of the signature "Smokin' Martinis," which give off a vapor to make them look steamy. When the novelty wears off, set your sights on the menu, which has standouts like ginger-crusted bigeye ahi tuna with panko-covered orange cilantro sticky rice and a tender filet mignon. If you're stuck on dessert, get another smoky martini.

Contemporary American. Dinner. Outdoor dining. Children's menu. Bar. $16-35

CHESTER'S KITCHEN & BAR

University Square, 111 S. Broadway, Rochester, 507-424-1211; www.chesterskb.com

Chester's offers a dimly lit dining room with dark wood tables and big booths in olive, gray and chocolate-brown. The cozy ambience sets the mood for the comfort food the restaurant dishes out. Start off with Chester's pizza—basil pesto, oven-roasted tomatoes, mozzarella and basil on lavash. Among the entrées, go for the rotisserie Minnesota chicken or the slow-smoked baby-back barbecue ribs. The made-to-order banana cream pie provides a comforting capper to the meal.

American, steak. Lunch, dinner, late-night, Sunday brunch. Outdoor dining. Children's menu. Bar. $16-35

MICHAEL'S FINE DINING

15 S. Broadway, Rochester, 507-288-2020; www.michaelsfinedining.com

Open since 1951, Michael's shows its Greek roots with comfort food like flaming saganaki cheese and gyros, but this is first and foremost a fine-dining destination. Meat and seafood get top billing with dishes like New York strip sirloin with garlic butter, caramelized scallops and roasted Long Island duckling. If you do crave some Greek cuisine, you can always follow up your meaty entrée with a sweet, flaky baklava.

Seafood, steak, Mediterranean. Lunch, dinner. Closed Sunday. Reservations recommended. Children's menu. Bar. $16-35

PRESCOTTS

Crossroads Shopping Center, 1201 S. Broadway, Rochester, 507-536-7775; www.prescottsgrill.com

Prescotts may be located in a strip mall, but you won't find any food court fare in the restaurant. Instead, the seasonal menu features starters like escargots and artichokes and main courses like crab-stuffed chicken breast. Locals especially like the restaurant's selection of house-made bread—which you can order for takeout—and its wine list. Don't miss the death by chocolate dessert. One bite of the popular flourless chocolate torte and you'll forget you're sitting in a mall.

American, French. Dinner. Closed Sunday. $16-35

SÖNTÉS

4 Third St. S.W., Rochester, 507-292-1628; www.sontes.com

Kick back in this airy wine bar decked out with white-linen-topped tables and local art on the walls. Of course, do it with a drink in your hand, and choose among the more than 40 by the glass and 100 by the bottle. Or design your own flight. Wine newbies can take advantage of Söntés' try-before-you-buy policy to ensure they're getting a palate-pleasing pour. Although wine is the focus here, don't forget the tapas menu from rising star chef Justin Schoville. It has everything from foie gras to pork and Laughing Bird shrimp rolls, along with a list of artisanal cheeses broken down into fun categories, such as "racy" and "stinky." To help you kick back even more, the wine bar features live music on the weekends.

Tapas. Dinner. Closed Sunday. Outdoor seating. Bar. $16-35

WELCOME TO WISCONSIN

FORESTS BLOTTED OUT THE SKY OVER WISCONSIN WHEN

the first French voyageurs arrived more than three centuries ago. Rich in natural resources, modern conservation concepts took strong root here—15,000 lakes, 2,200 streams and millions of acres of publicly owned forests. Native Americans called this land Ouisconsin, which means "where the waters gather."

Wisconsin is famous for breweries, universities, forests, paper mills, dairy products and diverse vacation attractions. Wisconsin is also the birthplace of the statewide primary election law, workers' compensation law, unemployment compensation and many other reforms that have since been widely adopted.

The Badger State acquired its nickname during the lead rush of 1827, when miners built their homes by digging into the hillsides like badgers. The state is America's dairyland, producing much of the nation's milk and more than 30 percent of all cheese consumed in the United States. It is a leader in the production of hay, cranberries and ginseng, and harvests huge crops of peas, beans, carrots, corn and oats. It is the leading canner of fresh vegetables and an important source of cherries, apples, maple syrup and wood pulp. A great part of the nation's paper products, agricultural implements and nonferrous metal products and alloys are manufactured here as well.

Wisconsin summers are balmy, and winter offers plenty of cold-weather activities, making the state a year-round vacationland that lures millions of visitors annually. This is a land of many contrasts: rounded hills and narrow valleys to the southwest, a huge central plain, rolling prairie in the southeast and the north filled with majestic forests, marshes and lakes.

BEST ATTRACTIONS

WISCONSIN'S BEST ATTRACTIONS

THE DELLS
The family-friendly Wisconsin Dells lays claim to being the waterpark capital of the world, making it the ultimate cold-weather destination. Slide down one of the 49 slides at Noah's Ark, the largest U.S. water park.

DOOR COUNTY
For a scenic getaway, head to Door County. Known as Cape Cod of the Midwest, the area is famous for its lovely foliage, picturesque villages and seemingly endless shoreline.

GREEN BAY
Football fanatics will want to hike over to Packers Country, otherwise known as Green Bay. The city is the home of legendary Lambeau Field and the Green Bay Packers Hall of Fame Museum.

MILWAUKEE
You'll learn a lot in the state's urban center. The Milwaukee Museum of Art gives a dose of culture, and Discovery World teaches about science and technology. But equally as important, the breweries churn out the city's famous beer.

NORTHERN WISCONSIN

Vacationers head to Northern Wisconsin to experience the state's northwoods, to join the throngs of fans cheering at Packer games and to relax along the water in beautiful Door County. But the region's many small towns are worth a visit.

Considered a gateway to the Apostle Islands, Bayfield is a charming community filled with orchards, inns, berry farms and a host of seasonal activities.

Headquarters of the Interstate State Park, St. Croix Falls has become a summer and winter resort area. Lions Park, north of town, has picnicking and boat launching, and there are many miles of groomed snowmobile trails in Polk County.

Crandon is the perfect destination for travelers searching for a rustic adventure. There are four lakes in Crandon, which offer opportunities for fishing, swimming and boating in summer. In winter, enjoy cross-country skiing and snowmobiling across the scenic terrain.

Minocqua is a four-season resort area known for its thousands of acres of lakes. The area contains one of the largest concentrations of freshwater bodies in America. Minocqua, the "Island City," was once completely surrounded by Lake Minocqua.

Located at the junction of the Wisconsin and Pelican rivers, Rhinelander is close to 232 lakes, 11 trout streams and two rivers. The logging industry, which built this area, still thrives and the many miles of old logging roads are excellent for hiking and mountain biking. Paved bicycle trails, cross-country skiing and snowmobiling are also popular in this northwoods area.

Door County's Sturgeon Bay sits at the farthest inland point of a bay where swarms of sturgeon were once caught and piled like cordwood along the shore. The historic portage from the bay to Lake Michigan, used for centuries by Native Americans and early explorers, began here. The Sturgeon Bay ship canal now makes the route a waterway used by lake freighters and pleasure craft.

Washington Island, six miles off the coast of Door County, is one of the oldest Icelandic settlements in the United States. Many Scandinavian festivals are still celebrated. The island may be reached by ferry.

For an urban getaway, Green Bay is the go-to spot in Northern Wisconsin. The oldest settlement in the state, Green Bay is a paper and cheese producing center as well as a hub for health care and insurance. But it's mostly famous for its professional football team, the mighty Green Bay Packers.

WHAT TO SEE

ALGOMA
VON STIEHL WINERY
115 Navarino St., Algoma, 920-487-5208, 800-955-5208; www.vonstiehl.com

Housed in a 140-year-old brewery, this is the oldest winery in Wisconsin. It offers wine, cheese and jelly tastings at the end of each tour. Be sure to try the semi-dry, fruity riesling, the winery's specialty.

May-October, daily; rest of year, Friday-Sunday.

ASHLAND
COPPER FALLS STATE PARK
Highway 169 and Copper Falls Road, Mellen, 715-274-5123; www.dnr.wi.gov

This 2,500-acre park has more than eight miles of river, plus nature and hiking trails that provide spectacular views of the gorge and the falls. Attractions include swimming, fishing, canoeing, backpacking, cross-country skiing, picnicking and a playground.

Daily.

BAYFIELD
APOSTLE ISLANDS NATIONAL LAKESHORE
415 Washington Ave., Bayfield, 715-779-3397; www.nps.gov

These 11 miles of mainland shoreline and 21 islands of varying size feature hiking, boating, fishing, plus primitive campsites on 18 islands.

Check out one of the two visitors centers, in Bayfield (daily) and at Little Sand Bay (Memorial Day-September).

LAKE SUPERIOR BIG TOP CHAUTAUQUA

Ski Hill Road, Bayfield, 715-373-5552, 888-244-8368; www.bigtop.org

At this outdoor venue, you can catch folk and bluegrass performances, musicals and theater.

Admission: varies. June-Labor Day, Wednesday-Sunday evenings; some Tuesday and matinee performances.

MADELINE ISLAND FERRY LINE

1 Washington Ave., Bayfield, 715-747-2051; www.madferry.com

The Island Queen, Nichevo II and the Madeline Bayfield make frequent trips between LaPointe and Bayfield.

Admission: varies. April-January, daily.

CHIPPEWA FALLS

BRUNET ISLAND STATE PARK

23125 255th St., Cornell, 715-239-6888; www.dnr.wi.gov

This 1,032-acre river island park features swimming, fishing, boating, canoeing, nature and hiking trails, cross-country skiing, picnicking, a playground and camping.

COOK-RUTLEDGE MANSION

505 W. Grand Ave., Chippewa Falls, 715-723-7181; www.cookrutledgemansion.com

This restored 1887 Victorian mansion offers guided tours. Listed on the National Register of Historic Places, the home showcases high Victorian Italianate architecture.

Admission: adults $5, children $1. June-August, Thursday-Sunday; September-May, by appointment.

LAKE WISSOTA STATE PARK

18127 County Highway O, Chippewa Falls, 715-382-4574; www.dnr.wi.gov

This 1,062-acre park offers swimming, waterskiing, fishing, boating, canoeing, hiking, cross-country skiing, picnicking, a playground and camping.

Daily.

CRANDON

CAMP FIVE MUSEUM AND "LUMBERJACK SPECIAL" STEAM TRAIN TOUR

Highway 8 and Highway 32, Laona, 715-674-3414, 800-774-3414; www.camp5museum.org

Take this old steam train ride to the Camp Five Museum complex, where you will find an active blacksmith shop, a 1900s country store, a logging museum with an audiovisual presentation, a nature center with a diorama featuring area wildlife and a 30-minute guided forest tour.

Mid-June-late August, four departures Monday-Saturday.

EAU CLAIRE

DELLS MILL AND MUSEUM

E. 18855 County Road V, Augusta, 715-286-2714; www.dellsmill.com

This historic five-story water-powered flour and grist mill was built in 1864 out of hand-hewn timbers.

Admission: varies. May-October, Daily.

HIGHLIGHT

WHAT ARE THE TOP THINGS TO DO?

GET A DRINK AT VON STIEHL WINERY

Take a tour the state's oldest winery, Von Stiehl. You'll get to see the century-old underground caverns where the wine is aged. Each tour ends with a wine, cheese and jelly tasting. Be sure to tipple the fruit wine, which uses Door County cherries.

VISIT RHINELANDER LOGGING MUSEUM

Learn about Wisconsin's history as a lumber center at this museum, the only authentic logging camp in the region. Also learn about the area's mythical hodag, and try to spot the spiky creature in the woods.

ESCAPE TO CHEQUAMEGON-NICOLET NATIONAL FOREST

Take a scenic drive through Wisconsin's northwoods. The 661,000-acre national forest has pine, spruce, fir, sugar maple, oak and birch trees. Keep an eye out for white-tailed deer scurrying by.

SPRINT OVER TO LAMBEAU FIELD

Hardcore pigskin fanatics should visit Lambeau Field, home of the Packers. Even if it's the offseason, you can head to the "Frozen Tundra" to see the Green Bay Packers Hall of Fame, which showcases the team's Super Bowl trophies.

PAUL BUNYAN LOGGING CAMP

Carson Park, 1110 Carson Park Drive, Eau Claire, 715-835-6200;
www.paulbunyancamp.org

See what life was like for an old-time logger. This restored 1890s logging camp has a bunkhouse, a cook shack, a blacksmith shop, a dingle, a filers shack, barn and heavy equipment display.

Admission: adults $5, children $2. First Monday in April-first Monday in October.

FISH CREEK

AMERICAN FOLKLORE THEATRE

Peninsula State Park Amphitheater, 9462 Shore Road, Fish Creek, 920-854-6117;
www.folkloretheatre.com

See original folk musical productions such as *Guys and Does,* based on American lore and literature at this theater.

July-August.

PENINSULA STATE PARK

9462 Shore Road, Fish Creek, 920-868-3258; www.dnr.state.wi.us

This 3,763-acre park has nine miles of waterfront, including sandy and cobble-stone beaches, caves and cliffs and an observation tower. Swimming, fishing, boating, waterskiing, hiking, bicycle trails, cross-country skiing, snowmobiling, picnic grounds, a playground, concessions and camping are all available.

GREEN BAY

GREEN BAY BOTANICAL GARDENS

2600 Larsen Road, Green Bay, 920-490-9457; www.gbbg.org

If the botanical gardens look familiar, it may be because you saw it on *The Bachelorette.* Single lady Ali Fedotowsky went there on a date. Bring your own date to go to see GBBG's formal rose, children's and four-season garden.

Admission: adults $7, seniors $5, children 5-12 $2, children 4 and under free. May-October, Daily; November-April, Monday-Friday.

GREEN BAY PACKERS (NFL)

Lambeau Field, 1265 Lombardi Ave., Green Bay, 920-469-7500; www.packers.com

Probably the most storied football venue in the NFL, Curly Lambeau Field is home to the Green Bay Packers. Site of the famous Ice Bowl, the stadium is known for its harsh weather (it's commonly referred to as the "frozen tundra of Lambeau Field"), as well as for the "Lambeau Leaps" that Packer players take into the waiting arms of cheesehead fans in the front row of the end zone.

GREEN BAY PACKERS HALL OF FAME

Lambeau Field Atrium, 1265 Lombardi Ave., Green Bay, 920-499-4281, 888-442-7225; www.packers.com

This museum chronicles the history of the Green Bay Packers from 1919 to present and also houses a unique collection of multimedia presentations, memorabilia, hands-on activities and NFL films. Feast your eyes on the holiest of football awards—a Super Bowl trophy. You can see three of them here.

Admission: adults $10, seniors and students $8, children 6-11 $5, children 5 and under free. Monday-Saturday 9 a.m.-6 p.m., Sunday 10 a.m. to 5 p.m.

HERITAGE HILL STATE PARK

2640 S. Webster Ave., Green Bay, 920-448-5150; www.heritagehillgb.org

The park includes a 40-acre living history museum and a complex of 26 historical buildings that illustrate the development of northeast Wisconsin. You can check out everything from a courthouse and hospital to a cheese factory and maple sugaring house.

Admission: adults $8, seniors $7, children 5-17 $6, children 4 and under free. Memorial Day-late-October, Daily; December, Friday-Saturday. Christmas festival, Friday-Sunday in December.

ONEIDA NATION MUSEUM

W892 County Road EE, De Pere, 920-869-2768; museum.oneidanation.org

Permanent and hands-on exhibits tell the story of the Oneida Nation. See handmade crafts from the Oneida and how the tribe has helped the country during times of war and peace.

Admission: adults $2, seniors and children $1. September-May, Tuesday-Friday; June-August, Tuesday-Saturday.

MANITOWISH WATERS
CRANBERRY BOG TOURS
Community Center, Highway 51 Airport Road, Manitowish Waters, 715-543-8488; www.manitowishwaters.org

Begin your tour with a video while sampling juice and dried cranberry samples. Then follow guides in your own vehicle up to the bogs, where you can go off and explore on your own or buy some cranberry goodies in the gift shop.

Late July-early October, Friday.

MENOMONIE
MABEL TAINTER MEMORIAL BUILDING
205 Main St. E., Menomonie, 715-235-0001, 715-235-9726; www.mabeltainter.com

This hand-stenciled and ornately carved cultural center looks like a castle. It was constructed in 1889 by lumber baron Andrew Tainter in memory of his daughter Mabel. The building contains a 313-seat Victorian-era theater that hosts various performances on its stage.

Tours: adults $5, seniors and students $4, children 6-12 $3, children 5 and under free. Guided tours daily.

WILSON PLACE MUSEUM
101 Wilson Circle, Menomonie, 715-235-2283

This Victorian mansion is the former residence of Sen. James H. Stout, founder of the University of Wisconsin. Nearly all furnishings are original.

Admission: adults $5, students $3.50, children 12 and under $2. Guided tours Memorial Day-Labor Day, Friday-Sunday afternoons.

MINOCQUA
JIM PECK'S WILDWOOD
10094 State Highway 70, Minocqua, 715-356-5588; www.wildwoodwildlifepark.com

This wildlife park features hundreds of tame animals and birds native to the area. Many of them can be pet at the baby animal nursery. The more than 500 animal residents include a wolf, tiger, black bear and wallaby.

Admission: adults $12, children 8. May-mid-October, daily.

MINOCQUA WINTER PARK NORDIC CENTER
12375 Scotchman Lake Road, Minocqua, 715-356-3309; www.skimwp.org

This center has more than 35 miles of groomed and tracked cross-country trails, two groomed telemarking slopes and more than one mile of lighted trails for night skiing (Thursday-Friday only).

December-March, Thursday-Tuesday.

NORTHERN LIGHTS PLAYHOUSE
5611 Highway 51, Hazelhurst, 715-356-7173; www.nl-playhouse.com

Set in the northwoods, this professional repertory theater presents Broadway plays, musicals and comedies and also offers a children's theater.

Memorial Day-early October.

RHINELANDER
RHINELANDER LOGGING MUSEUM
810 Keenan St., Rhinelander, 715-369-5004; www.rhinelanders-morningside.com

The most complete displays of old-time lumbering in the Midwest are found here. On the grounds are the Five Spot, which is the last narrow-gauge railroad locomotive to work Wisconsin's northwoods, and a restored depot dating from the late 1800s. The museum also displays the "hodag"—called "the strangest animal known to man" because, well, it's a hoax. The creature—which supposedly is hairy, covered with horns and sports tusks—has become the symbol of the city.

Admission: free. Memorial Day-Labor Day, daily.

ST. CROIX FALLS
GOVERNOR KNOWLES STATE FOREST
325 Highway 70, Grantsburg, 715-463-2898; www.dnr.state.wi.us

A 33,000-acre expanse extending north and south along the St. Croix River, this forest offers fishing, boating, canoeing, hiking, a bridle path, snowmobile and cross-country ski trails, picnicking and group camping.

Daily.

INTERSTATE STATE PARK
Highway 35, St. Croix Falls, 715-483-3747; www.dnr.wi.gov

At 1,325 acres, this is Wisconsin's oldest state park. It offers swimming, fishing, boating, canoeing, picnicking, camping, hiking and cross-country ski trails. The Ice Age National Scientific Reserve operates a visitors center here.

Daily.

STURGEON BAY
ROBERT LA SALLE COUNTY PARK
1015 Green Bay Road, Sturgeon Bay, 800-527-3529; www.doorcounty.com

This site is where La Salle and his band of explorers were rescued from starvation by friendly Native Americans. A monument marks the location of La Salle's fortified camp.

THE FARM
4285 State Highway 57, Sturgeon Bay, 920-743-6666; www.thefarmindoorcounty.com

The Farm is like an outdoor museum of rural farm life. You can pet animals and fowl in natural surroundings, plus you can check out a pioneer farmstead and wildlife display.

Admission: adults $8, children 4-12 free, children 3 and under free. Memorial Day-Mid-October, daily.

SUPERIOR
BRULE RIVER STATE FOREST
6250 S. Ranger Road, Brule, 715-372-5678; www.dnr.wi.gov

On 40,218 acres, this forest offers fishing, boating, canoeing and nature, hiking, snowmobile and cross-country ski trails.

HIGHLIGHT

WHAT IS THERE TO DO IN DOOR COUNTRY?

Famous for its foliage and 250 miles of shoreline, Door County is a peninsula with Green Bay on the west and Lake Michigan on the east. Its picturesque villages, rolling woodlands, limestone bluffs and beautiful vistas are the reason the area is often referred to as the Cape Cod of the Midwest.

Door County offers year-round attractions. Spring and summer bring fishing, sailing, beachcombing, camping, hiking, biking and horseback riding. Thousands of acres of apple and cherry blossoms color the landscape in late May. There is excellent scuba diving in the Portes des Mortes (Death's Door) Straits at the tip of the peninsula, where hundreds of shipwrecks lie in the shifting freshwater sands. Fall colors can be viewed from the endless miles of trails and country roads, which become cross-country ski routes in winter.

Many artists reside here, as evidenced by the towns' shops, galleries and boutiques. Summertime theater and concerts also attract tourists.

The taste of the peninsula is unquestionably the legendary fish boil. Trout or whitefish and potatoes and onions are cooked in a cauldron over an open fire. When the fish has almost finished cooking, kerosene is thrown onto the fire, creating a huge flame and causing the unwanted oils to boil out and over the pot.

PATTISON STATE PARK

6294 Highway 35 S., Superior, 715-399-3111; www.dnr.state.wi.us

This state park has 1,476 acres of sand beach and woodlands. Head here for swimming, fishing, canoeing, a nature center, playgrounds, hiking and cross-country ski trails. The outstanding park attraction is Big Manitou Falls, which at 165 feet is the highest waterfall in the state. Little Manitou Falls, a 31-foot drop, is upstream of the main falls.

Daily.

THREE LAKES

CHEQUAMEGON-NICOLET NATIONAL FOREST

4364 Wall St., Eagle River, 715-479-2827; www.fs.fed.us

This forest has 661,000 acres and is 62 miles long and 36 miles wide; the elevation ranges from 860 feet to 1,880 feet. It is noted for scenic drives through pine, spruce, fir, sugar maple, oak and birch trees.

Daily.

WASHINGTON ISLAND

ROCK ISLAND STATE PARK

Little Lake Road, Washington Island, 920-847-2235; www.dnr.state.wi.us

This 912-acre park was the summer home of electric tycoon C.H. Thordarson. It features buildings in Icelandic architectural style, and it provides plenty of recreational activities, including swimming, fishing, boating, nature trails and more than nine miles of hiking and snowmobile trails.

Daily

WHERE TO STAY

BAYFIELD

★★★OLD RITTENHOUSE INN

301 Rittenhouse Ave., Bayfield, 888-611-4667, 800-779-2129; www.rittenhouseinn.com

Travelers looking for something a bit different can find it in this whimsical and charming inn. Considered by many as the preferred lodging for romance and weekend getaways, the inn consists of the lovely Victorian Old Rittenhouse Inn itself, which also houses a restaurant. Guests can enjoy the comfortably appointed guest rooms, all of which feature lovely antiques, and enjoy fine dining that covers everything from hearty breakfasts to elegant dinners. Most rooms have fireplaces and whirlpool tubs. Take time to sit on the wrap-around porch and admire the nice views of Lake Superior.

19 rooms. Restaurant. Complimentary breakfast. $60-150

EAU CLAIRE

★★★FANNY HILL VICTORIAN INN & DINNER THEATER

3919 Crescent Ave., Eau Claire, 715-836-8184, 800-292-8026; www.fannyhill.com

A beautiful river view is the claim to fame at this elegant inn, which has a classic flair. Each room has Victorian touches, like carved oak headboards, that cap off the romantic surroundings. You needn't leave the property for entertainment; take a walk through the Victorian garden overlooking the Chippewa River or buy a ticket to the dinner theater to see productions like Neil Simon's *Last of the Red Hot Lovers* and *Noises Off*.

11 rooms. Restaurant, bar. Complimentary breakfast. $151-250

FISH CREEK

★★★WHITE GULL INN

4225 Main St., Fish Creek, 920-868-3517, 888-364-9542; www.whitegullinn.com

Built in 1896, this longstanding charmer features antiques in the lovely suites, rooms and cottages. Accommodations have been fully restored (fireplaces and whirlpool baths are common) and the seven houses and cottages offer distinctly period details, like a maple canopied bed or French doors leading to a private deck. Have a candlelight dinner at the onsite restaurant, which serves dishes such as herbed lamb shank and Parmesan-dusted halibut fillet. Don't miss the traditional fish boil.

17 rooms. Restaurant, bar. Complimentary breakfast. $151-250

RECOMMENDED

GREEN BAY

ALOFT GREEN BAY

465 Pilgrim Way, Green Bay, 920-884-0800; www.starwoodhotels.com

If you are coming to Green Bay and want to stay near Lambeau Field but not be in the thick of the action, try Aloft. It's two miles from the famed football field. When you need a break from cheesehead madness, hang in the cozy riverside hotel for a more chill setting. Choose between the lounge with a four-panel LCD television and a pool table or the intimate backyard with dim lights, candles and plenty of seating. The rooms use space well, providing both comfy, modern digs with light wood and a work area that has a connectivity station that recharges your gadgets and links to the 42-inch LCD TV. The bathrooms have Bliss Spa toiletries and oversized showerheads. Bonus: The entire hotel is equipped with free WiFi, so it won't only appeal to Packers fans but techies as well.

105 rooms. Bar. Business center. Fitness center. Pool. $61-150

HOTEL SIERRA

333 Main St., Green Bay, 920-432-4555; www.hotel-sierra.com

When you step into this boutique hotel's lobby and see the open eight-story atrium with 20-foot lit palm trees, porcelain tiles, oversized lamps and zebra wood, you'll forget you're in Packers country. The rooms in the all-suite hotel are devoid of Packers green and yellow; instead there's soothing natural shades like olive and beige. Plus, they have full kitchens with stainless-steel appliances, microwaves and small refrigerators, and the living spaces come with 32-inch flat-panel televisions and pullout sofas. Take advantage of the free breakfast, which includes made-to-order omelets, before you run off to the adjacent KI Convention Center or Lambeau Field, which is about four miles away.

240 rooms. Restaurant, bar. Complimentary breakfast. Business center. Fitness center. Pool. Spa. $61-150

RICE LAKE

★★★★CANOE BAY

Off Hogback Road, Rice Lake, 715-924-4594; www.canoebay.com

Canoe Bay is rather like a luxurious camp for adults, with gourmet dining, an award-winning wine cellar and extensive amenities. Situated on 280 acres in northwestern Wisconsin, the resort's three private, spring-fed lakes are perfect for a multitude of recreational opportunities. Test out the waters using the hotel's canoeing, kayaking and row-boating equipment. The wilderness trails are ideal for hiking in summer months, while snowshoeing and cross-country skiing are popular during the winter. The resort has no telephones or televisions, not to mention a no-kids policy, so that you won't be distracted from the peaceful setting. Choose from either well-appointed rooms at the lodge and inn or cozy private cottages. Linger over dinner in the candlelit Dining Room, where dishes are

---

WHAT ARE THE BEST WATERFRONT HOTELS?

Canoe Bay:
This beautiful hotel sits on 280 acres along with three private lakes. Aside from admiring the lakeside vista from your room, you can hit the water and do some canoeing, kayaking or row boating.

Old Rittenhouse Inn:
This charming Victorian inn gives you a front-seat view of Lake Superior. Sit in the swing on the wrap-around porch to gaze at the water, or stroll the grounds to get up close to the lake.

WHAT ARE THE BEST STEAK HOUSES?

Black & Tan Grille:
This grill serves up succulent steaks. Its namesake Black & Tan makes use of one of Wisconsin's best products: cheese. The tenderloin comes with gorgonzola brochettes and a chèvre demi swirl.

Republic Chophouse:
At this Green Bay chophouse, steaks get V.I.P. treatment. The signature Irish New Yorker is a N.Y. strip marinated in Guinness and whiskey, among other things. Even better, the dish comes with a shot of Jameson.

prepared with organic produce from the garden and locally produced ingredients.

19 rooms. Restaurant. Complimentary breakfast. Fitness center. No children allowed. $351 and up

WHERE TO EAT

RECOMMENDED
GREEN BAY

BLACK & TAN GRILLE
130 E. Walnut St., Green Bay, 920-430-7700;
www.blackandtangrille.com

Housed in the historic Bellin Building, Black & Tan offers a seasonal menu, but the specialty is the steaks. Try the signature Black & Tan, a tenderloin served on top of gorgonzola brochettes and topped with caramelized onions. The rack of lamb offers a Mediterranean spin, with an olive tapenade stuffed inside and a sauce made with Greek yogurt. The second-floor dining room gives a view of the Fox River and downtown Green Bay. After your meal, head down to the first-floor lounge for an Irish Funeral—Starbucks coffee liqueur, Baileys Irish Cream and Jameson whiskey—or another selection from the extensive martini list.

American. Dinner. Bar. $16-35

BRETT FAVRE'S STEAKHOUSE
1004 Brett Favre Pass, Green Bay, 920-499-6874;
www.brettfavresteakhouse.com

Football fans will chow down at this steakhouse in hopes of seeing former Packer Brett Favre. Even if the quarterback is a no-show, you can still look at the Packers memorabilia and Favre's trophies, which tastefully adorn the dining room. Steak is the winner here; go for the London broil with cracked pepper and sautéed button mushrooms or the slow-roasted prime rib with horseradish sauce. Before the Packers' home games, come to the restaurant for its big outdoor tailgating shindig. The restaurant, only two blocks from Lambeau Field, offers unlimited food and beverages, including brats, burgers, jambalaya, beer and Bloody Marys.

American, steakhouse. Dinner. Bar. $16-35

HINTERLAND BREWERY
313 Dousman St., Green Bay, 920-438-8050;
www.hinterlandbeer.com

Although this restaurant is inside a brewery, you won't find cheese curds and brats on the menu. Instead, the menu is filled with upscale and unusual combinations, like seared diver scallops and pork belly appetizer, or a wood-fire grilled striped marlin with andouille sausage or sockeye salmon with bacon for entrées. Whichever you choose, make sure you pair it with the Hinterland Pale Ale or one of the other beers brewed onsite.

American. Dinner. Closed Sunday. Reservations recommended. Bar. $16-35

REPUBLIC CHOPHOUSE
218 N. Adams St., Green Bay, 920-430-7901; www.republicchophouse.com

The food at this house of meat gets a special touch from chef Abbey Steffen; each cut gets seasoned with a top-secret spice recipe to make it stand out. This is a chophouse, so you have to go for the carnivorous dishes. Order the Irish New Yorker—a New York strip steak marinated in Guinness, whiskey, garlic, onion, oregano and sesame oil—which also comes with a shot of Jameson. The Moroccan lamb rib chops are marinated in Moroccan spices and served with a cilantro-lime crème fraîche. Cap off the meal with the four-layer red velvet cake drizzled with chocolate.

American, steakhouse. Dinner. Closed Sunday. Children's menu. Bar. $28-70

MILWAUKEE

Thriving and progressive, Milwaukee has retained its gemutlichkeit (German for "coziness"), though today's conviviality is as likely to be expressed at a soccer game or at a symphony concert as at the beer garden. Though it is still the beer capital of the nation, its leading single industry is not brewing but the manufacture of X-ray apparatus and tubes.

Milwaukee's Teutonic personality has dimmed, becoming only a part of the local color of a city long famous for good government, a low crime rate and high standards of civic performance. With a history going back to the days when Native Americans called this area Millioki, or "gathering place by the waters," Milwaukee is a city of 96.5 square miles on the west shore of Lake Michigan, where the Milwaukee, Menomonee and Kinnickinnic rivers meet. As a result of the St. Lawrence Seaway, Milwaukee has become a major seaport on America's new fourth seacoast. Docks and piers handle traffic of 10 lines of oceangoing ships.

The city provides abundant tourist attractions, including professional and college basketball, hockey, football and baseball, soccer and auto racing. Milwaukee has art exhibits, museums, music programs, ballet and theater, including the Marcus Center for Performing Arts. Its many beautiful churches include the Basilica of St. Josaphat, St. John Cathedral and the Gesu Church.

WHAT TO SEE

BETTY BRINN CHILDREN'S MUSEUM
O'Donnell Park, 929 E. Wisconsin Ave., Milwaukee, 414-390-5437; www.bbcmkids.org

Kids 10 and under will have a blast at this interactive museum, where they can enter a digestion tunnel and hear what their body sounds like as it's processing food, or create their own racetrack and test drive golf ball-shaped push carts on different road surfaces.

BEST ATTRACTIONS

WHAT ARE THE TOP THINGS TO DO IN MILWAUKEE?

BRING THE KIDS TO DISCOVERY WORLD

Little ones will like playing with the 150 interactive exhibits in this museum, which focuses on science and technology. But music-fan parents will have their own fun checking out legendary guitarist Les Paul's memorabilia in his "House of Sound."

SPEED OVER TO THE HARLEY-DAVIDSON MUSEUM

Learn all about Harleys and the people who ride them at this museum. Exhibits feature hogs that date back to 1903. Stunt riders often come to the museum to give action-packed shows.

MAKE IT MILLER TIME AT THE FAMOUS BREWERY

Take a tour of Miller Brewery, one of Milwaukee's last-remaining large-scale beer-making facilities. The best part of the free tour is that it ends with samples of suds for the adults and root beer for the kiddies.

PERUSE THE MILWAUKEE ART MUSEUM

You could spend the day exploring the various works inside the MAM. But the museum building, designed by architect Santiago Calatrava, is a work of art itself, with the wing-like Burke brise soleil changing positions twice daily.

EAT AT THE MILWAUKEE PUBLIC MARKET

Taste local produce at this daily indoor market. Wisconsin staples like cheese and beer are offered, but you can also buy fresh bread, soups and various ethnic dishes and eat them in the second-floor Palm Garden.

Admission: adults and children 1 and up $6, seniors $5, children under 1 free. Tuesday-Saturday 9 a.m.-5 p.m., Sunday noon-5 p.m.; June-August, Monday 9 a.m.-5 p.m.

CAPTAIN FREDERICK PABST MANSION

2000 W. Wisconsin Ave., Milwaukee, 414-931-0808; www.pabstmansion.com

This magnificent 1893 house once owned by the Pabst beer baron features exquisite woodwork, wrought iron and stained glass, plus a restored interior. Guided tours are available daily on the hour.

Admission: adults $9, seniors and students $8, children 6-17 $5, children 5 and under free. Monday-Saturday 10 a.m.-4 p.m., Sunday noon-4 p.m.

CITY HALL

200 E. Wells St., Milwaukee, 414-286-3285; www.ci.mil.wi.us

This Milwaukee landmark is of Flemish Renaissance design. The Common Council Chamber and Anteroom retain their turn-of-the-century character featuring ornately carved woodwork, leaded glass, stenciled ceilings, two large stained-glass windows and ironwork balconies surrounding the eight-story atrium.

Monday-Friday.

DISCOVERY WORLD: THE JAMES LOVELL MUSEUM OF SCIENCE, ECONOMICS AND TECHNOLOGY

815 N. James Lovell St., Milwaukee, 414-765-9966; www.discoveryworld.org

Discovery World, aimed at kids 14 and under, is filled with 150 interactive exhibits. At the 4Cast Center, try your hand at weather forecasting with live Doppler Radar, the Lightning Track and a seismograph. In "Les Paul's House of Sound," find out about the Wisconsin native's life, see one of the largest collections of his sound equipment and guitars, and learn how this guitarist used technology to change the sound of music.

Admission: adults $16.95, seniors $14.95, students $9.95, children 3-17 $12.95, children 2 and under free. Tuesday-Friday 9 a.m.-4 p.m., Saturday-Sunday 10 a.m.-5 p.m.

HAGGERTY MUSEUM OF ART

530 N. 13th St., Milwaukee, 414-288-7290; www.marquette.edu

On the Marquette campus, this museum includes paintings, prints, drawings, sculpture and decorative arts. The permanent collection boasts works from artists such as Rembrandt, Andy Warhol, Jacob Lawrence, Helen Frankenthaler and Robert Rauschenberg

Admission: free. Monday-Wednesday, Friday-Saturday 10 a.m.-4:30 p.m., Thursday 10 a.m.-8 p.m., Sunday noon-5 p.m.

HARLEY-DAVIDSON MUSEUM

400 W. Canal St., Milwaukee; www.harley-davidson.com

Go hog wild at this 20-acre museum, which tells the story behind the motorcycle company and the culture it has created. You'll learn about Harley-Davidson's history through photos, videos and apparel, but you're here to see the motorcycles. And the museum delivers, showcasing rides from 1903 through today. Check out the exhibit on women riders and the Experience Gallery, where you can actually sit in a Harley's saddle and ride it, albeit virtually through a video screen.

Admission: adults $16, children 5-17 $10, children 4 and under free; tour prices vary. Monday, Wednesday, Friday-Sunday 9 a.m.-6 p.m.; Tuesday, Thursday 9 a.m.-8 p.m.

IROQUOIS BOAT LINE TOURS

445 W. Oklahoma Ave., Milwaukee, 414-294-9450

View the lakefront, harbor, lighthouse, breakwater and foreign ships in port.

Admission: varies. Early June-August, daily.

MARCUS CENTER FOR THE PERFORMING ARTS

929 N. Water St., Milwaukee, 414-273-7206; www.marcuscenter.org

This strikingly beautiful structure, overlooking the Milwaukee River, has four theaters, reception areas and a parking facility connected by a skywalk. You can catch Broadway productions like *Wicked* and *Jersey Boys* on the stages.

MILLER BREWERY TOUR
4251 W. State St., Milwaukee, 414-931-2337, 800-944-5483; www.millercoors.com

Milwaukee is synonymous with beer, so take the one-hour guided tour of one of America's most well-known brewery. MillerCoors is Milwaukee's sole remaining large-scale brewery and the nation's second largest. At the end of the tour, adults can tipple free beer samples while kids can chug root beer. During summer, visit the outdoor beer garden.

Admission: free. Labor Day-Memorial Day, Monday-Saturday 10 a.m.-5 p.m., October-April, 10 a.m.-5:30 p.m., last tour at 3:30 p.m.

MILLER FIELD
1 Brewers Way, Milwaukee; milwaukee.brewers.mlb.com

The Milwaukee Brewers baseball team blessed Miller Field in spring 2001. Since then, the ballpark, along with its red-brick façade and fan-shaped convertible roof, has become a second home to Brewers fans everywhere. To get up close, go on one of the public tours (April-September).

MILWAUKEE ART MUSEUM
700 Art Museum Drive, Milwaukee, 414-224-3200; www.mam.org

Among the more than 25,000 works at the MAM, you'll find paintings from Giacometti, Picasso and Kandinsky and photography from Diane Arbus, Irving Penn and Robert Mapplethorpe. But the museum's building may be the most eye-catching piece of art. Famed architect Santiago Calatrava designed the Burke brise soleil, a moveable sunscreen that's become the museum's trademark. When the 217-foot sunscreen wings fold and unfold against the backdrop of Lake Michigan, the museum looks like a bird ready to take flight.

Admission: adults $12, seniors and students $10, children free. Tuesday-Wednesday, Friday-Sunday 10 a.m.-5 p.m., Thursday 10 a.m.-8 p.m.

MILWAUKEE COUNTY ZOO
10001 W. Blue Mound Road, Milwaukee, 414-771-3040; www.milwaukeezoo.org

See 2,500 mammals, birds, reptiles and fish at the Milwaukee County Zoo, which is renowned for displaying predators next to their prey. The zoo features an animal health center with a public viewing area; if you aren't the squeamish type, catch a treatment procedure or surgery (mornings are best). The sea lion show, miniature zoo train, zoomobile with guided tours and carousel are all available for a fee.

Admission: adults $11.75, seniors $10.25, children 3-12 $8.75, children 2 and under free. May-September, Monday-Saturday 9 a.m.-5 p.m., Sunday and holidays 9 a.m.-6 p.m.; October-April, daily 9 a.m.-4:30 p.m.

MILWAUKEE PUBLIC MARKET
400 N. Water St., Milwaukee, 414-336-1111; www.milwaukeepublicmarket.org

For a real taste of Milwaukee, bring your recyclable shopping bags to the Milwaukee Public Market. The year-round indoor market offers goods from local vendors, everything from handmade candy to fresh seafood. And of

SPECIAL EVENT

SUMMERFEST

Henry Maier Festival Grounds, 200 N. Harbor Drive, Milwaukee, 800-273-3378;
www.summerfest.com

Milwaukee's premier event, this popular festival goes on for 11 days and includes 11 different music stages and scores of food stands. It has such a big following that many people take the train in from Chicago. More than 800 bands perform at the summertime ritual. Past performers include everyone from Sheryl Crow to Lady Antebellum.
Late June-early July.

course this is Wisconsin, so you'll find cheese and beer here as well. Enjoy your treats in the second-floor Palm Garden. The market also offers classes with noted celebrity chefs like Rick Bayless and Aria Kagan.
Monday-Friday 10 a.m.-8 p.m., Saturday 8 a.m.-7 p.m., Sunday 10 a.m.-6 p.m.

MILWAUKEE PUBLIC MUSEUM

800 W. Wells St., Milwaukee, 414-278-2700; www.mpm.edu

This natural and human history museum features unique "walk-through" dioramas, exhibits and life-size replicas of dinosaurs. Among the displays is the fossils of a Hebior mammoth. There's also an IMAX theater and planetarium at the museum.
Admission: adults $12, seniors and children 13-17 $10, children 3-12 $8, children 2 and under free. Monday, Wednesday-Saturday 9 a.m.-4 p.m., Sunday 10 a.m.-4 p.m.

MITCHELL PARK HORTICULTURAL CONSERVATORY

524 S. Layton Blvd., Milwaukee, 414-649-9800; www.county.milwaukee.gov

The superb modern design here features three self-supporting domes—tropical, arid and show domes—which host outstanding seasonal shows and beautiful exhibits all year. Each dome is almost half the length of a football field in diameter and nearly as tall as a seven-story building.
Admission: adults $6.50, children $5. Monday-Friday 9 a.m.-5 p.m., Saturday-Sunday 9 a.m.-4 p.m.

PABST THEATER

144 E. Wells St., Milwaukee, 414-286-3663; www.pabsttheater.org

The center of Milwaukee's earlier cultural life, this restored theater has excellent acoustics and hosts musical and drama events.
Tours: Saturday.

PARK SYSTEM

9480 W. Watertown Plank Road, Milwaukee, 414-257-6100; www.county.milwaukee.gov

One of the largest in the nation at 14,681 acres, this system includes 137 parks and parkways, community centers, five beaches, 19 pools, 16 golf courses, 134 tennis courts and winter activities such as cross-country skiing, skating and sledding.

ST. JOAN OF ARC CHAPEL

14th Street and Wisconsin Avenue, Milwaukee, 414-288-6873; www.marquette.edu

Brought from France and reconstructed on Long Island, New York, in 1927, this 15th-century chapel was brought here in 1964.

Tours daily.

VILLA TERRACE DECORATIVE ARTS MUSEUM

2220 N. Terrace Ave., Milwaukee, 414-271-3656; www.villaterracemuseum.org

This Italian Renaissance-style house serves as a museum for decorative arts from the 15th to 18th centuries. Guided tours are offered.

Admission: adults $5, seniors $3, children free. Wednesday-Sunday 1-5 p.m.

WHERE TO STAY

★★★HILTON MILWAUKEE CITY CENTER

509 W. Wisconsin Ave., Milwaukee, 414-271-7250, 800-774-1500; www.hiltonmilwaukee.com

Those looking to stay in the downtown area will enjoy all this comfortable hotel has to offer, with its location near local theaters, museums and major businesses. This hotel has been restored to its 1920s splendor with chandeliers, woodwork and marble floors. The traditionally designed rooms are pleasant and spacious. The hotel offers a few places where you can kick back. For a hearty meal, Milwaukee Chophouse features steaks and seafood. In true Wisconsin style, there's even a 20,000-square-foot indoor waterpark on the grounds.

730 rooms. Restaurant, bar. Pool. $61-150

★★★HILTON MILWAUKEE RIVER

4700 N. Port Washington Road, Milwaukee, 414-962-6040, 800-445-8667; www.milwaukeeriver.hilton.com

Overlooking the banks of the Milwaukee River, this Hilton is within striking distance of nearly everything Milwaukee has to offer. Rooms are spacious and well-appointed with amenities that aim to give you a good night's rest, including a pillow menu and blackout curtains. A few of them face the river, but if you get stuck in a room without a view, head to The Anchorage. The seafood restaurant offers a stately spot overlooking the river.

161 rooms. Restaurant, bar. Business center. Fitness center. Pool. $151-250

★★★HOTEL METRO

411 Mason Ave., Milwaukee, 414-272-1937; www.hotelmetro.com

This all-suite European-style boutique hotel is within walking distance of several of Milwaukee's main attractions, including the Milwaukee Art Museum and the Milwaukee Public Market. The various rooms—all equipped with refreshment bars and Aveda bath products—range from master suites with separate sitting areas and whirlpool baths to the even more spacious 600-square-foot deluxe suites. The rooftop spa has everything from a saltwater hot tub and fitness equipment to a sun garden. Metro Bar & Café offers upscale bistro fare using seasonal, fresh ingredients and a selection of more than 60 wines.

65 rooms. Restaurant, bar. Fitness center. Pets accepted. $151-250

★★★HYATT REGENCY MILWAUKEE

411 E. Mason St., Milwaukee, 414-276-1234, 800-233-1234;
www.milwaukee.hyatt.com

This hotel delights with spacious guest rooms dressed in mustard, tan, navy and dark wood. It also offers Milwaukee's only revolving rooftop restaurant, which affords panoramic views of the city's skyline. Oversized work stations and wireless Internet make this a good choice for business travelers.

484 rooms. Restaurant, bar. $151-250

★★★INTERCONTINENTAL MILWAUKEE

139 E. Kilbourn Ave., Milwaukee, 414-276-8686, 800-996-3426;
www.intercontinentalmilwaukee.com

Located in Milwaukee's charming theater district, this elegant hotel is actually within the same building complex as the Milwaukee Repertory and Pabst theaters. So if you're in town for a show, this hotel is your best bet. Well-appointed tan-filled rooms overlook the Milwaukee River and guests are within walking distance of the Marcus Center, City Hall and plenty of shopping and dining.

220 rooms. Restaurant, bar. Business center. Fitness center. $151-250

★★★THE PFISTER HOTEL

424 E. Wisconsin Ave., Milwaukee, 414-273-8222, 800-558-8222; www.thepfisterhotel.com

The Pfister has been a perennial favorite of Milwaukee natives since 1893. The hotel embraces its past with a museum-quality collection of Victorian artwork. The artsy hotel even has an artist-in-residence program that features a working studio that's open to the public. The rooms have a touch of Old World elegance, with dark wooded headboards and muted floral textiles. The views of the city and Lake Michigan are particularly alluring, and the restaurants and lounges are the places to see and be seen in the city. Sunday brunch at Café Rouge is popular with guests and locals, while Blu spices up the scene with special martinis and flights of wine.

307 rooms. Restaurant, bar. Business center. Fitness center. Pool. Spa. $151-250

★★★SHERATON MILWAUKEE BROOKFIELD HOTEL

375 S. Moorland Road, Brookfield, 262-786-1100,
800-325-3535; www.sheraton.com

The traditional guest rooms have flat-screen TVs, high-speed Internet access and floor-to-ceiling

---

WHAT ARE THE BEST BOUTIQUE HOTELS IN MILWAUKEE?

Hotel Metro
This all-suite hotel forces you to relax. Whether it's your room's whirlpool bath, slippers and robe; the gym's saltwater hot tub with cascading water; or the rooftop Zen garden replete with waterfall and pond, this is the perfect place to unwind.

The Pfister Hotel
The Pfister is like the Milwaukee Art Museum of hotels. It has an admirable collection of Victorian artwork, and the hotel even employs an artist-in-residence who works in an onsite studio that's open to the public.

windows. The signature Sweet Sleeper bed guarantees a restful night's sleep, though the down pillows and comforter don't hurt, either. Downtown area shopping and nightlife are close at hand here, as well as Brookfield Hills Golf Club. But shoppers will like the hotel's location adjacent to Brookfield Square Mall, which contains more than 100 shops.

389 rooms. Restaurant. Pool. Fitness center. Pets accepted. $151-250

WHERE TO EAT

★★★BARTOLOTTA'S LAKE PARK BISTRO

3133 E. Newberry Blvd., Milwaukee, 414-962-6300;
www.lakeparkbistro.com

This restaurant serves authentic French dishes and many wood-fired oven specialties in a Parisian-style dining room. Such dishes as steamed mussels in a creamy white wine broth with garlic and shallots, filet mignon au poivre and roasted halibut with caramelized fennel, sautéed spinach and a Provencal-style olive tapenade show off chef Adam Siegel's talent. The sizeable wine list is worth perusing.

*French. Lunch, dinner, Sunday brunch. Children's menu. Bar.
$16-35*

★★★MIMMA'S CAFÉ

1307 E. Brady St., Milwaukee, 414-271-7337; www.mimmas.com

This family-run restaurant has grown from an eight-seat eatery to a 150-seat, fine Italian restaurant with impressive faux-marble walls, paintings, chandeliers and polished-tile flooring. Try inventive dishes such as lemon-pepper fettuccini with mussels, tomatoes, basil and garlic, or black pasta with scallops, shrimp, crab and sun-dried tomatoes in a porcini cream sauce.

Italian. Dinner. Outdoor seating. Bar. $16-35

★★★OSTERIA DEL MONDO

Knickerbocker on the Lake, 1028 E. Juneau Ave., Milwaukee, 414-291-3770; www.osteria.com

Chef-owner Marc Bianchini changes up the German landscape of Wisconsin with this authentic Italian café, located in the Knickerbocker hotel. The wine, food—for example, bucatini with onions and Italian bacon—and desserts transport you to Italy. The wine bar adds a lively touch to this casual yet intimate restaurant.

Italian. Dinner. Reservations recommended. Outdoor seating. Bar. $16-35

★★★PANDL'S BAYSIDE

8825 N. Lake Drive, Milwaukee, 414-352-7300; www.pandls.com

This restaurant serves up a wonderfully cozy

atmosphere in an attractive setting with an elaborate salad bar, family-friendly brunches and good value. Enjoy fresh fish, steaks and the ever-popular duckling with raspberry sauce.

American. Lunch, dinner. Children's menu. Bar. $36-85

★★★SANFORD
1547 N. Jackson St., Milwaukee, 414-276-9608; www.sanfordrestaurant.com

The site, once a grocery store owned by the Sanford family, houses a modern, sophisticated dining room offering New American cuisine from an à la carte menu. There is also a four-course seasonal menu and an additional, five-course ethnic tasting menu offered on weeknights. The menu changes frequently, but you can expect inventive dishes like grilled sturgeon on crab hash and pancetta, or a caraway-and-paprika-crusted veal loin.

American. Dinner. Closed Sunday. Reservations recommended. $36-85

CENTRAL WISCONSIN

Located in the heart of the state, this region is surrounded by hills, lakes and forests. Though there are several larger cities to balance it out.

On the more rustic side, there's Elkhart Lake, famous for its good beaches. It is one of the state's oldest vacation spots. Meanwhile, in the winter, travelers head to Wautoma and its surrounding areas for cross-country skiing and snowmobiling trails, miles of bike routes and plenty of areas to camp.

The small towns with big-city amenities are both household names. Kohler, a small town near Sheboygan, has gained a reputation as one of the region's top resort and spa destinations. The entire town was built by the Kohler fixtures family and offers unparalleled relaxation in a charming, quiet setting. Many come here to play the four world-class golf courses within Blackwolf Run and Whistling Straits, both designed by the legendary Pete Dye and host to several memorable PGA and LPGA events. The courses are both challenging and beautiful, a combination of American wilderness and Irish links style ruggedness.

The other well-known town in the area is Oshkosh, named for the chief of the Menominee. Oshkosh is located on the west shore of Lake Winnebago, the largest freshwater lake within the state. The city is known for the many recreational activities offered by its lakes and rivers. This is the original home of the company that produces the famous overalls that helped make "Oshkosh" a name brand.

WHAT TO SEE

APPLETON
THE BUILDING FOR KIDS
100 W. College Ave., Appleton, 920-734-3226; www.kidmuseum.org

The hands-on exhibits here include operating in the doll hospital, climbing through a human heart, playing with oversized veggies in the New Happy Baby Garden or climbing the Story Tree, the museum's centerpiece that has five tree forts.

Admission: $7.25, children under 1 free. Tuesday-Friday 9 a.m.-5 p.m., Saturday 10 a.m.-5 p.m., Sunday noon-5 p.m.

BEST ATTRACTIONS

WHAT ARE THE TOP THINGS TO DO?

BERGSTROM-MAHLER MUSEUM
This unusual museum specializes in glass paperweights. It boasts a permanent collection of more than 3,000 of the colorful objects, which come in various shapes, sizes and designs.

THE BUILDING FOR KIDS
Children will have a field day at this kiddie museum. Tots can play with oversized vegetables in the New Happy Baby Garden, while older kids will climb the Story Tree to hang out in one of the forts.

EAA AIRVENTURE MUSEUM
This aviation museum showcases more than 250 aircraft, including antiques, classics, ultralights, aerobatic and rotary-winged planes. You can take a ride in a vintage airplane at Pioneer Airport, which is located behind the museum.

THE HISTORY MUSEUM AT THE CASTLE
330 E. College Ave., Appleton, 920-735-9370; www.myhistorymuseum.org

The major exhibit themes at this museum on the Fox Valley community include electricity, papermaking, agriculture, transportation and communications. There is also an extensive exhibit devoted to Appleton native Harry Houdini.
Admission: adults $7.60, seniors and students $5.50, children 5-17 $3.50, children 4 and under free. Tuesday-Sunday.

MUSIC-DRAMA CENTER
420 E. College Ave., Appleton, 920-832-6611; www.lawrence.edu

The center at Lawrence University houses the Cloak Theater, an experimental arena playhouse, and Stansbury Theater, a 500-seat space. You can catch concerts and plays here during the academic year.

ELKHART LAKE
BROUGHTON-SHEBOYGAN COUNTY MARSH
W7039 County Road SR, Elkhart Lake, 920-876-2535; www.elkhartlake.com

This 14,000-acre wildlife area offers fishing, boating, canoeing, duck hunting, camping and a lodge and restaurant.

LITTLE ELKHART LAKE

Elkhart Lake, www.co.sheboygan.wi.us

Bring your fishing gear to Little Elkhart Lake. The 131-acre lake has heavy concentrations of pike, walleye, bass and panfish.

OLD WADE HOUSE HISTORIC SITE

W7824 Center Road, Greenbush, 920-526-3271; www.wisconsinhistory.org

The restored Old Wade House is an early stagecoach inn with a nearby smokehouse, blacksmith shop and mill dam site. Plus, it includes the Jung Carriage Museum, which houses more than 100 restored horse- and hand-drawn vehicles.

Admission: adults $11, seniors and students $9.25, children 5-17 $5.50, children 4 and under free. May-October.

FOND DU LAC

GALLOWAY HOUSE AND VILLAGE

336 Old Pioneer Road, Fond du Lac, 920-922-6390, 920-922-0991; www.fdl.com

This restored 30-room Victorian mansion has four fireplaces, carved woodwork and stenciled ceilings. The village features 24 buildings, including a one-room schoolhouse, a print shop, a general store, an operating gristmill, a museum with a collection of Native American artifacts, war displays and other area artifacts.

Admission: adults $7, seniors $6, children $5. Memorial Day-Labor Day, daily; rest of September, Saturday-Sunday.

ICE AGE VISITOR CENTER

N2875 Highway 67, Campbellsport, 920-533-8322; www.dnr.state.wi.us

Films, slides and panoramas show you how glaciers molded Wisconsin's terrain; naturalists are there to answer your questions.

Daily.

NORTHERN UNIT

N1765 Highway G, Campbellsport, 262-626-2116; www.dnr.state.wi.us

The forest is being developed as part of an Ice Age National Scientific Reserve. Its 30,000 acres include Long and Mauthe Lake Recreation Areas and scenic Kettle Moraine Drive.

OCTAGON HOUSE

276 Linden St., Fond du Lac, 920-922-1608; www.marlenesheirlooms.com

This 12-room octagonal house was built in 1856 by Isaac Brown and designed by Orson Fowler. It has a hidden room, secret passageways and an underground tunnel, plus period antiques, dolls, and spinning-wheel demonstrations. It is supposedly one of the state's most haunted spots.

Tours: $15. Monday, Wednesday, Friday afternoons.

ST. PAUL'S CATHEDRAL

51 W. Division St., Fond du Lac, 920-921-3363; www.stpaulsfdl.org

The English Gothic limestone structure has wood carvings from Oberammergau, Germany, rare ecclesiastical artifacts and a variety of stained-glass windows. Take a walk in the cloister garden. Self-guided tours by appointment.

KOHLER

JOHN MICHAEL KOHLER ARTS CENTER

608 New York Ave., Kohler, 920-458-6144; www.jmkac.org

Visit here for changing contemporary art exhibitions, galleries, a shop, a historic house, theater and dance and concert series. The exhibitions emphasize craft-related forms, installation works, photography, new genres, ongoing cultural traditions and the work of self-taught artists.

Admission: free. Daily.

OLD PLANK ROAD RECREATIONAL TRAIL

101 Upper Road, Kohler, 920-457-3699; www.us.kohler.com

Bike along Lake Michigan all the way to the Kettle Moraine State Forest on this 17-mile trail. The concierge at the American Club can hook you up with a bike, helmet, map and even a boxed lunch to take with you on your scenic trip.

RIVER WILDLIFE

411 Highland Drive, Kohler, 920-457-0134, 800-344-2838

This "country club in the woods" is a private recreational center and dining club located on a 500-acre wildlife preserve. If you're staying at the American Club, you can buy a pass that allows you to get away from it all and enjoy a secluded morning with Mother Nature, or get in a day of hiking, horseback riding, canoeing, kayaking, fishing and more. Afterward, relax in the rustic log cabin, which is just as you may picture it, replete with a massive fieldstone fireplace, pine floors and antique wood furnishings. You'll definitely want to stick around for dinner, too. The menu features regionally inspired cuisine that includes such hearty bites as wild mushroom bruschetta and pan-seared elk medallions. Members also have access to four hike-in campsites and the Tomczyk, a secluded one-room lodging cabin with a wood-burning sauna. The cabin sleeps up to eight people and can only be reached by a half-mile hike. Advanced reservations are required for most activities and dining.

MARSHFIELD

WILDWOOD PARK AND ZOO

1800 S. Central Ave., Marshfield, 715-384-4642, 800-422-4541; www.ci.marshfield.wi.us

This free zoo houses a variety of animals and birds, mostly native to Wisconsin. Come see timber wolves, grizzly bears, bald eagles, bison and elk.

Admission: free. Mid-May-late September, daily; October-April, Monday-Friday.

NEENAH-MENASHA

BARLOW PLANETARIUM

1478 Midway Road, Menasha, 920-832-2848; www.uwfox.uwc.edu

This planetarium's 3-D projections explain the stars in shows that look at astronomy myths and the planets. There are also laser shows that rock out with music from groups like U2 and Pink Floyd. Kids get their own star shows with pretend campfire stories that explore the constellations.

Thursday-Friday evening, Saturday-Sunday.

BERGSTROM-MAHLER MUSEUM

165 N. Park Ave., Neenah, 920-751-4658; www.bergstrom-mahlermuseum.com

The glass museum's prize exhibit is the more than 3,000 colorful glass paper-weights. It also showcases antique German glass, American regional paintings and changing exhibits.

Admission: free. Tuesday-Saturday 10 a.m.-4:30 p.m., Sunday 1-4:30 p.m.

HIGH CLIFF GENERAL STORE MUSEUM

N7630 State Park Road, Sherwood, 920-989-1106; www.dnr.state.wi.us

The museum depicts life in the area from 1850 to the early 1900s.

Mid-May-September, Friday-Sunday.

OSHKOSH
EAA AIRVENTURE MUSEUM

3000 Poberezny Road, Oshkosh, 920-426-4818; www.airventuremuseum.org

More than 250 aircraft are on display at this museum, including home-built aircraft, antiques, classics, ultralights, aerobatic and rotary-winged planes. It also features a special World War II collection and extensive collections of aviation art and photography. Antique airplanes fly on weekends.

Admission: adults $12.50, seniors $10.50, children 6-17 $9.50, children 5 and under free. May-October. Daily.

GRAND OPERA HOUSE

100 High Ave., Oshkosh, 920-424-2350; www.grandoperahouse.org

This restored 1883 Victorian theater offers a variety of performing arts. The oldest-operating theater building in the state, the Grand Opera House is the home of the Water City Chamber Orchestra.

OSHKOSH PUBLIC MUSEUM

1331 Algoma Blvd., Oshkosh, 920-424-4731; www.oshkoshmuseum.org

Housed in a turn-of-the-century, Tudor-style mansion with Tiffany stained-glass windows and interior, this museum also occupies an adjacent addition. Exhibits include a china and glassware collection and life-sized dioramas depicting French exploration, British occupation, pioneer settlement and native wildlife.

Admission: adults $7, seniors $5, children 6-17 $3.50, children 5 and under free. Tuesday-Saturday 10 a.m.-4:30 p.m., Sunday 1-4:30 p.m.

SHEBOYGAN
KOHLER ANDRAE STATE PARK

1020 Beach Park Lane, Sheboygan, 920-451-4080; www.dnr.wi.gov

This park includes 1,000 acres of woods and sand dunes and offers swimming, nature and cross-country ski trails, picnicking, playgrounds, concessions and camping.

STEVENS POINT
STEVENS POINT BREWERY

2617 Water St., Stevens Point, 715-344-9310; www.pointbeer.com

Take a tour of this historic 1857 brewery, which includes a trip to the tasting room, where you'll get to try the newest brews. Afterward, pick up some

HIGHLIGHT

WHAT ARE KOHLER'S GOLF COURSES?

As a frequent host of some of the country's top golf tournaments, including the PGA Championship and U.S. Women's Open, Kohler has the regions top links. Here's where to go to get in a few good games while visiting Kohler.

WHISTLING STRAITS

THE STRAITS

This 560-acre course was designed to emulate the old seaside links in Ireland, down to the herds of Scottish Blackface Sheep that were imported to roam the ground and graze in the rough. The course runs two miles along the coastline, through dunes and plateaus. In fact, it has been described as looking like the surface of the moon, with intimidating cavernous bunkers, 40-foot high dunes and rock-hard fairways and greens made from fescue grass. Plus, every single hole has a breathtaking view of Lake Michigan. But don't let the tranquil setting fool you. Renowned for hosting the 2004 PGA Championship, the course, which is only for walkers, is a true test of your skills. After your round, relax in the cozy, Irish country farmhouse, which serves as the clubhouse.

IRISH COURSE

Four meandering streams run through the bunkering and rolling dunes and grassland of this traditional, challenging course. The par-3 13th is the most memorable hole, featuring a blind shot over dunes to a huge 14,000-square-foot green.

BLACKWOLF RUN

The 36 holes of Blackwolf Run are located in a river basin, which was formed by melting glaciers back in the Ice Age. Playing here affords stunning views of the Sheboygan River Valley and you might even spot pheasant, deer, fox, hawk and eagle, as the area is populated with wildlife.

THE RIVER COURSE

Carved through rolling terrain and flatlands, with natural glacial lakes, the River Course may have hosted the 1998 U.S. Women's Open, but it can make a grown man cry. Dynamic and difficult, this woodsy 7,000-yard course has dramatic elevation changes—with some tee boxes located on bluffs up to 100 feet high—and giant sand traps.

MEADOW VALLEYS

Although it's the easiest of the four, players of all skill levels will enjoy this wide-open, Scottish links-style course. Fairways wind through beautiful fields and across gulches, and many holes require shots over grassy hills. Watch out for frequent sand traps and water hazards.

INSTRUCTION

The Kohler Golf Academy offers one-, two-, three- and four-day schools and state-of-the-art video analysis to improve your swing. The Golf Academy for Women features 11 hours of lessons during a three-night stay, including two hours of on-course instruction on the River, Meadow Valleys or Irish courses.

RESERVATIONS

If you book a room at the American Club, which we recommend, you can go ahead and reserve your tee time anytime for any of the courses. If you're staying somewhere else, keep in mind that reservations for the Straits and River may be placed a maximum of 14 days in advance. There's a 72-hour cancellation policy.

of the Point Belgian White, which won a gold medal in the World Beer Championships.

Tours: adults $3, children 5-11 $1, children 4 and under free. Monday-Saturday, reservations suggested.

UNIVERSITY OF WISCONSIN-STEVENS POINT

2100 Main St., Stevens Point, 715-346-0123; www.uwsp.edu

Across the entire front of the four-story Natural Resources Building is the world's largest computer-assisted mosaic mural. The onsite Museum of Natural History has one of the most complete collections of preserved birds and bird eggs in the country.

TWO RIVERS

POINT BEACH STATE FOREST

9400 County Trunk O, Two Rivers, 920-794-7480; www.dnr.wi.gov

A 2,900-acre park with heavily wooded areas, sand dunes and a beach along Lake Michigan, Point Beach offers nature, hiking, snowmobile and cross-country ski trails, and ice skating.

Daily.

ROGERS STREET FISHING VILLAGE MUSEUM

2102 Jackson St., Two Rivers, 920-793-5905

The museum features relics of the commercial fishing industry, a 60-year-old diesel engine, artifacts from sunken vessels, life-size woodcarvings and arts and crafts galleries featuring work from area artists.

Admission: adults $4, children $2. June-August, daily.

WAUPACA

HARTMAN CREEK STATE PARK

N2480 Hartman Creek Road, Waupaca, 715-258-2372; www.dnr.state.wi.us

This 1,400-acre park has a 300-foot sand beach on Hartman Lake, which makes it a good place for swimming, fishing, boating and canoeing. If you'd prefer to stick to dry land, check out the nature, hiking, snowmobile and cross-country ski trails.

WAUPUN

HORICON NATIONAL WILDLIFE REFUGE

W4279 Headquarters Road, Mayville, 920-387-2658; www.fws.gov

Horicon is the largest freshwater cattail marsh in the country, with more than 32,000 acres. Large flocks of Canada geese and various species of ducks can be seen October, November, March and April.

Monday-Friday.

WAUSAU

MARATHON COUNTY HISTORICAL MUSEUM

403 McIndoe St., Wausau, 715-848-6143; www.marathoncountyhistory.com

This former home of early lumberman Cyrus C. Yawkey has Victorian-period rooms, a model railroad display and changing theme exhibits.

Admission: adults $7, seniors $6, children 6 and older $5, children 5 and under free. Tuesday-Thursday 9 a.m.-4:30 p.m., Saturday-Sunday 1-4:30 p.m.

SPECIAL EVENTS

BRAT DAYS

Kiwanis Park, 17th and New Jersey streets, Sheboygan, 920-457-9491; www.sheboyganjaycees.com
This festival pays homage to the area's German heritage and the city's most famous food. The food fest began in 1953, and is the biggest festival in Sheboygan each year.
Early August.

EXPERIMENTAL AIRCRAFT ASSOCIATION AIR VENTURE

3000 Poberezny Road, Oshkosh, 920-426-4800; www.airventure.org
Held at Wittman Regional Airport, this is one of the nation's largest aviation events with more than 500 educational forums, workshops and seminars; daily air shows; exhibits; and more than 12,000 aircraft.
Late July-early August.

HOLLAND FEST

118 Main St., Cedar Grove, 920-457-9491; www.hollandfest.com
A celebration of Dutch traditions, Holland Fest includes wooden-shoe dancing, street scrubbing, a folk fair, food, music, an art fair and a parade.
Last Friday-Saturday in July.

KOHLER FOOD & WINE EXPERIENCE

110 Upper Road, Kohler, 800-344-2838; www.destinationkohler.com
This annual event features cooking demonstrations, food and wine tastings and seminars. Past participants include siblings and *Top Chef* season-six competitors Michael and Bryan Voltaggio as well as noted French chef and author Jacques Pépin.
Three days in late October.

POLAR BEAR SWIM

712 Riverfront Drive, Suite 101, Sheboygan, 920-457-9491; www.sheboygan.org
More than 350 swimmers brave Lake Michigan's icy winter waters to raise money for charity.
January 1.

ROAD AMERICA

N7390 Highway 67, Elkhart Lake, 800-365-7223; www.roadamerica.com
Located on 525 rolling, wooded acres, this racecourse is a closed-circuit four-mile sports car track with 14 turns. One of the most popular events of the season is the CART Indy race, which draws top-name race teams.
June-September.

TRADITIONAL HOLIDAY ILLUMINATION

419 Highland Drive, Kohler, 920-457-8000; www.destinationkohler.com
More than 200,000 lights on trees surrounding Kohler hospitality facilities create a winter fantasyland in the Kohler Village.
Thanksgiving-February.

RIB MOUNTAIN STATE PARK
4200 Park Road, Rib Mountain Drive, Wausau, 715-842-2522; www.dnr.wi.gov

Part of an 860-acre park, the summit of Rib Mountain is one of the highest points in the state. Hiking trails wind past rocky ridges and natural oddities in quartzite rocks.

Daily.

WAUTOMA
NORDIC MOUNTAIN SKI AREA
W5806 County Road West, Wautoma, 920-787-3324, 800-253-7266; www.nordicmountain.com

The longest run here is one mile with a vertical drop of 265 feet. The ski area also features 13 miles of cross-country trails, rentals and a ski school.

Night skiing: December-mid-March, Thursday-Tuesday.

WHERE TO STAY

RECOMMENDED
APPLETON
COPPERLEAF HOTEL
300 W. College Ave., Appleton, 920-749-0303, 877-303-0303; www.copperleafhotel.com

This European-style boutique hotel creates an inviting atmosphere. The sage, mocha, and tangerine rooms come with microwaves and refrigerators, and the bathrooms have Aveda soaps and whirlpool tubs. Suites get a little cozier with electric fireplaces. After dining at the onsite Black & Tan Grille, which serves up a mean steak, borrow a DVD from the free library at the front desk. There's nothing more cozy than snuggling in bed and watching a movie.

73 rooms. Restaurant, bar. Complimentary breakfast. Fitness center. Spa. $116-180

GREEN LAKE
★★★HEIDEL HOUSE RESORT & CONFERENCE CENTER
643 Illinois Ave., Green Lake, 920-294-3344; www.heidelhouse.com

Set on 20 acres on Green Lake, Heidel House offers something for everyone no matter the season, including hiking trails, an ice rink in winter, fishing charters, yacht cruises and plenty of activities for children. From the Main Lodge to the lofty Estate Rooms, accommodations are comfortable and well-appointed. Gadget-loving guests will want to stay in either the Main Lodge or Lac Verde, whose rooms have free WiFi and Nintendo. And three restaurants—Grey Rock, the Sunroom and Boathouse—offer an array of dining options for every taste. Everyone will agree to some dessert at the Pump House Parlor, an ice cream shop.

205 rooms. Restaurant. Business center. Fitness center. Pool. Spa. $151-250

KOHLER
★★★★THE AMERICAN CLUB
419 Highland Drive, Kohler, 920-457-8000, 800-344-2838; www.americanclub.com

Located in the charming village of Kohler, the American Club is a cozy country getaway. In addition to access to world-class golf, you get friendly, warm service and a relaxing spot in which to lounge around. The rooms are simple but elegant and comfortable with wood-beamed ceilings, white duvets and bathrooms with

Kohler bath and shower accessories. The Kohler spa is the centerpiece of the resort and sets the relaxing, happy atmosphere. You'll find guests walking around in spa robes throughout the day and into the evening, when everyone mingles in the lobby over wine, cheese and other nibbles. Afterward, you can easily pop around to the different restaurants; many are in walking distance or you can hop on a shuttle.
240 rooms. Restaurant, bar. Spa. Beach. Golf. Tennis. $251-350

SHEBOYGAN
★★★BLUE HARBOR RESORT & CONFERENCE CENTER
725 Blue Harbor Drive, Sheboygan, 920-452-2900, 866-701-2583; www.blueharborresort.com

This massive four-story resort also houses a 54,000-square-foot indoor entertainment area and waterpark and the Northern Lights Arcade. The Lake Michigan location gives inspiration to the nautical-themed rooms. The rooms in the all-suite hotel have microwaves, mini-refrigerators, coffee makers and living areas with sofa sleepers. Elements Spa is a lovely adult retreat for an aroma body wrap or massage. The 12-and-under set can get pampered at Scooops Kid Spa with a chocolate-brownie mani-pedi, which comes with free ice cream. If you're looking for a casual meal with the family, head to On the Rocks Bar & Grille and the Rusty Anchor Buffet. For more upscale options, try Blue Point Wine & Tapas Bar or Weissgerber's Seabird Restaurant.
183 rooms. Restaurants, bar. Spa. $151-250

WHERE TO EAT

KOHLER
★★★★THE IMMIGRANT RESTAURANT
419 Highland Drive, Kohler, 920-457-8888, 800-344-2838; www.destinationkohler.com

The remnants of Walter J. Kohler Sr.'s boarding house are the basis for the opulent yet inviting Immigrant Restaurant and Winery Bar. No expense was spared when it came to the creation of the building. The Immigrant Restaurant is divided into six rooms, each of which represents the nationalities that populated Wisconsin in its early days—Dutch, German, Norman, Danish, French and English. The wonderful dishes include pan-seared scallops with heirloom carrot purée and vodka-caviar butter,

---

WHICH HOTEL HAS THE BEST SPA?

The American Club: The jewel in the American Club's crown is its Kohler Waters Spa. The spa offers a full menu of treatments, but the ones that sparkle are those involving water, such as the RiverBath, which bathes you in different colored lights amid strong whirlpool jets.

or slow-cooked Wagyu beef cheeks with celery root. For those who want to try a little bit of everything, the restaurant offers a sampling menu, with such delectable items as deep fried quail eggs with sweet chili sauce and sirloin carpaccio with garlic chips. Paired with one of the excellent wines, this may be just the ticket. Afterward, head to the bar, a popular gathering spot, and order yet another exquisite wine and enjoy a dessert, such as vanilla-and-Armagnac-roasted bananas, lemon-raspberry cake or the chocolate trilogy. While you're here, ask about wine and cheese tastings.

American. Dinner. Closed Sunday. Reservations recommended. Jacket required. Bar. $36-85

RECOMMENDED

CUCINA
725 E. Woodlake Road, Kohler, 920-457-8888

Fill up on hearty plates of pasta at this casual Italian restaurant with a domed ceiling and Roman columns overlooking Wood Lake. There's nothing fancy about the tortelloni or the seafood linguini, which is makes a great choice when you don't feel like making a fuss.

Italian. Lunch, dinner, Sunday brunch. Reservations recommended. $16-35

THE WISCONSIN ROOM
119 Highland Drive, Kohler, 920-457-8888

The professional service and the nostalgic setting, with antique chandeliers and leaded glass windows, will draw you in to this restaurant. The original dining hall of immigrant workers for Kohler, the Wisconsin Room features regional Midwestern fare, including pepper-crusted venison steak with wild mushroom risotto, braised red cabbage and blackberry preserves; grilled tenderloin with a delicious foyot sauce; and cinnamon-lavender duck breast. Friday nights feature a seafood buffet.

American. Breakfast, dinner, Sunday brunch. Reservations recommended. $36-85

SPA

KOHLER
★★★★KOHLER WATERS SPA
The American Club, 419 Highland Drive, Kohler, 920-457-8000; www.destinationkohler.com

Kohler Waters Spa takes full advantage of its namesake's long history in the fixture and bath business. Water plays a part in just about everything at this spa, from the design—waterfalls abound from the relaxation pool to some treatment rooms—to the services—where water therapies such as aroma-therapy baths are the highlight. The spa recently renovated its signature wet treatment rooms, where you can take a rejuvenating Acoustic Bath with music and sound vibrations or a Harmony Bath with an exfoliation and hydromas-sage, among other services. A glass-enclosed rooftop deck includes both an outdoor sunning space and an indoor lounge. The spa offers a complete menu for couples and specialty treatments for men, including scrubs, baths and a golfer's massage.

WHERE TO SHOP

SHOPS AT WOODLAKE
Kohler, 920-459-1713; www.destinationkohler.com

Pick up clothing, fly-fishing supplies, furniture, home accessories and other specialty goods at this small shopping center in Kohler village.

Monday-Friday 10 a.m.-6 p.m., Saturday 10 a.m.-5 p.m., Sunday noon-5 p.m.

SOUTHERN WISCONSIN

When people want a full-out water-filled vacation, they head to Southern Wisconsin. The biggest destination, especially in the summer, is the Wisconsin Dells. Until 1931, this city was called Kilbourn, but it changed its name in the hope of attracting tourists to the nearby Dells. It seems to have worked—the Wisconsin Dells has become the state's prime tourist attraction. Although some aspects of the Dells lean toward the tacky side, the overall feel is good clean fun.

The region offers a wide selection of campgrounds, bed and breakfasts, hotels, motels, resorts, condos and cottages. Of these, 17 house indoor water parks. But man-made and natural attractions keep visitors from lingering too long at area accommodations.

Families can explore the Upper and Lower Dells on a Dells Boat Tour or the water- and land-based environs on an original World War II Duck. Take to the water at Noah's Ark, America's largest water park, housing 5 million gallons of water and three miles of water slides. Uncover the enchantment under the Big Top at Circus World Museum in nearby Baraboo, take a wagon tour through a working elk ranch, or ride the rails through the Baraboo Hills at the Mid-Continent Railway Museum.

College town Madison, home of the University of Wisconsin-Madison, draws a different crowd. But tourists also come to the city to see the rich architectural heritage left by Frank Lloyd Wright, who led the Prairie School movement here. There are a number of Wright buildings; many are private homes and not open to the public. Another city with a Frank Lloyd Wright connection is Spring Green. Its claim to fame is that the famous architect grew up in this community, built his home, Taliesin East, here and established the Taliesin Fellowship for the training of apprentice architects.

Another popular getaway is Lake Geneva, an attractive four-season resort area. Recreational activities include boating, fishing, swimming, horseback riding, camping, hiking, biking, golf, tennis, skiing, cross-country skiing, ice fishing, snowmobiling and ice boating. Chicagoans come here to escape the city and relax on the beach.

WHAT TO SEE

BARABOO
CIRCUS WORLD MUSEUM
550 Water St., Baraboo, 608-356-8341; www.circusworldmuseum.com

This museum has 50 acres and eight buildings filled circus lore and is the original summer quarters of Ringling Bros. Circus. Live circus acts perform

BEST ATTRACTIONS

WHAT ARE THE TOP THINGS TO DO?

GO UNDER THE BIG TOP AT THE CIRCUS WORLD MUSEUM

This museum was the original summer quarters of the Ringing Bros. Circus. See live acts perform and the daily circus parade. You'll also learn about all of the lore surrounding one of the greatest shows on earth.

PLACE YOUR BETS AT HO-CHUNK CASINO & BINGO

When you need to give your sunburned skin a reprieve from days spent under the sun in the Dells, take a break at this gaming casino. There are blackjack tables, slot machines, video poker and more.

VISIT THE ANGEL MUSEUM

If you like angels, you must visit this museum. It boasts the world's largest angel collection with more than 13,000 angels. Angel-loving Oprah Winfrey donated a number of pieces from her personal collection.

RELAX AT BIG FOOT BEACH STATE PARK

Chicagoans retreat to Lake Geneva for a quick getaway. They plant themselves on the sandy shores of Big Foot Beach State Park. The park also offers fishing, picnicking and camping.

GET WET AT NOAH'S ARK WATERPARK

Noah's Ark claims to be the biggest waterpark in America. You can cool off on its 49 water rides, two wave pools and two rivers. Children have their own designated waterplay areas where they can frolic.

under the Big Top, plus there is a daily circus parade, a display of parade wagons, steam calliope concerts, a P.T. Barnum sideshow, a wild animal menagerie, a carousel and a band organ.

Admission for May-August: adults $14.95, seniors $12.95, children 5-11 $7.95, children 4 and under free; September: adults $7.95, seniors $6.95, children 5-11 $3.50, children 4 and under free. Early May-mid-September, daily.

HO-CHUNK CASINO & BINGO

S3214A Highway 12, Baraboo, 800-746-2486; www.ho-chunk.com

When you tire of the outdoor fun in the Dells, try your luck in this gaming casino. Ho-Chunk features 48 blackjack tables, 1,200 slot machines, video poker and keno.

Daily, 24 hours.

MID-CONTINENT RAILWAY MUSEUM

E8948 Diamond Hill Road, North Freedom, 608-522-4261; www.midcontinent.org

This restored 1894 depot is a complete 1900 rail environment with steam locomotives, coaches, a steam wrecker and snowplows, plus artifacts and historical exhibits. Entry includes a train ride and access to the museum.

Admission: adults $15, seniors and students $13, children 3-12 $9, children 2 and under free.
Daily 9:30 a.m.-5 p.m.; trains depart at 11 a.m., 1 and 3 p.m.

MIRROR LAKE STATE PARK

E10320 Fern Dell Road, Baraboo, 608-254-2333; www.mirrorlakewisconsin.com

This 2,050-acre park features swimming, fishing, boating and canoeing, plus hiking, cross-country skiing, picnicking, a playground and camping.

Daily.

SAUK COUNTY HISTORICAL MUSEUM

531 Fourth Ave., Baraboo, 608-356-1001; www.saukcounty.com

This museum houses 19th-century household goods, textiles, toys, china, military items, a pioneer collection, Native American artifacts, circus memorabilia, a natural history display and photos.

Admission: free. Tuesday-Saturday noon-5 p.m.

BELOIT

ANGEL MUSEUM

656 Pleasant St., Beloit, 608-362-9099; www.angelmuseum.com

This museum features a collection of more than 13,000 angels made from everything from leather to china. Oprah Winfrey has donated more than 500 angels from her private collection.

Admission: adults $7, seniors $6, children 5-17 $4, children 4 and under free. Tuesday-Saturday 10 a.m.-4 p.m.; June-August, Sunday 1-4 p.m.

BELOIT COLLEGE

700 College St., Beloit, 608-363-2000; www.beloit.edu

Noted for the Theodore Lyman Wright Museum of Art, Beloit College also houses the Logan Museum of Anthropology, which has changing displays of Native American and Stone Age artifacts. The campus also contains prehistoric mounds.

Campus tours by appointment.

BLACK RIVER FALLS

BLACK RIVER FALLS STATE FOREST

910 Highway 54 E., Black River Falls, 715-284-1406; www.dnr.wi.gov

A 66,000-acre area, this state forest offers swimming, fishing, boating, canoeing, hiking, cross-country skiing, snowmobiling, a bridle trail, picnicking, a playground and camping. There is also a lookout tower and wildlife.

Daily.

BURLINGTON
SPINNING TOP EXPLORATORY MUSEUM
533 Milwaukee Ave., Burlington, 262-763-3946; www.wisconline.com

You don't have to worry about fooling around in this museum; it's encouraged. Find exhibits and displays dealing with tops, yo-yos and gyroscopes, plus top games, demonstrations, hands-on experiments and video presentations. Make an appointment to tour the facility and meet a tops expert from MGM.

Admission: $11. Appointments only.

CEDARBURG
CEDAR CREEK SETTLEMENT AND WINERY
N70W6340 Bridge Road, Cedarburg, 262-377-8020, 800-827-8020; www.cedarcreeksettlement.com

This stone woolen mill was converted into a winery and houses shops, art studios and restaurants. The winery makes strawberry, cranberry and grape wines, and there is a museum of antique wine-making tools.

Daily.

DODGEVILLE
GOVERNOR DODGE STATE PARK
4175 Highway 23, Dodgeville, 608-935-2315; www.dnr.state.wi.us

A 5,029-acre park with 95-acre and 150-acre lakes, Governor Dodge includes rock formations and white pine and offers swimming; fishing; boating and canoeing; bicycle, hiking and bridle trails; cross-country skiing; snowmobiling; picnicking; playgrounds; concessions; camping; backpack campsites; and a horse campground.

Nature programs: June-August, daily.

FORT ATKINSON
DWIGHT FOSTER HOUSE
407 Merchants Ave., Fort Atkinson, 920-563-7769; www.hoardmuseum.org

The historic home of the city's founder, this five-room, two-story Greek Revival frame house has period furnishings and many original pieces.

Tuesday-Saturday.

HOARD HISTORICAL MUSEUM
401 Whitewater Ave., Fort Atkinson, 920-563-7769; www.hoardmuseum.org

Housed in a historic home, this museum features pioneer history and archaeology of the area, period rooms, an antique quilt, a bird room, old costumes and clothing, antique firearms, a reference library and permanent and changing displays.

Admission: free. Tuesday-Sunday 9:30 a.m.-4:30 p.m.

GALESVILLE
MERRICK STATE PARK
S2965 Highway, 101 S. Webster St., 608-687-4936; www.dnr.state.wi.us

A 324-acre park along the Mississippi River, Merrick features canoeing and camping.

Daily.

PERROT STATE PARK

W26247 Sullivan Road, Trempealeau, 608-534-6409;
www.dnr.state.wi.us

Trempealeau Mountain, a beacon for voyageurs for more than 300 years, is in this 1,425-acre park. French fur trader Nicolas Perrot, after whom the park was named, set up winter quarters here in 1686. A French fort was built on the site in 1731.

Daily.

JANESVILLE
MILTON HOUSE MUSEUM

18 S. Janesville St., Milton, 608-868-7772; www.miltonhouse.org

This hexagonal building was constructed of grout. The Underground Railroad had a stop here, and a tunnel connects it with the original log cabin.

Admission: adults $6, seniors $5, children 5-12 $3, children 4 and under free. Memorial Day-Labor Day, daily 10 a.m.-5 p.m.; May and September-mid-October, weekends, also Monday-Friday by appointment.

KENOSHA
BONG STATE RECREATION AREA

26313 Burlington Road, Kansasville, 262-878-5600; www.dnr.state.wi.us

This 4,515-acre area offers swimming, fishing, boating, hiking, bridle and off-road motorcycle trails, cross-country skiing, snowmobiling, picnicking, guided nature hikes, a nature center, a special events area and camping.

KEMPER CENTER

6501 Third Ave., Kenosha, 262-657-6005; www.kempercenter.com

Composed of approximately 11 acres, this area houses several buildings, including an Italianate Victorian mansion. The complex has more than 100 different trees, a rose collection, a mosaic mural, outdoor tennis courts, a picnic area and the Anderson Art Gallery (Thursday-Sunday afternoons).

RAMBLER LEGACY GALLERY

220 51st Place, Kenosha, 262-654-5770; www.kenoshahistorycenter.org

This eclectic gallery features Lorado Taft dioramas of famous art studios; Native American, Oceanic and African arts; Asian ivory and porcelain; Wisconsin folk pottery; a mammals exhibit and a dinosaur display.

Tuesday-Sunday.

LA CROSSE
HIXON HOUSE

429 N. Seventh St., La Crosse, 608-782-1980; www.lchsweb.org

This 15-room home features Victorian and Asian furnishings. A visitor information center and gift shop is in the building that once served as a wash house.

Admission: adults $8.50, seniors $7.50, students $6, children $4.50. Memorial Day-Labor Day, Tuesday-Sunday.

LA CROSSE QUEEN CRUISES

La Crosse, 608-784-2893; www.lacrossequeen.com

This sightseeing cruise on the Mississippi River is aboard a 150 passenger, double-deck paddle wheeler.

Admission: varies. Early May-mid-October, daily. Dinner cruise: Friday night, Saturday-Sunday.

PUMP HOUSE REGIONAL ARTS CENTER

119 King St., La Crosse, 608-785-1434; www.thepumphouse.org

Find regional art exhibits and performing arts here. The art center has three galleries and a 140-seat theater. The theater puts on productions such as *Waiting for Lefty* by Clifford Odets.

Tuesday-Saturday, afternoons.

LAKE GENEVA

BIG FOOT BEACH STATE PARK

1452 Highway H, Lake Geneva, 262-248-2528; www.dnr.state.wi.us

This 272-acre beach park on Geneva Lake offers swimming (lifeguard on duty mid-June-Labor Day, weekends only), fishing, picnicking, a playground, winter sports and camping.

Daily.

MADISON

GEOLOGY MUSEUM

1215 W. Dayton St., Madison, 608-262-2399; www.geology.wisc.edu

Exhibits include a six-foot rotating globe, rocks, minerals, a black-light display, a walk-through cave, meteorites and fossils, including the skeletons of a giant mastodon and dinosaurs.

Admission: free. Monday-Friday 8:30 a.m.-4:30 p.m., Saturday 9 a.m.-1 p.m.

HENRY VILAS PARK ZOO

702 S. Randall Ave., Madison, 608-258-9490; www.vilaszoo.org

World famous for successful orangutan, Siberian tiger, spectacle bear, penguin and camel breeding programs, this free zoo has exhibits with 600 specimens consisting of 140 species.

Admission: free. Daily 9:30 a.m.-5 p.m.

LAKE KEGONSA STATE PARK

2405 Door Creek Road, Stoughton, 608-873-9695; www.dnr.wi.gov

This 343-acre park offers swimming, waterskiing, fishing, boating, hiking and nature trails, picnicking, a playground and camping.

Daily.

MADISON CHILDREN'S MUSEUM

100 State St., Madison, 608-256-6445; www.madisonchildrensmuseum.com

At this hands-on museum, kids can show their artistic side at an art studio where they can make their own sculptures, paintings and drawings. Or they can get creative at "Possible-opolis," an exhibit that encourages children to use their noggins to create a city.

Admission: adults and children $6.95, seniors $5.95. Tuesday-Wednesday, Friday-Sunday 9:30 a.m.-5 p.m.; Thursday 9:30 a.m.-8 p.m.

STATE CAPITOL

Capital Square, 2 E. Main St., Madison, 608-266-0382; www.wisconsin.gov

A focal point of the city, the white granite capitol building has a classic dome topped by Daniel Chester French's gilded bronze statue *Wisconsin*.

Tours: daily.

STATE HISTORICAL MUSEUM

30 N. Carroll St., Madison, 608-264-6555; www.wisconsinhistory.org/museum

Permanent exhibits explore the history of Native American life in Wisconsin and a gallery features changing Wisconsin and U.S. history exhibits.

Tuesday-Saturday.

UNIVERSITY OF WISCONSIN-MADISON

716 Langdon St., Madison, 608-263-2400; www.wisc.edu

The 929-acre campus extends for more than two miles along the south shore of Lake Mendota.

MAUSTON

BUCKHORN STATE PARK

W8450 Buckhorn Park Ave., Necedah, 608-565-2789; www.dnr.wi.gov

A 2,504-acre park, Buckhorn has facilities for swimming, water-skiing, fishing, boating, canoeing, hunting, hiking, nature trails, picnicking and a playground.

Daily.

MENOMONEE FALLS

HARLEY-DAVIDSON TOUR

W156 N9000 Pilgrim Road, Menomonee Falls, 877-883-1450; www.harley-davidson.com

Milwaukee is Hog Heaven, so it's only fitting to tour the propeller-factory-turned-Harley-facility and see transmission and engine assembly from start to finish. Tickets for the 30-minute tours are handed out at 9 a.m. on a first-come, first-served basis; arrive early.

Admission: free. Monday 9 a.m.-2 p.m.

PRAIRIE DU CHIEN

FORT CRAWFORD MUSEUM

717 S. Beaumont Road, Prairie du Chien, 608-326-6960; www.fortcrawfordmuseum.com

This museum features relics of 19th-century medicine, Native American herbal remedies, drugstores and dentist and physicians' offices.

Admission: adults $5, seniors $4, children $3. May-October, daily.

STONEFIELD

12195 County Road W., Cassville, 608-725-5210; stonefield.wisconsinhistory.org

Named for a rock-studded, 2,000-acre farm that Nelson Dewey (the first elected governor of Wisconsin) established on the bluffs of the Mississippi River, Stonefield is an agricultural museum that contains displays of farm machinery. The site also features a re-creation of an 1890 Stonefield Village comprising a blacksmith, a general store, a print shop, a school, a church and 26 other buildings.

Admission: adults $8, seniors and students $6.75, children 5-17 $4, children 4 and under free. Memorial Day-early September, daily; early September-mid-October, Saturday-Sunday.

VILLA LOUIS

521 N. Villa Louis Road, Prairie du Chien, 608-326-2721; villalouis.wisconsinhistory.org

Built on site of Fort Crawford, this restored 1870 home contains original furnishings and a collection of Victorian decorative arts.

Admission: adults $9, seniors and students $7.75, children 5-17 $4.50, children 4 and under free. May-October, daily 10 a.m.-4 p.m.

WYALUSING STATE PARK

13081 State Park Lane, Bagley, 608-996-2261; www.dnr.state.wi.us

A 2,654-acre park at the confluence of the Mississippi and Wisconsin rivers, Wyalusing features the Sentinel Ridge, which provides a commanding view of the area. Other features include fishing, boating, canoeing as well as 18 miles of nature, hiking and cross-country ski trails.

Daily.

SPARTA

ELROY-SPARTA STATE TRAIL

113 White St., Kendall, 608-337-4775; www.wiparks.net

Built on an old railroad bed, this 32-mile hard-surfaced trail passes through three tunnels and over 23 trestles.

April-October, daily.

SPRING GREEN

HOUSE ON THE ROCK

5754 Highway 23, Spring Green, 608-935-3639; www.thehouseontherock.com

Designed and built by Alexander J. Jordan atop a chimney-like rock, House on the Rock sits 450 feet above a valley. Waterfalls and trees are located throughout house along with collections of antiques and oddities. Inside the house, you'll find a larger-than-life sea creature, *Titanic* memorabilia, a carousel and more.

Admission: adults $28.50, seniors $26.50, children 4-17 $15.50, children 3 and under free. Mid-March-late October, daily.

TALIESIN

Highways 23 and C, Spring Green, 608-588-7900; www.taliesinpreservation.org

Architecture master Frank Lloyd Wright built his home, Taliesin—a Welsh term for "shining brow"—in Spring Green. The National Historic Landmark went through a number of incarnations, due to fires, but you can tour the restored home and other Wright-designed buildings on this 600-acre estate.

Tours: prices vary. October-May.

TOWER HILL STATE PARK

5808 County Highway C, Spring Green, 608-588-2116; www.dnr.state.wi.us

This state park includes 77 acres of wooded hills and bluffs overlooking the Wisconsin River. The site has a pre-Civil War shot tower and lead-mining village of Helena.

Daily.

HIGHLIGHT

WHAT IS THERE TO DO IN DEVIL'S LAKE STATE PARK?

Located in Baraboo, these 11,050 acres—with spring-fed Devil's Lake as the greatest single attraction—form one of Wisconsin's most beautiful state parks. Remnants of an ancient mountain range surround the lake, providing unique scenery. The lake, 1.25 miles long, is in the midst of sheer cliffs of quartzite that rise as high as 500 feet above the water. Unusual rock formations may be found at the top of the bluffs.

Aside from the scenery, the park offers plenty to keep you busy. Sandy swimming beaches with bathhouses, concessions and boat landings are at either end. The park also provides hiking and cross-country skiing trails, picnic grounds, improved tent and trailer facilities and a nature center. Make a trip to see the Native American mounds, which include the Eagle, Bear and Lynx mounds. General tourist supplies are available at the north and south shores. The park has a naturalist in residence who may be contacted for information concerning year-round nature hikes and programs.

TOMAH
MILL BLUFF STATE PARK
15819 Funnel Road, Camp Douglas, 608-427-6692; www.dnr.wi.gov
This park has 1,258 acres with rock bluffs, swimming, picnicking and camping.
Daily.

NECEDAH NATIONAL WILDLIFE REFUGE
W7996 20th St. W., Necedah, 608-565-2551; www.fws.gov
Water birds may be seen during seasonal migrations with lesser numbers present during the summer. Resident wildlife includes deer, wild turkeys, ruffed grouse, wolves and bears.
Daily.

WILDCAT MOUNTAIN STATE PARK
E13660 State Highway 33, Ontario; www.dnr.wi.gov., Ontario, 608-337-4775
This park has 3,470 acres of hills and valleys and offers trout fishing in Kickapoo River and Billings and Cheyenne creeks, canoeing and nature, hiking, bridle and cross-country ski trails. Observation points provide a panoramic view of the countryside.
Daily.

WATERTOWN
OCTAGON HOUSE AND FIRST KINDERGARTEN IN USA
919 Charles St., Watertown, 920-261-2796; www.watertownhistory.org
Completed in 1854, the 57-room mansion has a 40-foot spiral cantilever-hanging staircase, Victorian-style furnishings throughout and many original pieces. The grounds include a restored kindergarten founded in 1856 and a 100-year-old barn with early farm implements.
Admission: adults $7, seniors $6, children $4. May-October, daily.

WAUKESHA
OLD WORLD WISCONSIN
S103W 37890 Highway 67, Eagle, 262-594-6300;
oldworldwisconsin.wisconsinhistory.org

This museum fills 576 acres with more than 65 historic structures reflecting various ethnic backgrounds of Wisconsin history. Restored buildings include a church, a town hall, a schoolhouse, a stagecoach inn, a blacksmith shop and 10 complete 19th-century farmsteads. All buildings are furnished with period artifacts and staffed by costumed interpreters.

Admission: adults $16, seniors and students $14, children 5-17 $9, children 4 and under free. May-October, daily.

WISCONSIN DELLS
BEAVER SPRINGS FISHING PARK AND RIDING STABLES
600 Trout Road, Wisconsin Dells, 608-254-2735; www.beaverspringsfun.com

Guided one-hour rides tour spring-fed ponds stocked with trout, catfish, bass and other fish.

April-October, daily.

DELLS DUCKS
1550 Wisconsin Dells Parkway, Wisconsin Dells, 608-254-6080; www.dellsducks.com

The one-hour land/water tour offers views of scenic rock formations along the Wisconsin River.

Late May-late October, daily.

H.H. BENNETT STUDIO AND HISTORY CENTER
215 Broadway, Wisconsin Dells, 608-253-3523; www.hhbennett.com

The oldest photographic studio in the United States features the landscape and nature photography of H. H. Bennett that helped make the Dells area famous. The studio is still in operation and it is possible to purchase enlargements made from Bennett's original glass negatives.

Memorial Day-late October, daily; November-April, by appointment.

NOAH'S ARK WATERPARK
1410 Wisconsin Dells Parkway ,Wisconsin Dells, 608-254-6351; www.noahsarkwaterpark.com

With 49 water rides, two wave pools, two rivers and four kiddie waterplay areas, Noah's Ark calls itself the largest waterpark in the nation. The newest ride is the Scorpion's Tail, a nearly vertical waterslide loop that's 10 stories high.

Admission: adults and children $35.99, seniors $28.79, children 2 and under free. Memorial Day-Labor Day, daily.

RIVERVIEW PARK & WATERWORLD
Highway 12, Wisconsin Dells, 608-254-2608; www.riverviewpark.com

Waterworld features more than 30 rides, including a wave pool, speed slides, tube rides and kids' pools. The park portion offers go-carts on a Grand Prix track and Kidz Zone, a track and go-karts made especially for the kiddies.

Admission: $10, children 5 and under $5. Park: late May-early September, Waterworld: late May-early September, daily.

TOMMY BARTLETT'S ROBOT WORLD & EXPLORATORY

560 Wisconsin Dells Parkway, Wisconsin Dells, 608-254-2525; www.tommybartlett.com

More than 150 hands-on exhibits at this science museum explore principles of light, sound and motion. Check out the world's only Russian Mir Space Station core module. Robot-guided tours are offered daily.

Admission: adults $12, seniors $9.60, children 6-11 $9, children 5 and under free. June-August, daily 9 a.m.-9 p.m.; September-May 10 a.m.-4 p.m.

WHERE TO STAY

FONTANA
★★★THE ABBEY RESORT

269 Fontana Blvd., Fontana, 800-709-1323; www.theabbeyresort.com

Situated on 90 lush acres and set on the water's edge, this elegant resort and spa delights with its restaurants; try the Mediterranean cuisine at Porto. The rooms look like little cottages, with either beamed or vaulted ceilings, outdoor balconies, wall-mounted LCD televisions and sleeper sofas. The atmosphere of quiet elegance makes for an enjoyable stay.

334 rooms. Restaurant, bar. Business center. Pool. Spa. Tennis. $60-150

LAKE GENEVA
★★★GRAND GENEVA RESORT & SPA

7036 Grand Geneva Way, Lake Geneva, 262-248-8811, 262-248-2556, 800-558-3417; www.grandgeneva.com

This resort and spa is situated on 1,300 acres of wooded meadowland with a private lake. A 36-hole golf course, the luxurious Well Spa and a host of dining options makes this spot a treat. Guest rooms are equipped with upscale amenities, including Aveda products, TVs embedded in the bathroom mirrors, 37-inch LCD flat-screen televisions in the room and balconies. Well Spa offers a full range of treatments, from various massages to hydrotherapy. Hitting upon delicious food is easy at one of the resort's three main rest aurants: Ristorante Brissago, Geneva ChopHouse and Grand Café.

355 rooms. Restaurant, bar. Fitness center. Spa. Golf. Tennis. $151-250

★★★THE LODGE AT GENEVA RIDGE

W4240 Highway 50, Lake Geneva, 262-248-9121, 800-225-5558; www.genevaridge.com

Outdoor enthusiasts will want to check into the Lodge, which offers golf, various water sports, horseback riding, hayrides, hot-air balloon rides and a petting zoo nearby. When you need a break from the action, relax in your room, which has warm woods, natural tones, flat-panel TVs and refrigerators. Or make an appointment at the full-service spa, which offers an extensive menu of treatments and services. Try the volcanic stone massage to ease away any tension. The country-style fare in the dining room offers hearty meals, though you can find something lighter at the Lake View Lounge.

146 rooms. Restaurant, Bar. Spa. Tennis. $151-250

★★★TIMBER RIDGE LODGE & WATERPARK

7020 Grand Geneva Way, Lake Geneva, 262-249-8811, 866-636-4502;
www.timberridgeresort.com

Moose Mountain Falls Waterpark resides here, but there's plenty more to take advantage of at this all-season, all-suite resort. The kitchenettes have full-size fridges, stoves dishwashers and double sinks, and rooms come with cozy amenities, such as whirlpool baths, covered balconies and fireplaces. The 1,300-acre spread is known for its spacious suites and its proximity to nearby cities—it's just an hour's drive from Milwaukee. The Spa & Sport Center, along with the championship golf course, keeps guests moving. There's a diverse set of dining options, such as Smokey's Bar-B-Que House and the Hungry Moose Food Court. And a full lineup of children's activities makes this place perfect for families.

225 rooms. Restaurant, bar. Golf. $151-250

RECOMMENDED

FRENCH COUNTRY INN

W4190 West End Road, Lake Geneva, 262-245-5220; www.frenchcountryinn.com

This historic inn is only 15 feet from the lake. You can enjoy the view while noshing on the free breakfast in the lakeside dining room. The bathed-in-white guestrooms with light-colored wood and French doors leading to balconies or patios make you feel like you're in a French country inn. Portions of the guest house were built in Denmark and shipped to the United States for the Danish exhibit at the 1893 Columbian Exposition in Chicago.

124 rooms. Restaurant. Complimentary breakfast. Pool. $251-350

MADISON

★★★EDGEWATER HOTEL

666 Wisconsin Ave., Madison, 608-256-9071, 800-922-5512; www.theedgewater.com

Lakeview rooms await guests at this getaway on Lake Mendota. You can hang out at the pier and get cabana service or you can dine in the Admiralty restaurant, which offers an upscale menu in a setting that provides some of the best vistas available. Enjoy a cocktail in the Cove Lounge or outdoor dining at Café on the Pier.

108 rooms. Restaurant, bar. Business center. Fitness center. Pets accepted. $61-150

★★★MADISON CONCOURSE HOTEL & GOVERNOR'S CLUB

1 W. Dayton St., Madison, 608-257-6000, 800-356-8293; www.concoursehotel.com

The Madison Concourse is situated in the heart of downtown Madison. The Dayton Street Café and Ovations provide reliable dining, and guest rooms are all well-appointed for business travelers with free WiFi and desks. The hotel doesn't have a spa, but if you snag one of the whirlpool air tub suites, the two-person tub's air streams provide a soothing spa-like soak. The Governor's Club Executive Level, which encompasses the top three floors of the hotel, provides views of the State Capital and the city skyline, plus complimentary top-shelf cocktails, hors d'oeuvres and other special amenities.

356 rooms. Restaurant, bar. Pool. $61-150

★★★SHERATON MADISON HOTEL

706 John Nolen Drive, Madison, 608-251-2300, 800-325-3535; www.sheraton.com

The stately exterior of this Sheraton is a welcome sight for business and pleasure travelers alike. Rooms are comfortable, especially because of the Sheraton's new beds, and the hotel is centrally located. It's about two miles from the Madison Children's Museum and three miles from the University of Wisconsin-Madison. Lobby WiFi stations are convenient and there's a heated indoor pool if you have some free time.

239 rooms. Restaurant, bar. Pets accepted. Pool. $61-150

RECOMMENDED

SPRING GREEN
HOUSE ON THE ROCK RESORT

5754 Highway 23, Spring Green, 608-935-3639; www.houseontherock.com

This resort is part of the sprawling House on the Rock complex, an unusual structure that was built on top of a chimney-like rock. The all-suite resort's rooms overlook the 27-hole championship golf course, plus they have refrigerators, microwaves and whirlpool baths. For more active pursuits, play some tennis or jump in the indoor pool. You also can choose to unwind in the onsite spa.

80 rooms. Restaurant, bar. Pool. Spa. Tennis. $151-250

WAUKESHA
★★★MILWAUKEE MARRIOTT WEST

W231N 1600 Corporate Court, Waukesha, 262-574-0888, 800-228-9290;
www.marriott.com

This modern, comfortable hotel overlooks an attractive small pond. You can take in the view from large picture windows in your room. In case you are traveling for business, rooms have good-sized desks. For a change of scenery, bring your laptop into the upscale lobby and make use of its WiFi. The hotel offers convenient access to highways and area activities, but if you prefer to stick nearby, the hotel has an indoor pool and whirlpool.

281 rooms. Restaurant, bar. Business center. Fitness center. Pool. $61-150

WISCONSIN DELLS
★★★WILDERNESS HOTEL & GOLF RESORT

511 E. Adams St., Wisconsin Dells, 608-253-9729, 800-867-9453; www.wildernessresort.com

Although you're in the Dells, this hotel takes its cues from the northwoods for its rustic-inspired décor. It's not that rustic, though, since the recently renovated rooms have flat-screen TVs, microwaves and refrigerators. Duffers bring their game here to play on the challenging 18-hole course. But an even bigger draw may be the for-guests-only indoor and outdoor water parks that equal about 12 football fields. In fact, the resort is more of an amusement park, complete with go-karts, mini-golf and even a zip line.

483 rooms. Restaurant, bar. Golf. $151-250

RECOMMENDED

SUNDARA INN & SPA
920 Canyon Road, Wisconsin Dells, 888-735-8181; www.sundaraspa.com

Located just outside the popular Wisconsin Dells, Sundara means "beautiful" and that is exactly what the location of this luxurious getaway surrounded by lush pine trees is. The intimate resort is made up of 26 suites and 12 villas. Each suite offers a king featherbed, spa bathroom and fireplace, while villas have luxurious amenities and up to 1,700 square feet of space. While the accommodations are supremely comfortable, the beautiful infinity pool, cozy outdoor fireplace and inviting spa will easily draw you out of your room. The spa offers an extensive selection of treatments, including the Warming Glow massage where warm candle wax made of essential oils is melted and then used during the massage. All guests are invited to participate in the Purifying Bath Ritual, a seven-step process that will leave you feeling completely relaxed. All meals can be enjoyed in-suite, poolside or in the Radiance Rotunda which offers pretty nature views.

26 rooms, 12 villas. Restaurant. Fitness Center. Pool. Spa. $251-350

WINTERGREEN RESORT AND CONFERENCE CENTER
60 Gasser Road, Wisconsin Dells, 608-254-2285, 800-648-4765; www.wintergreen-resort.com

When you're not stuck in the hotel's convention center working, make a beeline for the adjacent Tanger Outlet Center for some serious discount shopping. Or kick back at the indoor or outdoor water parks. Along with the waterpark offerings, families will like the spacious rooms with microwaves, fridges and WiFi.

111 rooms. Restaurant, bar. Pool. $60-150

WHERE TO EAT

LAKE GENEVA
★★★RISTORANTE BRISSAGO
Grand Geneva Resort & Spa, 7036 Grand Geneva Way, Lake Geneva, 262-248-8811; www.grandgeneva.com

Named after a town on Lake Maggiore in the Italian-Swiss countryside, this restaurant enjoys a Midwestern, countryside home all its own. Executive chef Robert Fedorko turns fresh ingredients imported from Italy into delicious dishes such as pasta marinara with garlic shrimp, filet mignon in a Gorgonzola crust and Parmesan mashed potatoes or pizza with four cheeses. The dining room is just one of the options at the Grand Geneva Resort & Spa.

Italian. Dinner. Closed Monday. Bar. $36-85

RECOMMENDED

POPEYE'S GALLEY AND GROG
811 Wrigley Drive, Lake Geneva, 262-248-4381; www.popeyesonlakegeneva.com

If you are looking for some comfort food, you can chow down on barbecue at Popeye's Galley and Grog. You'll find everything from brisket to baby-back ribs slathered in the delicious sauce. The smoked meats are another specialty; try the flame-roasted rotisserie chicken. On Fridays, fill up at the all-you-can-eat fish fry.

American. Lunch, dinner. Children's menu. Bar. $16-35

MADISON

★★★ADMIRALTY

The Edgewater Hotel, 666 Wisconsin Ave., Madison, 608-256-9071; www.theedgewater.com

This dining room boasts spectacular sunset views over Lake Mendota and a classic, international menu with dishes like filet mignon with foie gras and applewood-smoked bacon. The space carries Old World charm with its leather chairs, framed photographs and tableside preparations of dishes.

International. Breakfast, lunch, dinner, Sunday brunch. Outdoor seating. Bar. $16-35

★★★L'ETOILE

1 S. Pinckney St., Madison, 608-251-0500; www.letoile-restaurant.com

Chef Tory Miller and his wife, Traci, are at the helm of this landmark Madison restaurant, where the focus is on local, sustainable products. Menus change seasonally and ingredients are sourced from a variety of local, small-scale farmers. Come here to experience some of this university town's best dining, with dishes like rib-eye with cabernet jus and bone marrow-blue cheese compound butter. Don't miss the outstanding cheese course, offering a choice of artisan Wisconsin selections like 15-year aged cheddar and Havarti.

French. Dinner. Closed Sunday. Bar. $36-85

MENOMONEE FALLS

★★★FOX AND HOUNDS

1298 Friess Lake Road, Hubertus, 262-628-1111; www.foxandhoundsrestaurant.com

This renowned spot, located a few miles west of Milwaukee, is set in an 1845 log cabin that was built by the first clerk of Washington County. Meat and seafood are the house specialties, with choices like a T-bone with au jus and shrimp-stuffed salmon with crabmeat dressing. It's worth planning ahead for a reservation at the all-you-can-eat Friday fish fry.

American. Dinner, Saturday-Sunday lunch. Children's menu. Bar. $36-85

MINERAL POINT

★★★RAY RADIGAN'S

11712 S. Sheridan Road, Pleasant Prairie, 262-694-0455; www.foodspot.com

Just three miles from town, this popular stop has been a beloved local institution since 1933, dishing out superb steaks. The lobster Thermidor and the LeBlanc special, a prime blue ribbon T-bone steak, are both standouts.

American. Lunch, dinner. Closed Monday. Reservations recommended. Children's menu. Bar. $16-35

OCONOMOWOC

★★★GOLDEN MAST INN

W349 N5253 Lacy's Lane, Okauchee, 262-567-7047; www.weissgerbers.com

This local restaurant offers a wide array of entrées with a German flair. Try sauerbraten, red cabbage and spaetzle or authentic Wiener schnitzel.

American, German. Dinner, brunch. Closed Monday. Reservations recommended. Outdoor seating. Children's menu. Bar. $36-85

WAUWATOSA

★★★RISTORANTE BARTOLOTTA

7616 W. State St., Wauwatosa, 414-771-7910; www.bartolottaristorante.com

A classic representation of trattoria-style dining, this restaurant features a menu that highlights fresh and authentic ingredients. Go for the hand-cut pappardelle with slow-braised duck ragu or the mixed seafood grill teeming with shrimp, scallops, calamari, baby octopus and fish. The eatery has a loyal following and delivers a casual dining experience.

Italian. Dinner. Reservations recommended. Outdoor seating. Children's menu. Bar. $16-35

WELCOME TO ONTARIO

WHILE THE REST OF CANADA LOVES TO TEASE TORONTO FOR
its big-city gravity, this metropolitan hub and its surrounding province justify its ego. A colorful and endless mishmash of wilderness adventure, diverse cultures, urbane cosmopolitanism and rustic rural scenery, the province of Ontario has it all.

Ontario can be divided into north and south—the far northern wilderness is dominated by lakes, forests and logging camps, while the southern is an agricultural, industrial and commercial hive inhabited by 90 percent of the population.

Toronto, the provincial capital, and Ottawa, the nation's capital, offer tourists a wide spectrum of vibrant and world-class theater, restaurants, galleries, museums and recreational facilities. The Stratford Festival in Stratford and the Shaw Festival in Niagara-on-the-Lake are not to be missed, and the same goes for the spectacular Niagara Falls. Ontario's many recreational areas, such as Algonquin and Quetico provincial parks and St. Lawrence Islands National Park, offer a bounty of camping, hiking and all varieties of outdoor adventure. To the north lie Sudbury and Sault Ste. Marie; to the northwest, Thunder Bay, Fort Frances and Kenora, which offer canoeing, fishing and hunting. Perhaps more appealing than any one attraction is the vast, unspoiled nature of the province itself. More than 400,000 lakes and magnificent forests form a huge vacationland just a few miles from the U.S. border stretching all the way to Hudson Bay.

BEST ATTRACTIONS

ONTARIO'S BEST ATTRACTIONS

NIAGARA FALLS

The awe-inspiring Niagara Falls are a must-visit for any traveler. Whether you see them during the day or lit-up at night, the robust Falls are a sight. More than 12 million come out each year to marvel at Niagara Falls.

OTTAWA

As Canada's capital, Ottawa provides a major political arena for the country. But the beautiful city also has a robust cultural scene with a bevy of art, music and other cultural offerings.

TORONTO

This cosmopolitan city has it all: vibrant and diverse neighborhoods, chic shops, excellent restaurants and plenty of tourist attractions. It is even home to one of the Seven Wonders of the Modern World, the CN Tower.

EASTERN ONTARIO

Amid the rolling hills, rocky highlands and sand dunes in this region, you'll find a mix of charming small towns and hopping big cities. In the heart of the Thousand Islands, Gananoque is home base for endless boating, sailing, canoeing, kayaking, jet skiing, scuba diving, water taxis and charters. St. Lawrence Islands National Park, made up of nearly two-dozen beautiful islands, features nature trails, parks, beaches and island camping.

Nestled where the Rideau Canal and the St. Lawrence River meet Lake Ontario, Kingston is a freshwater sailor's dream, a city that exquisitely blends history and modern sophistication. Stroll through the bustling downtown and its boutiques and bistros, through its meandering waterfront with heritage-filled neighborhoods and breathtaking parklands.

The biggest city in Eastern Ontario is the nation's capital, Ottawa. With its parks full of flowers, universities, museums and diplomatic embassies, Ottawa is one of Canada's most beautiful cities. Ottawa is also a city of waterways, including the majestic Ottawa River, the fast-flowing Gatineau and the placid Rideau. But no waterway has defined Ottawa like the Rideau Canal, the oldest continuously operated canal in North America. It's a playground for skaters in winter and for boaters in summer. Filled with festivals, buskers, theater, music and dance, Ottawa also prides itself on a superb collection of museums—such as the National

Gallery of Canada, which has one of the country's best art collections, and the Bytown Museum, which depicts Ottawa's rowdy, lumberjack past. The capital city showcases Canada's art, music, people and politics with grace and verve—in both English and French.

WHAT TO SEE

GANANOQUE
1000 ISLANDS CAMPING RESORT
1000 Islands Parkway, Gananoque, 613-659-3058; www.1000islandsinfo.com

This beautiful campground area features a pool. Tent and trailer sites are available, and there's a playground, nature trails and miniature golf.

1000 ISLANDS SKYDECK
Hill Island, Lansdowne, 613-659-2335; www.1000islandsskydeck.com

The 400-foot tower offers views of the 1000 Islands and the St. Lawrence River. Visitors ride an elevator that takes 40 seconds to reach the first of three observation decks.

Admission: adults $9.75, children 6-12 $5.75, children 5 and under free. Mid-April-May, September-October, daily 9 a.m.-6 p.m.; June-August, daily 9 a.m.-8 p.m.

GANANOQUE BOAT LINE
6, Water St., Gananoque, 613-382-2144; www.ganboatline.com

Get out on the open water with a three-hour tour through the 1000 Islands with a stop at Boldt Castle.

Admission: varies. Mid-May-mid-October, schedule varies.

ST. LAWRENCE ISLANDS NATIONAL PARK
2 County Road 5, 14 miles east of Gananoque, Mallorytown, 613-923-5261, 800-839-8221; www.pc.gc.ca

Established in 1904, this park lies on a 50-mile stretch of the St. Lawrence River between Kingston and Brockville. It consists of 20 island areas and a mainland headquarters at Mallorytown Landing. The park offers boat-launching facilities, beaches, natural and historic interpretive programs, island camping, picnicking, hiking and boating. A visitor reception center and the remains of an 1817 British gunboat are at Mallorytown Landing and open mid-May to mid-October. The islands can be accessed by water taxi or by rental boats at marinas along both the Canadian and American sides.

Monday-Friday 8 a.m.-4:30 p.m.

KINGSTON
AGNES ETHERINGTON ART CENTRE
University Avenue and Queen's Crescent, Kingston, 613-533-2190; www.aeac.ca

This family-friendly art center hosts ever-changing exhibitions of contemporary and historical art. In the permanent collection, check out the paintings from Rembrandt and other Dutch artists and the African art offerings.

Admission: adults $4, seniors $2.50, children free. Tuesday-Friday 10 a.m.-4:30 p.m., Saturday-Sunday 1-5 p.m.

HIGHLIGHT

WHAT ARE THE TOP THINGS TO DO?

ENJOY THE OUTDOORS AT ST. LAWRENCE ISLANDS NATIONAL PARK

You'll have to take a water taxi or other boat to many of the 20 islands that make up St. Lawrence Islands National Park. But the scenic spot is worth it. The park has a beach, hiking, camping and more.

GET INTO THE GAME AT THE INTERNATIONAL ICE HOCKEY FEDERATION MUSEUM

Ice hockey is the national sport of Canada. Head to this museum to learn about the game's history and to see rare memorabilia, such as Wayne Gretzky's jersey from his inaugural season with the Edmonton Oilers.

GO SHOPPING AT THE BYWARD MARKET

Get ready to do some shopping at ByWard, one of Canada's largest public markets. Vendors peddle everything from produce to local crafts. Be sure to stop by the BeaverTails kiosk to sample the famous doughnut-like pastry.

TAKE IN THE ART AT THE NATIONAL GALLERY OF CANADA

The museum hosts a number of traveling exhibits, but it also has a vast permanent collection that includes European paintings, Inuit art, contemporary works and Canadian art.

BELLEVUE HOUSE NATIONAL HISTORIC SITE

35 Centre St., Kingston, 613-545-8666; www.pc.gc.ca

This 1840 Italianate villa was home of Sir John A. Macdonald, the first prime minister of Canada, and is replete with restored and furnished period pieces. Have afternoon tea in the garden or see multimedia displays and video presentations at the visitors center.

Admission: adults $3.90, seniors $3.40, children $1.90. April-May, daily 10 a.m.-5 p.m., June-Labor Day, daily 9 a.m.-6 p.m.; Labor Day-October, daily 10 a.m.-5 p.m.

FORT HENRY

1 Fort Henry Drive, Kingston, 613-542-7388, 800-437-2233; www.forthenry.com

One of Ontario's most spectacular historic sites, Fort Henry was built in the 1830s and restored during the 1930s. During the guided tour, you'll see 19th-century British infantry and artillery drills; military pageantry; exhibits

of military arms, uniforms and equipment; and explore garrison-life activities.
Admission: varies. Mid-May-early October, daily 10 a.m.-5 p.m.

GRAND THEATRE

218 Princess St., Kingston, 613-530-2050; www.whatsonkingston.com

This century-old, renovated theater hosts live plays, dance, symphonic and children's performances by professional companies and local groups. The stage has hosted everything from a production of *Sweeney Todd* to the Eagles. There is also a nice summer theater program.
Monday-Saturday 10:30 a.m.-5:30 p.m.

INTERNATIONAL ICE HOCKEY FEDERATION MUSEUM

277 York St., Kingston, 613-544-2355; www.ihhof.com

Hockey is a big deal in Canada, and this museum proves it with displays tracing the history of the game from its beginning in Kingston in 1885 to the present.
Admission: adults $5, seniors $4, students $3, children 6-12 $2, children 5 and under free.
Monday-Saturday 10 a.m.-4 p.m., Sunday noon-4 p.m.

MARINE MUSEUM OF THE GREAT LAKES AT KINGSTON

55 Ontario St., Kingston, 613-542-2261; www.marmuseum.ca

Ships have been built in Kingston since 1678. This museum explores the tales, adventures and enterprise of Inland Seas history. The museum features a ship-building gallery, an 1889 engine room with dry dock engines and pumps and artifacts and changing exhibits. The Museum Ship Alexander Henry, a 3,000-ton icebreaker, is open for tours and bed and breakfast accommodations.
Admission: adults $5, children $4.50. Daily 10 a.m.-4 p.m.

OTTAWA

BEAVERTAILS

69 George St., 613-241-1230;

This popular Canadian pastry resembles the tail of a beaver and comes with a variety of sweet and salty toppings. The original kiosk that began serving this pastry still operates in the ByWard Market district. The pastry is based on an ancient North American Voyageur recipe and is a descendant of the quick bread the Voyageurs baked. The tasty flat doughnut-like treat comes topped with things like chocolate, fruit and candy.
Daily 10 a.m.-11 p.m.

BYTOWN MUSEUM

540 Wellington St., Ottawa, 613-234-4570; www.bytownmuseum.com

Located in the heart of downtown, the museum occupies Ottawa's oldest stone building and includes artifacts, documents and pictures relating to Colonel By, Bytown and the history and social life of the region. Tours by appointment only.
Admission: adults $6, seniors and students $4, children 5-12 $3, children 4 and under free.
April-May 16, Thursday-Monday 10 a.m.-2 p.m.; May 17-October 12, daily 10 a.m.-5 p.m.;
October 13-November, Thursday-Monday 10 a.m.-2 p.m.; December-March, Monday-Friday
by appointment only.

BYWARD MARKET

55 ByWard Market Square, Ottawa, 613-562-3325; www.byward-market.com

One of Canada's oldest and largest public markets, ByWard offers a traditional outdoor farmer's market with vendors hawking food and produce, arts and crafts and more (they are here year-round but hours vary). The other part of the market takes up four blocks with boutiques, restaurants, salons, museums, bars, art galleries and outdoor cafés, including the famous BeaverTails pastry kiosk.

Farmer's market: May-October, daily 7 a.m.-6 p.m.; ByWard Market: daily, hours vary.

CANADIAN MUSEUM OF NATURE

Metcalf and McLeod streets, Ottawa, 613-566-4700, 800-263-4433; www.nature.ca

The exhibits at this museum focus on nature and the environment. You'll learn about dinosaurs, insects, gems and minerals, birds and mammals of Canada and the evolution of the planet. The museum underwent a renovation in 2010 and opened new spots like the RBC Blue Water Gallery, whose star exhibit is the skeleton of a blue whale, the world's largest animal.

Admission: adults $10, seniors and students $8, children 4-12 $6, children 3 and under free. Mid-May-August, Monday-Wednesday, Saturday-Sunday 9 a.m.-6 p.m., Thursday-Friday 9 a.m.-8 p.m.; September-April, Tuesday-Wednesday, Friday-Sunday 9 a.m.-6 p.m., Thursday 9 a.m.-8 p.m.

CANADIAN PARLIAMENT BUILDINGS

Wellington Street on Parliament Hill, Ottawa, 613-996-0896; www.parl.gc.ca

Neo-Gothic architecture dominates this part of the city. This is where the House of Commons and Senate meet; visitors may request free tickets to both chambers when Parliament is in session. A guided tour includes the House of Commons, Senate Chamber, and Parliamentary Library. The Centennial Flame, lit in 1967 as a symbol of Canada's 100th birthday, is also here, as is the Memorial Chapel, dedicated to Canadian servicemen who lost their lives in the Boer War, WWI, WWII and the Korean War. An observation deck is located atop the Peace Tower.

CENTRAL EXPERIMENTAL FARM

88 Prince of Wales Drive, Ottawa, 613-991-3044

This farm contains approximately 1,200 acres of field crops, ornamental gardens and an arboretum. View a showcase of herds of beef and dairy cattle, sheep, swine, and horses. There is also a tropical greenhouse, the Canada Agricultural Museum (www.agriculture.technomuses.ca), Clydesdale horse-drawn wagon and sleigh rides available at this not-so-typical farm.

Admission: adults $6, seniors and students $5, children 3-14 $3, children under 3 free. March-October, daily 9 a.m.-5 p.m.; barn: daily 9 a.m.-5 p.m. Tropical Greenhouse: daily 9 a.m.-4 p.m. Gardens: daily.

NATIONAL ARTS CENTRE

53 Elgin St., Ottawa, 613-947-7000; www.nac-cna.ca

This center for performing arts houses a concert hall and two theaters for music, dance, variety and drama. It is the home of the National Arts Centre Orchestra, and features more than 800 performances each year. There is also a canal-side café and landscaped terraces with panoramic view of Ottawa.

NATIONAL AVIATION MUSEUM

Rockcliffe Airport, 11 Aviation Parkway, Ottawa, 613-990-1985, 800-463-2038; www.aviation.technomuses.ca

More than 100 historic aircraft, 49 of which are on display in the Walkway of Time, can be viewed here. Displays demonstrate the development of aircraft in peace and war, emphasizing Canadian aviation.

Admission: adults $9, seniors and students $6, children 4-15 $5, children 3 and under free. May-August, daily 9 a.m.-5 p.m.; September-April, Wednesday-Sunday 10 a.m.-5 p.m.

NATIONAL GALLERY OF CANADA

380 Sussex Drive, Ottawa, 613-990-1985, 800-319-2787; www.national.gallery.ca

The gallery's permanent exhibits include European paintings from the 14th century to the present; Canadian art from the 17th century to the present; contemporary and decorative arts, prints, drawings, photos; and Inuit art. A reconstructed 19th-century Rideau convent chapel with Neo-Gothic fan-vaulted ceiling is the only known example of its kind in North America. There are also gallery talks, films, restaurants and a bookstore.

Admission: adults $9, seniors and students $7, children 12-19 $4, children 11 and under free. May-September, daily 10 a.m.-5 p.m., Thursday 10 a.m.-8 p.m.; October-April, Tuesday-Sunday 10 a.m.-5 p.m., Thursday 10 a.m.-8 p.m.

NATIONAL MUSEUM OF SCIENCE AND TECHNOLOGY

1867 St. Laurent Blvd., Ottawa, 613-991-3044; www.sciencetech.technomuses.ca

Explore more than 400 exhibits with many do-it-yourself experiments. Canada's role in science and technology are shown through displays on space, transportation, agriculture, computers, communications, physics and astronomy. The unusual open restoration bay allows viewing of various stages of artifact repair and refurbishment.

Admission: adults $9, seniors and students $6, children 4-14 $4, children 3 and under free. Labor Day-April, Tuesday-Sunday 9 a.m.-5 p.m.; May-Labor Day, Monday-Sunday 9 a.m.-5 p.m.

RIDEAU CANAL

34A Beckwith St. S., runs 125 miles between Kingston and Ottawa, Ottawa, 613-992-8142, 800-230-0016; www.pc.gc.ca

This canal was constructed under the direction of Lt. Col. John By of the Royal Engineers between 1826 and 1832 as a safe supply route to Upper Canada. Its purpose was to bypass the St. Lawrence River in case of an American attack. There are 24 lock stations where visitors can picnic, watch boats pass through the hand-operated locks and see wooden lock gates, cut stone walls and many historic structures. In summer, there are interpretive programs and exhibits at various locations. Areas of special interest include Kingston Mills Locks, Jones Falls Locks off Highway 15, Smith Falls Museum off Highway 15, Merrickville Locks on Highway 43 and Ottawa Locks. Boating is popular (mid-May-mid-October) here, and ice skating takes off when the weather turns cold (mid-December-late February).

ROYAL CANADIAN MINT

320 Sussex Drive, Ottawa, 613-993-8990, 800-276-7714; www.rcmint.ca

See how Canadian coins are produced at the mint's headquarters in this historic building. You'll also get to check out the expansive collections of coins and medals. Guided tours will explain the detailed process of minting coins and printing bank notes.

Admission: Monday-Friday: adults $5, seniors $4, children 5-17 $3, children 4 and under free; Saturday-Sunday: adults $3.50, seniors $2.80, children 5-17 $2, children 4 and under free. Mid-May-September, Monday-Friday 9 a.m.-6 p.m., Saturday-Sunday 9 a.m.-4:30 p.m.; early May-August, Monday-Sunday 9 a.m.-4 p.m.

VICTORIA MEMORIAL MUSEUM BUILDING

240 McLeod St., Ottawa, 613-566-4700; www.nature.ca

This castle-like structure houses a museum that interrelates man and his natural environment. It also is the site for the Canadian Museum of Nature. Natural history exhibits from dinosaurs to present-day plants and animals can be viewed as well as an outstanding collection of minerals and gems.

WHERE TO STAY

GANANOQUE

★★★GANANOQUE INN

550 Stone St. S., Gananoque, 613-382-2165, 800-465-3101; www.gananoqueinn.com

This historic inn sits on the banks of the St. Lawrence River in the heart of the Thousand Islands. Many of the rooms have fireplace and Jacuzzis, and all are heavy on personalized charm and coziness. For some privacy, book the Cedar Knoll. The gingerbread-trimmed Victorian house has a private deck that affords a gorgeous view of the Thousand Islands.

57 rooms. Restaurant, bar. Spa. $61-150

★★★TRINITY HOUSE

90 Stone St. S., Gananoque, 613-382-8383, 800-265-4871; www.trinityinn.com

In the heart of the famous Thousand Islands, this fully restored 1859 home has antiques mixed together with modern amenities. The guest rooms all have different décor. One of the most popular rooms sports a Chinois theme, with deep-blue walls with white woodwork and a black-and-gold inlaid screen. Wander through Victorian perennial gardens with herbs and flowers used by the chef in preparing the evening meals. Or sit in a rocking chair in the open-air porch.

8 rooms. Restaurant, bar. Complimentary breakfast. Spa. $61-150

KINGSTON

★★★MERRILL

343 Main St. E., Picton, 613-476-7451; www.merrillinn.com

This Victorian house was built in 1878 for Edwards Merrill, one of Canada's top barristers. A sprinkling of period antiques gives the otherwise contemporary rooms a touch of Old World elegance. You'll be greeted with iced tea and chocolate-chip cookies at check-in, and the innkeepers will make you feel like family.

13 rooms. Restaurant. Complimentary breakfast. $151-250

OTTAWA

★★★THE FAIRMONT CHATEAU LAURIER

1 Rideau St., Ottawa, 613-241-1414, 800-441-1414;
www.fairmont.com

This impressive castle enchants visitors with its setting overlooking Parliament Hill, the Rideau Canal and the Ottawa River. It is conveniently located in the city center. The traditional rooms have dark wood; a color palette of tan, gray and blue; and valences framing the windows. Enjoy elegant dining at Wilfrid's, while Zoe's Lounge is a more casual alternative. Guest services include a full-service fitness club with a stunning Art Deco pool and the ability to check out with your BlackBerry.

429 rooms. Restaurant, bar. Business center. Fitness center. Pool. Spa. Pets accepted. $151-250

★★★THE FAIRMONT LE CHATEAU MONTEBELLO

392 rue Notre Dame, Montebello, 819-423-6341, 800-441-1414; www.fairmont.com

Stretched out along the banks of the Ottawa River, this log cabin-style lodge charms with spectacular scenery. The rooms have a similar rustic vibe, with dark wood and plaid bedspreads and drapes. From hiking, biking and boating, the recreational pursuits offered here are endless. Sybaritic-minded visitors enjoy the pampering treatments at the spa, while gastronomes savor the cuisine at the resort's dining rooms. Aux Chantignoles turns out French fare like escargot casserole with roasted garlic cream sauce.

210 rooms. Restaurant, bar. Business center. Pool. Spa. Pets accepted. Golf. Tennis. $151-250

★★★GASTHAUS SWITZERLAND INN

89 Daly Ave., Ottawa, 613-237-0335; www.ottawainn.com

Tucked inside a restored 1872 house, this charming inn provides traditional Swiss hospitality. Some of the rooms are small, but they all offer personalized touches and comfortable beds. Plus, they all come equipped with 32-inch flat-screen LCD televisions and complimentary WiFi.

22 rooms. Restaurant. Complimentary breakfast. No children under 12. $61-150

★★★HILTON LAC-LEAMY

3 Blvd. Du Casino, Hull, 819-790-6444;
www.hiltonlacleamy.com

This hotel has an appealing location. It is on the shore of Lake Leamy and Des Carrieres Lake, it's connected to Casino Lac-Leamy, and it is close to

---

WHICH OTTAWA HOTELS HAVE THE MOST UNIQUE DÉCOR?

The Fairmont Chateau Laurier

From the outside, the Fairmont Chateau Laurier Ottawa doesn't look like a hotel. You'd easily mistake it for a magnificent fairytale castle. After all, the hulking limestone building does have turrets.

The Fairmont Le Chateau Montebello

Who knew that log cabins could be chic? The Fairmont Le Chateau Montebello is supposed to look like a red cedar log cabin, and the hotel even mimics the theme in its rugged rooms, but this sprawling chateau is all about luxury, not roughing it.

Gatineau's shopping district and near an all-season walking/biking trail. When dinnertime comes around, various dining options include the French-style bistro, Le Cellier, or a fine dining experience at Le Baccara. The rooms are what you would expect from a Hilton: comfortable and well-appointed.

349 rooms. Restaurant, bar. Business center. Pool. $151-250

★★★MARRIOTT OTTAWA

100 Kent St., Ottawa, 613-238-1122, 800-853-8463; www.ottawamarriott.com

Located in the heart of downtown, the hotel is close to local attractions such as Canada's Parliament Buildings, the Rideau Canal, the Ottawa Congress Centre and the National Gallery of Canada. Enjoy a panoramic view of the city with your meal at the Merlot Rooftop Grill, a revolving restaurant. Your brood will keep busy in the fun-for-all-ages Kids' Zone, which has an activity center for kids, a tree house, a pool table, a foosball table, an Xbox 360 and a Wii.

480 rooms. Restaurant, bar. Business center. Pool. Pets accepted. $151-250

★★★MINTO PLACE SUITE HOTEL

185 Lyon St. N., Ottawa, 613-232-2200, 800-267-3377; www.mintosuitehotel.com

Minto Place Suite Hotel offers a convenient location, as just outside its doors you can explore Parliament Hill, the Casino Lac-Leamy and the historic ByWard Market. Use the hotel's free bike rentals to pedal around and explore the area. Rooms in the all-suite hotel have luxurious bedding, 42-inch televisions and fully equipped kitchenettes. If you don't feel like cooking, head to Prime 360, the hotel's steakhouse.

417 rooms. Restaurant, bar. Fitness center. Pool. $251-350

★★★THE WESTIN OTTAWA

11 Colonel By Drive, Ottawa, 613-560-7000, 800-937-8461; www.westin.com

Located only blocks from Parliament Hill and the ByWard Market, this hotel is connected to the Rideau Center Shopping Complex and the Ottawa Congress Center. You can see the bustle of the city from the rooms' big-picture windows. Guest rooms are decorated in soothing neutral tones and many of them have soaking tubs.

487 rooms. Restaurant, bar. Business center. Pool. Spa. Pets accepted. $151-250

WHERE TO EAT

RECOMMENDED
KINGSTON
AUNT LUCY'S

1399 Princess St., Kingston, 613-542-2729; www.auntlucysdinnerhouse.com

This homestyle restaurant serves up meaty dishes that mom would make, including pot roast, meatloaf and turkey. Try the thick slabs of steaks or the shrimp doused in garlic-chardonnay sauce. End your meal with the from-scratch black raspberry cheesecake. Mom would approve.

Seafood, steak. Lunch, dinner, Sunday brunch. $16-35

OTTAWA

★★★JOHN TAYLOR AT DOMUS CAFÉ

87 Murray St., Ottawa, 613-241-6007; www.domuscafe.ca

Under chef John Taylor, this café offers innovative dishes using local meats and produce. A member of the Slow Food movement, the restaurant uses the freshest ingredients to prepare your meal. Enjoy dishes such as pan-roasted halibut with red-skin potatoes, warm wilted greens, zucchini and Swiss chard chutney; and grass-fed grilled Kerr farm flatiron steak with sweet corn polenta, wilted greens, mushrooms and tomato-apple chutney. The café also offers an extensive award-winning wine list and a hefty single-malt Scotch menu. Go for Canada's Glen Breton Scotch.

French bistro. Lunch, dinner. Reservations recommended. Bar. $36-85

CENTRAL ONTARIO

This region of Ontario is known for one of the most popular tourist attractions: Niagara Falls. More than 12 million people head to Niagara Falls each year, and not just to see the roaring waters. The area is also home to more than 70 award-winning wineries. Visitors will also find dozens of excellent golf courses and more than 124 miles of spectacular cycling and hiking trails. You'll also get a better view of Niagara Falls from this side of the border.

Near Niagara Falls there's a picturesque town that is often called the loveliest in Ontario. In Niagara-on-the-Lake, beautiful old homes line the tree-shaded streets and the town's attractions include theater, historic sites, beautiful gardens and Queen Street's shops, hotels and restaurants. Delightful in any season, this is one of the best-preserved and prettiest remnants of the Georgian era.

Hamilton, linked to Toronto by the majestic Skyway Bridge, is a vibrant community with excellent dining, galleries and shopping. Emerging artists make their home downtown, a bustling engine of creative energy with a thriving gallery scene. Browse for antiques and collectibles, or wander through cobbled streets for a nightlife scene that swings till the wee hours. The waterfront is a mecca for hikers, boarders and water-sports enthusiasts, while buyers flock to the cornucopia of ethnic food stores and shops on Ottawa Street. Circling the cosmopolitan pleasures of the city is the splendor of the Royal Botanical Gardens, the famous Bruce Trail and an abundance of conservation areas, water parks and walking paths.

One of the biggest draws to Ontario is its capital. Toronto is one of Canada's leading industrial, commercial and cultural centers. Having earned its name from the native word for "meeting place," Toronto is an awesome cosmopolitan place—the United Nations recently deemed it the world's most ethnically diverse city. A performing arts powerhouse, the city presents everything from Broadway musicals to standup comedy and opera to dance. Good shopping can be found throughout the city, but Torontonians are most proud of their Underground City, a series of subterranean malls linking more than 300 shops and restaurants in the downtown area. The other source of the city's pride is its professional sports teams, including the Maple Leafs (hockey), Blue Jays (baseball), Raptors (basketball) and Argonauts (football).

WHAT TO SEE

HAMILTON
AFRICAN LION SAFARI

1386 Cooper Road, Flamborough, 519-623-2620, 800-461-9453; www.lionsafari.com

Drive through this active wildlife park and spy exotic animals and bird shows, as well as training demonstrations. Along the safari trail, you may see lions, baboons, zebras, white rhinos and giraffes roaming.

Admission: adults $29.95, seniors $27.95, children 3-12 $24.95. May-late June, Monday-Friday 10 a.m.-4 p.m., Saturday-Sunday 10 a.m.-5 p.m.; late June-early September, daily 10 a.m.-5:30 p.m.; early September-early October, Monday-Friday 10 a.m.-4 p.m.

ART GALLERY OF HAMILTON

123 King St. W., Hamilton, 905-527-6610; www.artgalleryofhamilton.on.ca

This gallery boasts a collection of more than 9,000 sculptures and photographs covering several centuries by American, Canadian, British and European artists.

Admission: adults $10, seniors $8, children 6-17 $4, children 5 and under free. Tuesday-Wednesday noon-7 p.m., Thursday-Friday noon-9 p.m., Saturday-Sunday noon-5 p.m.

BATTLEFIELD HOUSE AND MONUMENT

77 King St., Stoney Creek, 905-662-8458; www.battlefieldhouse.ca

Devoted to the Battle of Stoney Creek, this 1795 settler's home and monument honors one of the most significant encounters of the War of 1812. Some rooms are furnished as a farm home of the 1830s and guides are dressed in period costumes.

Admission: adults $6.50, seniors and students $5.50, children 6-12 $4.50, children 5 and under. June 15-Labor Day, Tuesday-Sunday 11 a.m.-4 p.m.; Labor Day-June 14, Tuesday-Sunday 1-4 p.m.

CANADIAN FOOTBALL HALL OF FAME AND MUSEUM

58 Jackson St. W., Hamilton, 905-528-7566; www.cfhof.ca

Sports fans will rejoice once inside this national shrine to Canadian pigskin, which traces 120 years of football's history.

Admission: adults $7, seniors and students $3.50, children under 5 free. Tuesday-Saturday 9:30 a.m.-4:30 p.m.

CHILDREN'S MUSEUM

1072 Main St. E., Hamilton, 905-546-4848; www.myhamilton.ca

The Children's Museum is a participatory learning center where children ages 2 to 13 can expand sensory awareness of the world. Hands-on exhibits will keep kids occupied for hours. They can hunt for fossils in an archaeological dig or design mazes.

Admission: adults 41.50, children 1-13 $3.50, children under 1 free. April-September, Tuesday-Saturday 9:30 a.m.-3:30 p.m.; October-March, Wednesday-Saturday 9:30 a.m.-3:30 p.m., Sunday 11 a.m.-4 p.m.

DUNDURN CASTLE

610 York Blvd., Hamilton, 905-546-2872; www.hamilton.ca

Home of Sir Allan Napier MacNab, prime minister of the United Provinces of

BEST ATTRACTIONS

WHAT ARE THE TOP THINGS TO DO NEAR TORONTO?

SEE NIAGARA FALLS
The most famous site in these parts is the gorgeous Niagara Falls, and you can experience it up close via cable car, helicopter or boat. About 3,160 tons of water flows over the falls every second so there's no bad time to visit.

GO UP THE CN TOWER
The CN Tower is one of the world's tallest freestanding structures. Head to the outdoor observation deck or the glass-floor level for a breathtaking view of Toronto. For another way to see the city, dine in the restaurant, which rotates 360 degrees.

SHOP AT EATON CENTRE
When you're in the mood for a little shopping, come to Eaton Centre. The mall has more than 230 shops, but the impressive building itself is worth a look, with its glass roof, glass-enclosed elevators and fiberglass sculptures.

CHECK OUT THE EXHIBITS AT THE ROYAL ONTARIO MUSEUM
The ROM showcases natural history and world culture in its many exhibit halls. Peruse the popular Nubia Gallery, built after a ROM team discovered a new archaeological culture in Northern Sudan.

WALK AROUND THE ST. LAWRENCE MARKET
Not only is this Toronto's largest indoor market, where you can find everything from organic produce and specialty teas and coffee to locally made crafts, but the historic building is full of character.

Canada from 1854-1856, this 35-room mansion has been restored to its former splendor. Exhibits and programs run all year.
July-Labor Day, daily 10 a.m.-4 p.m.; Labor Day-July, Tuesday-Sunday noon-4 p.m.

FLAMBORO DOWNS
967 Highway 5 W., Flamborough, 905-627-3561; www.flamborodowns.com
Harness racing draws crowds here year-round with a grandstand that seats 3,000. The Confederation Cup race for the top three-year-old pacers in North America is held at Flamboro every August.
Wednesday-Friday, Sunday-Monday 6 p.m.

HAMILTON'S FARMERS MARKET
55 York Blvd., Hamilton, 905-546-2096; www.hamilton.ca

Fresh produce, flowers, meat, poultry, fish, cheese and baked goods are brought from all over the Niagara garden belt to this farmer's market.

Tuesday, Thursday 7 a.m.-6 p.m., Friday 8 a.m.-6 p.m., Saturday 6 a.m.-6 p.m.

ROYAL BOTANICAL GARDENS
680 Plains Road W., Hamilton, 905-527-1158; www.rbg.ca

Colorful gardens, natural areas and a wildlife sanctuary make up Hamilton's many gardens, including a rock garden with seasonal displays, a garden with herbaceous perennials, an arboretum containing world-famous lilacs in late May, a rose garden, a teaching garden, as well as woodland, scented and medicinal gardens. At Cootes Paradise Sanctuary, trails wind around more than 1,200 acres of water, marsh and wooded ravines.

Admission: adults $12.50, seniors and students $9.50, children 5-12 $7.25, children 4 and under free. Daily 10 a.m.-5 p.m.

NIAGARA FALLS
FALLSVIEW CASINO RESORT
6380 Fallsview Blvd., Niagara Falls, 888-325-5788; www.fallsviewcasinoresort.com

After you've conquered the Falls, you can spend your trip in places like this casino, which is perched on a cliff overlooking Horseshoe Falls. But you'll be too busy to notice the view; the casino offers more than 3,000 slots, 130 gaming tables and a poker room.

Daily.

GUINNESS WORLD OF RECORDS MUSEUM
4943 Clifton Hill, Niagara Falls, 905-356-2299, 866-656-0310; www.guinnessniagarafalls.com

Based on the popular book of records, the museum puts hundreds of original exhibits, artifacts, and laser video galleries on display, as well as re-creations of many of the world's greatest accomplishments.

Admission: adults $11.99, seniors and students $9.50, children $6.99. December-March, daily 10 a.m.-8 p.m.; April-May, daily 9 a.m.-midnight; June-August, daily 9 a.m.-2 a.m.; September-November, daily 10 a.m.-10 p.m.

IMAX THEATRE NIAGARA FALLS
6170 Fallsview Blvd., Niagara Falls, 905-358-3611, 866-405-4629; www.imaxniagara.com

This six-story-high movie screen shows *Legends and Daredevils*, a film high-lighting the Falls and the people who defied the treacherous waters, including a person who walked on a tightrope over the Falls and someone who survived the falling over in a barrel. Daredevil Adventure has displays, exhibits and some of the actual barrels used to traverse the Falls throughout history.

JOURNEY BEHIND THE FALLS
6650 Niagara Parkway, Queen Victoria Park, Niagara Falls, 905-354-1551; www.niagaraparks.com

An elevator descends to a point about 25 feet above the river, with excellent views of the Falls from below and behind. Don't worry about getting soaked; waterproof garments are supplied.

Admission: April-December: adults $12.75, children 6-12 $8.35, children 5 and under free. Open year-round; hours vary.

LOUIS TUSSAUD'S WAXWORKS

4960 Clifton Hill, Niagara Falls, 905-356-2238; www.ripleysniagara.com

Louis Tussaud's Waxworks is a collection of instantly recognizable, true-to-life wax figures. Life-size, historically costumed wax figures of the past and present are on display. Pose for pictures with Sarah Jessica Parker and John Lennon's doppelgängers. If you're looking for a scare, head into the Chamber of Horrors. *Admission: adults $14.68, children $7.90. Hours vary.*

MARINELAND

7657 Portage Road, Niagara Falls, 905-356-8250; www.marinelandcanada.com

At this theme park, see killer whales, dolphins and sea lions, and then visit wildlife displays with deer, bears, buffalo and elk. There are also thrill rides, including one of the world's largest steel roller coasters, as well as restaurants and picnic areas. *Admission: adults $40.95, children 5-9 $33.95. Hours vary.*

MINOLTA TOWER CENTRE

6732 Fallsview Blvd., Niagara Falls, 905-356-1501; www.niagaratower.com

This 325-foot tower offers a magnificent 360-degree view of the Falls and surrounding areas. There are eight levels at top with specially designed glass for ideal photography; a Minolta exhibit floor; the Waltzing Waters water and light spectacle; gift shops; an incline railway to the Falls and Top of the Rainbow dining rooms overlooking the Falls. Reservations are recommended.

NIAGARA FALLS AVIARY

5651 River Road, Niagara Falls, 905-356-8888, 866-994-0090; www.niagarafallsaviary.com

Wander through this 15,000-square-foot conservatory amid lush foliage. The environment simulates a tropical rainforest in which free-flying birds soar overhead. There are guided and self-guided tours and a restaurant. *Admission: adults $16.95, seniors $14.95, children $11.95. January-August, daily 9:30 a.m.-7 p.m.; September, Monday-Friday 10 a.m.-5 p.m., Saturday-Sunday 10 a.m.-6 p.m.; October-December, daily 10 a.m.-5 p.m.*

NIAGARA PARKS BOTANICAL GARDENS

2565 Niagara Parkway, Niagara Falls, 905-356-8554, 877-642-7275; www.niagaraparks.com

Come to the beautiful Botanical Gardens to sniff around the aromatic rose garden, which has more than 2,400 blooms. The grounds also include nearly 100 acres of horticultural exhibits and a nature shop. *Admission: free. Daily dawn-dusk.*

NIAGARA PARKS BUTTERFLY CONSERVATORY

2405 Niagara Parkway, Niagara Falls, 905-358-0025, 877-642-7275

Approximately 2,000 graceful butterflies make their home in this 11,000-square-foot, climate-controlled conservatory filled with exotic greenery and flowing water. Nearly 50 species of butterflies can be viewed from a 600-foot network of walking paths. There is an outdoor butterfly garden and a gift shop. *Admission: free. Daily dawn-dusk.*

NIAGARA SPANISH AERO CAR

850 Niagara Parkway, Niagara Falls, 905-354-5711; www.niagaraparks.com

The 1,800-foot cables support an antique car that crosses the whirlpool and rapids of the Niagara River. You'll get a great aerial view of the famous waters. It's a five-minute trip each way.

Admission: adults $11.75, children 6-12 $7.65, children 5 and under free. Mid-April-mid-October, daily.

OLD FORT ERIE

350 Lake Shore Road, Fort Erie, 905-871-0540

Fort Erie is the site of some of the fiercest fighting of the War of 1812. It has been restored to the period and offers guided tours of the Glengarry Light Infantry by interpreters dressed in uniform.

May-November, daily 10 a.m.-6 p.m.

SKYLON TOWER

5200 Robinson St., Niagara Falls, 905-356-2651, 866-434-4202; www.skylon.com

Skylon Tower soars 775 feet above the base of the Falls. To get a good view, you can choose between the three-level dome's indoor/outdoor observation deck or the revolving and stationary dining rooms served by three external, glass-enclosed Yellow Bug elevators. There are also specialty shops at base of tower.

NIAGARA-ON-THE-LAKE

BROCK'S MONUMENT

14184 Niagara River Parkway, Niagara, 905-468-4257

This monument is a massive, 185-foot memorial to Sir Isaac Brock, who was felled by a sharpshooter while leading his troops against American forces at the Battle of Queenston Heights in October 1812. A narrow, winding staircase leads to a tiny observation deck inside the monument. A walking tour of important points on the Queenston Heights Battlefield begins at Brock Monument. Brock and his aide-de-camp, Lt. Col. Macdonell, are buried here.

Mid-May-Labor Day, daily.

FORT GEORGE NATIONAL HISTORIC SITE

26 Queen St., Niagara-on-the-Lake, 905-468-4257; www.pc.gc.ca

Once the principal British post on the frontier, this fort saw much action during the War of 1812. There are 11 restored, refurnished buildings and massive ramparts.

April-October, daily 10 a.m.-5 p.m.; rest of year, by appointment.

MCFARLAND HOUSE

15927 Niagara Parkway, Niagara-on-the-Lake, 905-356-2241

This Georgian brick home was used as a hospital in the War of 1812 by both the American and British armies and is furnished in the Loyalist tradition.

Admission: adults $4.75, children 6-12 $3.65, children 5 and under free. July-Labor Day, daily; mid-May-June and Labor Day-September, Saturday-Sunday.

NIAGARA HISTORICAL SOCIETY MUSEUM

43 Castlereagh St., Niagara-on-the-Lake, 905-468-3912; www.niagarahistorical.museum

Opened in 1907, this is the earliest museum building in Ontario. Items from the time of the United Empire Loyalists, War of 1812, early Upper Canada and the Victorian era are all on display.

*Admission: adults $5, seniors $3, students $2, children $1. May-October, daily 10 a.m.-5 p.m.;
November-April, daily 1-5 p.m.; rest of year, Saturday-Sunday or by appointment.*

ST. MARK'S ANGLICAN CHURCH
47 Byron St., Niagara-on-the-Lake, 905-468-3123; www.stmarks1792.com

The original church was damaged by fire after being used as a hospital and barracks during the War of 1812. Rebuilt in 1822 and enlarged in 1843, the church contains an unusual three-layer stained-glass window. The churchyard dates from earliest British settlement.

July-August, daily; rest of year, by appointment.

ST. VINCENT DE PAUL ROMAN CATHOLIC CHURCH
73 Picton St., Niagara-on-the-Lake, 905-468-1383

St. Vincent is the first Roman Catholic parish in Upper Canada and an excellent example of Gothic Revival architecture. It was enlarged in 1965 and an older part was largely preserved.

TORONTO

ALLAN GARDENS
19 Horticultural Ave., Toronto, 416-392-7288; www.toronto.ca

More than 100 years old, these gardens cover more than 16,000 square feet of greenhouses. There are indoor and outdoor botanical displays, a wading pool and picnicking areas. The Palm House will transport you to a tropical locale with its bananas, bamboo and exotic screw pine tree.

Admission: free. Daily 10 a.m.-5 p.m.

BATA SHOE MUSEUM
327 Bloor St. W., Toronto, 416-979-7799; www.batashoemuseum.ca

When Sonja Bata's historical shoe collection began to surpass her storage space, the Bata family established the Bata Shoe Museum Foundation. Architect Raymond Moriyama's award-winning five-story, 3,900-square-foot building now holds more than 10,000 shoes, artfully arranged in four galleries to celebrate the style and function of footwear throughout 4,500 years of history. One permanent exhibition, "All About Shoes," showcases a collection of 20th-century celebrity kicks; artifacts on display range from ancient Egyptian sandals to Elton John's platforms.

*Admission: adults $14, seniors $12, students $8, children 5-17 $5, children 4 and under free.
Monday-Saturday 10 a.m.-5 p.m., Sunday noon-5 p.m.*

BLOOR/YORKVILLE AREA
Bounded by Bloor Street West, Avenue Road, Davenport Road and Yonge Street, Toronto, 416-928-3553; www.bloor-yorkville.com

The Bloor/Yorkville area is one of Toronto's most elegant shopping and dining sections, with nightclubs, music, designer couture boutiques and art galleries. The area itself is fun to walk around, with a cluster of courtyards and alleyways. There's also a contemporary park in the heart of the neighborhood with a huge piece of granite called The Rock. It was brought here from the Canadian Shield, a U-shaped region of ancient rock covering about half of Canada.

CASA LOMA
1 Austin Terrace, Toronto, 416-923-1171; www.casaloma.org

Take a self-guided multimedia tour of this domestic castle, built in 1911 over three years at a cost of $3.5 million. As romantic as he was a shrewd business-man, Sir Henry Pellatt, who founded the Toronto Electric Light Company, had an architect create this beautiful medieval castle. Soaring battlements, secret passageways, flowerbeds warmed by steam pipes, secret doors, servants' rooms and an 800-foot tunnel are just some of the treats you'll discover.

Admission: adults $18.19, seniors and children 14-17 $12.95, children 4-13 $10.02. Daily 9:30 a.m.-5 p.m.

COLBORNE LODGE
Colborne Lodge Drive and The Queensway, Toronto, 416-392-6916; www.city.toronto.on.ca

The successful 19th-century architect John Howard was just 34 when he completed this magnificent manor, named for the architect's first patron, Upper Canada Lt. Gov. Sir John Colborne. It remains an excellent example of Regency-style architecture, with its stately verandas that open to the garden and park.

Admission: adults $5.71, seniors and children 13-18 $2.62, children 4-12 $2.38. Hours vary.

CN TOWER
301 Front St. W., Toronto, 416-868-6937; www.cntower.ca

Toronto's CN Tower is one of the tallest freestanding structures in the world and on the list of the Seven Wonders of the Modern World. At 1,815 feet from the ground to the tip of its communications aerial, it towers over the rest of the city. Take the elevator to the top, where on a clear day it's said you can see the spray coming off Niagara Falls 62 miles away.

Daily 9 a.m-10 p.m., Friday-Saturday to 10:30 p.m.

ELGIN & WINTER GARDEN THEATRE CENTRE
189 Yonge St., Toronto, 416-872-5555; www.heritagefdn.on.ca

The 80-year history of these two theaters speaks more than any of the excellent productions they've hosted. Built in 1913, each theater was a masterpiece in its own right: The Elgin was ornate, with gold leaf, plaster cherubs and elegant opera boxes; the walls of the Winter Garden were hand-painted to resemble a garden, and its ceiling was a mass of beech bows and twinkling lanterns. Through the years, the stages saw the likes of George Burns and Gracie Allen, Edger Bergen and Charlie McCarthy, Milton Berle and Sophie Tucker.

The Ontario Heritage Foundation offers year-round guided tours on Thursdays at 5 p.m. and Saturdays at 11 a.m.

GEORGE R. GARDINER MUSEUM OF CERAMIC ART
111 Queen's Park, Toronto, 416-586-8080; www.gardinermuseum.on.ca

This museum contains one of the world's finest collections of Italian majolica, English Delftware and 18th-century continental porcelain.

HARBOURFRONT CENTRE
235 Queens Quay W., Toronto, 416-973-4600; www.harbourfrontcentre.com

This 10-acre waterfront community is alive with theater, dance, films, art shows, music, crafts and children's programs. Most events are free.

Admission: varies. Monday-Saturday 10 a.m.-11 p.m., Sunday 10 a.m.-9 p.m.

HIGH PARK

1873 Bloor St. W., Toronto, 416-392-1111; www.highpark.org

High Park is an urban oasis with expansive fields for sports, picnicking and cycling. Its large lake freezes in the winter and in the warmer months, you can check out the small zoo, swimming pool, tennis courts and bowling greens.

HISTORIC FORT YORK

100 Garrison Road, Toronto, 416-392-6907; www.city.toronto.on.ca

It may not have seen a lot of action—just one battle during the War of 1812—but Fort York's place in Toronto's history is secure. It is the birthplace of modern Toronto, having played a major role in saving York (now Toronto) from being invaded by 1,700 American soldiers. Fort York contains Canada's largest collection of original War of 1812 buildings and is a designated National Historic Site.

ICE SKATING AT GRENADIER POND

High Park, 1873 Bloor St. W., Toronto, 416-392-6916; www.toronto.ca

One of the most romantic ice-skating spots you'll find is Grenadier Pond in High Park, one of 25 parks offering free artificial rinks throughout the city. Warning: There's a sign warning people that ice skating isn't permitted in the pond, but locals openly flout the rule. In addition to vendors selling roasted chestnuts, there's a bonfire to keep you toasty. Other free ice rinks include Nathan Phillips Square in front of City Hall and an area at Harbor front Centre. Equipment rentals are available onsite.

Admission: free.

KENSINGTON MARKET

College Street and Spadina Avenue, Toronto

This maze of narrow streets is lined with food shops, vintage clothing stores, restaurants and jewelry vendors. There are bargain hunters haggling, café owners enticing diners and little stores brimming with items from Asia, South America, the Middle East and Europe.

KORTRIGHT CENTRE FOR CONSERVATION

9550 Pine Valley Drive, Woodbridge, 905-832-2289; www.kortright.org

This environmental center has trails, a bee house, a maple syrup shack, a wildlife pond and plantings. Naturalist-guided hikes are available, and there's cross-country skiing in winter. The site also includes a picnic area, café and theater.

Admission: adults $6, seniors $5, children free. Daily 10 a.m.-4:30 p.m.

LITTLE ITALY

West of Bathurst Street between Euclid Avenue and Shaw Street, Toronto;
www.littleitalyintoronto.com

After the British, Italians make up the largest cultural group in Toronto. Though the Italian community moved north as it grew, the atmosphere of Little Italy remains. Restaurants and bars open onto the sidewalks. Make like the locals and sit down at Café Diplomatico, or the Dip, for a cup of coffee and a cannoli while you people-watch.

MACKENZIE HOUSE

82 Bond St., Toronto, 416-392-6915; www.toronto.ca

The restored 19th-century Greek Revival home of William Lyon Mackenzie, first mayor of Toronto, includes furnishings and artifacts of the 1850s. There's also a re-created print shop on the premises.

Admission: adults $5.71, seniors $2.62, children 13-18 $2.62, children 5-12 $2.38, children 4 and under free. January-April, Saturday-Sunday noon-5 p.m.; May-Labor Day, Tuesday-Sunday noon-5 p.m.; Labor Day-December, Tuesday-Friday noon-4 p.m., Saturday-Sunday noon-5 p.m.

MARTIN GOODMAN TRAIL

Toronto, 416-392-8186; www.city.toronto.on.ca

Leave it to fitness-conscious Toronto not just to have a beautifully maintained waterfront but to build a trail that takes you from one end to the other. The Martin Goodman Trail is a public jogging, biking, walking and in-line skating path that connects all the elements of the waterfront, traversing 13 miles. It also travels past several spots for bike and skate rentals.

MEDIEVAL TIMES

Exhibition Place, Dufferin Gate, Toronto, 416-260-1234; www.medievaltimes.com

This 11th-century castle was created to replicate an 11th-century experience. While you gnaw on a big chicken leg and guzzle a goblet of mead, you'll watch knightly joust competitions and equestrian displays.

MOUNT PLEASANT CEMETERY

375 Mount Pleasant Road, Toronto, 416-485-9129; www.mountpleasantgroupofcemeteries.ca

One of the oldest burial grounds in North America, the Mount Pleasant Cemetery is the final resting place of many well-known Canadians, including Sir Frederic Banting and Charles Best, the discoverers of insulin; Glenn Gould, renowned classical pianist; and Prime Minister William Lyon Mackenzie King, who led Canada through World War II. The grounds have rare plants and shrubs as well as a Memorial Peony Garden.

ONTARIO PARLIAMENT BUILDINGS

Queen's Park, 111 Wellesley St. W., Toronto, 416-325-7500; www.parliamenthill.gc.ca

Guided tours of the Legislature Building and walking tour of grounds are available. You can also see the gardens, art collections and historic displays.

ONTARIO PLACE

955 Lakeshore Blvd. W., Toronto, 416-314-9900; www.ontarioplace.com

This is a 96-acre cultural, recreational and entertainment complex on three artificial islands in Lake Ontario. It includes an outdoor amphitheater for concerts, two pavilions with multimedia presentations, the Cinesphere theater with IMAX films year-round; three villages of snack bars, restaurants and pubs; miniature golf; lagoons, canals and two marinas; a 370-foot water slide, showboat, pedal and bumper boats and rides.

Mid-May-early September.

ONTARIO SCIENCE CENTRE

770 Don Mills Road, Toronto, 416-696-1000; www.ontariosciencecentre.ca

Ten huge exhibition halls in three linked pavilions are filled with displays on space and technology. Stand at the edge of a black hole; watch bees making honey; test your reflexes, heart rate or grip strength; use pedal power to turn on lights or raise a balloon; hold hands with a robot; or land a spaceship on the moon. Throughout the museum there are slide shows and films that demonstrate various aspects of science and two Omnimax theaters show films.

Admission: adults $18, seniors and students $13.50, children 4-12 $11, children 3 and under free. Daily 10 a.m.-5 p.m.

PARAMOUNT CANADA'S WONDERLAND

9580 Jane St., Vaughan, 905-832-8131; www.canadaswonderland.com

This 300-acre theme park is situated 30 minutes outside Toronto. You easily can spend the day scoping out its more than 140 attractions, including a 20-acre water park, live shows and more than 50 rush-inducing rides. The park is known for its roller coasters, from creaky old-fashioned wooden ones to The Fly, a coaster designed to make every seat feel as if it were in the front car.

Admission: adults $44.99, seniors and children $31.99. Hours vary.

PIER: TORONTO'S WATERFRONT MUSEUM

245 Queen's Quay W., Toronto

The original 1930s pier building on Toronto's celebrated waterfront includes two floors of hands-on interactive displays, rare historical artifacts, re-creations of marine history stories, an art gallery, a boat-building center, narrated walking excursions and children's programs.

Admission: adults $5, seniors and children $4. March-October, daily 10 a.m.-6 p.m.

QUEEN STREET WEST

From University Avenue to Bathurst Street, Toronto

Similar to New York's SoHo, Queen West is Toronto's hotbed of hip. Come here for vintage clothing stores, trendy home furnishings, retro grunge and street-vendor bohemia, as well as the handiwork of many up-and-coming fashion designers. In between the boutiques are antique stores, used bookstores and terrific bistros and cafés.

RIVOLI

334 Queen St. W., Toronto, 416-596-1908; www.rivoli.ca

This offbeat, artsy performance club was opened in 1982 on the site of Toronto's 1920s Rivoli Vaudeville Theatre. The focus is on eclectic and cutting-edge music and performances and includes everything from grunge and rock to poetry readings and comedy. The Indigo Girls, Tori Amos and Michelle Shocked all made their Toronto debuts here. Don't forget to check out the 5,000-square-foot pool hall with 13 vintage tables, including an 1870s Brunswick Aviator and a 1960s futuristic AMF seen in the Elvis movie *Viva Las Vegas.*

ROYAL ONTARIO MUSEUM

100 Queen's Park, Toronto, 416-586-5549; www.rom.on.ca

When the Royal Ontario Museum opened its doors to the public in 1914, its mission was to inspire wonder and build understanding of human cultures and the natural world. And its collections in archaeology, geology, genealogy, paleontology and sociology have moved in that direction ever since. One of the most-visited galleries is the Nubia Gallery, built in 1998 after a ROM team discovered a new archaeological culture in the Upper Nubia region of Northern Sudan, unearthing the remains of a settlement dating to 1000-800 B.C. The discovery has been officially recognized by UNESCO as "Canada's contribution to the United Nations' Decade for Cultural Development."

Admission: adults $24, seniors and students $21, children 4-14 $16, children 3 and under free. Monday-Thursday, Saturday-Sunday 10 a.m.-5:30 p.m., Friday 10 a.m.-9:30 p.m.

SPADINA HISTORIC HOUSE AND GARDEN

285 Spadina Road, Toronto, 416-392-6910; www.toronto.ca

Built for financier James Austin and his family, this 50-room house has been restored to its 1866 Victorian glory and is open to those who want to see how the upper crust spent quiet evenings at home. It's filled with the family's art, personal belongings and furniture. And until 1982, it was filled with the family itself; that's when the last generation of Austins left and the house was turned over to public ownership. Docents tend to the glorious gardens and orchard, which you can view in the summer.

ST. LAWRENCE MARKET

92 Front St. E., Toronto, 416-329-7120; www.stlawrencemarket.com

In 1803, Gov. Peter Hunt designated an area to be the "market block." Today, the St. Lawrence Market provides a good snippet of the way Toronto used to be. There are traces of the building's original architecture to make you feel as though the old city were alive and well. The market itself, Toronto's largest indoor market, sells 14 different categories of foods, including fresh seafood, poultry, meat, organic produce, baked goods, gourmet teas and coffees, plus fruits and flowers.

Tuesday-Thursday 8 a.m.-6 p.m., Friday 8 a.m.-7 p.m., Saturday 5 a.m.-5 p.m.

SAINTE-MARIE AMONG THE HURONS

East of Midland on Highway 12, Midland

This site is a reconstruction of the 17th-century Jesuit mission that was Ontario's first European community. Its 22 furnished buildings include native dwellings, workshops, a barn, a church and a hospital. There's also an orientation center and an interpretive museum. When you need a break, a café features period-inspired meals and snacks. Candlelight tours or canoe excursions are available here. The world-famous Martyrs' Shrine site of papal visit is across the highway.

Admission: adults $11.25, seniors $9.25, students $9.75, children 6-12 $8.50, children 5 and under free. Late April-mid-May, October, Monday-Friday 10 a.m.-5 p.m.; late May-September, daily 10 a.m.-5 p.m.

TASTE OF THE WORLD NEIGHBORHOOD BICYCLE TOURS AND WALKS
Station P Toronto, 416-923-6813; www.torontowalksbikes.com

Equal parts fact and food, the tour walks visitors through a forgotten hanging square, a hidden gallery and a lost pillory site. The food portion of the jaunt includes East Indian treats with new twists, decadent offerings with Belgian chocolate, sandwich samples at Carousel Bakery and a spread at St. Urbain Bagel. On Sundays, a different tour focuses on the contributions of 200 years of immigrant activity in the Kensington market, exploring Jewish and East Indian snacks, Lebanese goodies and chocolate truffles. The tour company suggests a light breakfast before the St. Lawrence Tour and no breakfast with the Kensington tour.

Daily 9:30 a.m.-1 p.m.

TORONTO ISLAND PARK
9 Queens Quay, Toronto, 416-392-8186; www.toronto.ca

Just seven minutes by ferry from Toronto lie 14 beautiful islands ripe for exploration. Centre Island is the busiest and home to Centreville, an old-fashioned amusement park with an authentic 1890s carousel and a flume ride. Within Centreville there's also a turn-of-the-century village complete with a Main Street, tiny shops, a firehouse and even a small working farm. All of the islands are great for renting bikes and traversing the 612 acres of shaded paths.

TORONTO MUSIC GARDEN
475 Queen's Quay W., Toronto, 416-973-3000; www.city.toronto.on.ca

In the mid-1990s, internationally renowned cellist Yo-Yo Ma worked with several other artists to produce a six-part film series inspired by the work of Johann Sebastian Bach's Suites for Unaccompanied Cello. The first film was titled The Music Garden and used nature to interpret the music of Bach's first suite. Toronto was approached to create an actual garden based on that movie and the result—Toronto Music Garden—now graces the waterfront, a symphony of swirls and curves and wandering trails. In the summertime, it hosts free concerts. Tours are offered, either with a guide or self-guided with a handheld audiotape.

TORONTO SYMPHONY ORCHESTRA
212 King St. W., Toronto, 416-598-3375; www.tso.ca

Founded in 1922, the Toronto Symphony features classical, pops and children's programs. There is wheelchair seating and audio enhancement for the hearing impaired.

TORONTO ZOO
361A Old Finch Ave., Scarborough, 416-392-5929; www.torontozoo.com

There are more than 5,000 animals representing more than 450 species at the Toronto Zoo. Well-designed and laid out, the zoo has four large tropical indoor pavilions and several smaller indoor viewing areas. Plus there are numerous outdoor exhibits that compose 710 acres of geographic regions, which can be explored on foot on the six miles of trails. Visit the 10-acre Tundra Trek to see the polar bears and reindeer. When you're tired of walking, take a ride on a pony, camel or a safari simulator.

Admission: adults $23, seniors $17, children 4-12 $13, children 3 and under free. Mid-May-early September, daily 9 a.m.-7:30 p.m.; mid-September-mid-October, daily 9 a.m.-6 p.m.; late October-December, daily 9:30 a.m.-4:30 p.m.

WOODBINE RACETRACK

555 Rexdale Blvd., Rexdale, 416-675-7223; www.woodbineentertainment.com

The only track in North America that can offer both standard-bred and thoroughbred racing on the same day, Woodbine is home to Canada's most important racecourse events. It hosts the $1 million Queens Plate, North America's oldest continuously run stakes race; the $1 million ATTO; the $1.5 million Canadian International; and the $1 million North America Cup for Standard-bred. It also has an outstanding grass course; it was here, in 1973, that racing legend Secretariat bid farewell to the sport with his win of the grass championship. Aside from the track action, Woodbine has 1,700 slot machines and many different dining options.

WHERE TO STAY

HAMILTON

★★★SHERATON HAMILTON HOTEL

116 King St. W., Hamilton, 905-529-5515, 888-627-8161; www.sheraton.com

Located in downtown Hamilton, this contemporary hotel has direct access to a shopping mall, the Convention Centre and Hamilton Place Concert Hall. Travelers here for work will appreciate the business center and the wireless Internet access. And if they stay in a club-level room, they also receive complimentary office supplies.

301 rooms. Restaurant, bar. Business center. Fitness center. Pool. Pets accepted. $151-250

NIAGARA FALLS

★★★DOUBLETREE FALLSVIEW RESORT & SPA BY HILTON-NIAGARA FALLS

6039 Fallsview Blvd., Niagara Falls, 905-358-3817, 800-222-8733; www.niagarafallsdoubletree.com

Cathedral ceilings with wood beams, slate floors and freshly baked chocolate chip cookies welcome guests at this rustic-themed hotel. The spacious guest rooms offer panoramic views of the upper Niagara River, and the property is only two blocks away from the Falls. For more nature, visit the in-house gallery, Ochre Art Gallery, which displays pieces inspired by the great Canadian outdoors. There are other options if you prefer spending time indoors; the Five Lakes Aveda Day Spa is the place to go for a deep-tissue massage or other treatment, and Buchanans Chophouse will take care of you for dinner. Plus, the Niagara Fallsview Casino is less than a quarter mile from the hotel.

224 rooms. Restaurant, bar. Business center. Fitness center. Pool. Spa. $151-250

★★★HILTON NIAGARA FALLS

6361 Fallsview Blvd., Niagara Falls, 905-354-7887, 888-370-0325; www.hiltonniagarafalls.com

Located in the heart of the bustling Niagara Falls tourist area, this hotel is near all the popular attractions. The Fallsview Casino is across the street, but you can get there via an enclosed glass walkway that connects the two buildings.

The Horseshoe Falls are only a quarter mile from the hotel. The dramatic lobby features lots of pale ochre marble and blond wood and many of the guest rooms offer outstanding views.

516 rooms. Restaurant, bar. Business center. Pool. $151-250

★★★MARRIOTT NIAGARA FALLS FALLSVIEW
6740 Fallsview Blvd., Niagara Falls, 905-357-7300, 888-501-8916;www.niagarafallsmarriott.com
Directly across from Horseshoe Falls, this is a prime Niagara Falls location. Area attractions, restaurants and shops are also nearby. The interior of this elegant hotel has a light, sunny feel. The Falls can be viewed from many of the guest rooms as well as right in the lobby.

432 rooms. Restaurant, bar. Business center. Fitness center. Pool. Spa. $151-250

★★★SHERATON FALLSVIEW HOTEL AND CONFERENCE CENTRE
6755 Fallsview Blvd., Niagara Falls, 905-374-1077, 800-618-9059; www.fallsview.com
With this hotel as your home base, you can easily walk to the Falls and numerous area attractions, like the Niagara Civic Convention Centre and the Fallsview Casino. The Sheraton is in smack-dab in the middle of the Fallsview Boulevard tourism district, so you'll have access to shops and restaurants as well. The large two-story lobby has a curved staircase with comfortable, casual seating. Guest rooms are attractive and feature deep-blue bed coverings, luxurious linens and comfortable mattresses.

402 rooms. Restaurant, bar. Business center. Pool. Pets accepted. $151-250

RECOMMENDED

EMBASSY SUITES HOTEL NIAGARA FALLS/FALLSVIEW
6700 Fallsview Blvd., Niagara Falls, 905-356-3600, 800-420-6980;
www.embassysuitesniagara.com
The top reason to stay at this all-suite hotel is that many of the rooms have an amazing vista of the Horseshoe and American Falls. That means you'll get a private—and dry—seat to see the seasonal fireworks illuminate Niagara Falls in a breathtaking evening light show. So if you book a room here, make sure it's a falls-view suite. Otherwise, dine at the ninth-floor Keg Steakhouse & Bar, whose floor-to-ceiling windows make you feel as though you're in the middle of the Falls.

512 rooms. Restaurant, bar. Complimentary breakfast. Pool. $61-150

NIAGARA-ON-THE-LAKE
★★★OBAN INN
160 Front St., Niagara-on-the-Lake, 905-468-2165, 888-669-5566; www.obaninn.ca
Once the home of a Scottish ship captain, this is now a modern hotel set in a wonderfully quaint, historic property. The grounds, which overlook Lake Ontario, feature charming English-style gardens. Individually decorated guest rooms have four-poster beds and antique furnishings with nice touches like turndown service, down comforters, LCD plasma televisions and Bose sound systems. Take advantage of the complimentary in-town shuttle service to go sightseeing. The hotel is a 15-minute drive from Niagara Falls.

26 rooms. Restaurant, bar. Complimentary breakfast. Spa. Pets accepted. $251-350

★★★PILLAR AND POST

48 John St., Niagara-on-the-Lake, 905-468-2123, 888-669-5566; www.vintageinns.com

This unique inn resides in a restored turn-of-the-century fruit-canning factory. The lobby is full of plants and antique furniture. But the tan-and-light-blue rooms have a more muted and contemporary feel. The fireplaces, which are in a number of rooms, and the nightly service that leaves a rose on your bed make your stay cozy. Don't miss a visit to the 100 Fountain Spa. Along with its long list of services, the spa has hot springs and a heated indoor saltwater pool.

122 rooms. Restaurant, bar. Business center. Pool. Spa. Pets accepted. $151-250

★★★PRINCE OF WALES

6 Picton St., Niagara-on-the-Lake, 905-468-3246, 888-669-5566; www.vintageinns.com

This historic treasure dates to 1864. Its unique character and formal charm make it one of Canada's most beloved hotels. The Victorian-inspired rooms are individually decorated, but they all have antiques, dark wood furniture and traditional brocades and tapestries. A cozy day spa celebrates the English countryside in its treatment rooms, and afternoon tea is a daily ritual. For sophisticated dining, visit Escabéche restaurant, where a modern French menu tempts and delights with dishes such as Canadian beef tenderloin with truffled forest mushrooms, sweet potato Dauphinoise, lobster butter and brandy jus.

112 rooms. Restaurant, bar. Business center. Fitness center. Pool. Spa. Pets accepted. $251-350

★★★QUEEN'S LANDING

155 Byron St., Niagara-on-the-Lake, 905-468-2195, 888-669-5566; www.vintageinns.com

Built with Victorian charm, this inn overlooks the Niagara River, opposite historic Fort Niagara. The Georgian-style theme carries from the lobby to the guest rooms with plush furnishings and wood detailing. The Tiara Restaurant offers peerless views of Niagara-on-the-Lake Harbour.

142 rooms. Restaurant, bar. Fitness center. Pool. Spa. $251-350

★★★WHITE OAKS CONFERENCE RESORT AND SPA

253 Taylor Road SS4, Niagara-on-the-Lake, 905-688-2550, 800-263-5766; www.whiteoaksresort.com

This large, modern resort has relaxation and comfort in mind. This is reflected in the guest room amenities such as Frette robes, nightly turndown service and pillow-topped mattresses. But for the full relaxation regimen, you'll have to stop by the full-service spa—where you can get everything from microdermabrasion to a "Nectar of Niagara" grape body wrap—and LIV, the resort's concept restaurant that uses seasonal, local ingredients.

220 rooms. Restaurant, bar. Business center. Fitness center. Pool. Spa. Golf. Tennis. $151-250

TORONTO

★★★DELTA CHELSEA

33 Gerrard St. W., Toronto, 416-595-1975, 800-243-5732; www.deltachelsea.com

Located in the heart of downtown Toronto, the Delta Chelsea puts guests within minutes of the city's best theater and attractions like the Royal Ontario Museum and the Art Gallery of Ontario. After a long day, send your brood to the Family Fun Zone, which has an indoor pool with a corkscrew waterslide, a teen lounge and kid center, while you unwind in the deep soaking tub in your elegant room.

1,590 rooms. Restaurant, bar. Business center. Fitness center. Pets accepted. $251-350

★★★FAIRMONT ROYAL YORK
100 Front St. W., Toronto, 416-368-2511, 866-540-4489; www.fairmont.com

The Royal York became known as a city within a city, with its 1.5 acres of public rooms, including a 12,000-book library; a concert hall with a 50-ton pipe organ; and 10 ornate passenger elevators. While the hotel is no longer as grand as it was in its heyday, the guest rooms and public spaces have been restored to their original elegance with hand-painted ceilings, the travertine pillars, crystal chandeliers and wall hangings.

1,365 rooms. Restaurants, bar. Business center. Fitness center. Pool. Pets accepted. $251-350

★★★★FOUR SEASONS HOTEL TORONTO
21 Avenue Road, Toronto, 416-964-0411; www.fourseasons.com

The Four Seasons Hotel Toronto is in a prime location in the upscale neighborhood of Yorkville. Guest rooms feature elegant colonial décor, plush furnishings and bay windows with charming views of Yorkville, or stunning vistas of the city'sdowntown. Business travelers aren't forgotten; they get pampered with the in-house business center and complimentary limousine service. If you aren't here for work, relax by the pools, sauna, whirlpool and fitness center.

380 rooms. Restaurant, bar. Business center. Fitness center. Pool. Pets accepted. $351 and up

★★★★THE HAZELTON HOTEL
118 Yorkville Ave., Toronto, 416-963-6300, 866-473-6301; www.thehazeltonhotel.com

Sleek luxury with hints of old Hollywood glam permeates the rooms and suites of the Hazelton hotel. You can almost get lost in the spacious rooms, each with an average of 620 square feet with 9-foot-tall ceilings, 80-square-foot dressing rooms and French doors that open up to balconies. They also come with perks like 42-inch plasma televisions with DVD players. The luxe experience extends beyond the rooms and into the Hazelton's signature Italian-influenced restaurant, One, led by chef Mark McEwan. The hotel even has its very own built-in elegant mini-movie theater that seats 25 on plush, leather seats.

77 rooms. Restaurant, bar. Business center. Fitness center. $351 and up

★★★HILTON TORONTO
145 Richmond St. W., Toronto, 416-869-3456, 800-445-8667; www.toronto.hilton.com

Guests will enjoy the location of this hotel in Toronto's financial and entertainment districts. It's across the street from the Four Seasons Centre of Performing Arts and a short walk to the CN Tower. As far as restaurants, there's an outpost of the popular Ruth's Chris Steakhouse chain right inside the hotel. The rooms are draped in neutral tones and include work stations for busy business travelers.

600 rooms. Restaurant, bar. Business center. Fitness center. Pool. Pets accepted. $151-250

★★★HOTEL LE GERMAIN
30 Mercer St., Toronto, 416-345-9500, 866-345-9501; www.germaintoronto.com

Sleek lines, modern architecture and a two-level lobby define this stylish hotel. Cozy up to the open-hearth fireplace in the library with a drink from the complimentary cappuccino bar. Or get some fresh air in the rooftop terrace. Four suites have fireplaces and private terraces, while all rooms come with goose-down comforters, Aveda toiletries, flat-screen televisions and DVD players.

122 rooms. Complimentary breakfast. Restaurant, bar. Pets accepted. Fitness center. $151-250

★★★INTERCONTINENTAL TORONTO CENTRE
225 Front St. W., Toronto, 416-597-1400, 800-422-7969; www.intercontinental.com

The downtown InterContinental caters to business travelers who need meeting space, business support, WiFi and proximity to the adjacent Metro Toronto Convention Centre. The hotel is great for leisure travelers, too, who want to stay close to theater, dining and shopping venues. The CN Tower is a block away, and the Distillery District is three blocks from the hotel. The rooms are sizeable and pet-friendly, so Fido can come along.

586 rooms. Restaurant, bar. Business center. Fitness center. Pool. Spa. Pets accepted. $351 and up

★★★INTERCONTINENTAL TORONTO YORKVILLE
220 Bloor St. W., Toronto, 416-960-5200, 888-567-8725; www.intercontinental.com

Located in the exclusive Yorkville neighborhood, this modern hotel has guest rooms designed to be both inviting and efficient with bay windows, marble bathrooms with separate showers and pillow-top mattresses. Thoughtful details are offered throughout the hotel, such as an international newspaper service and limo service.

208 rooms. Restaurant, bar. Business center. Fitness center. Pool. Pets accepted. $151-250

★★★LE ROYAL MERIDIEN KING EDWARD
37 King St. E., Toronto, 416-863-9700, 800-543-4300; www.lemeridien-kingedward.com

Le Royal Meridien King Edward is the grande dame of Toronto. This historic landmark opened in 1903 and has been hosting the world's elite ever since. On its first floor, the hotel offers a gallery featuring sculptures and paintings. The stately rooms have modern updates like 42-inch plasma TVs and iPod docking stations. Sharing the hotel's affinity for England in its décor, the Cafe Victoria and Consort Bar are essential elements of the superb King Edward experience.

298 rooms. Restaurant, bar. Business center. Fitness center. Spa. Pets accepted. $251-350

★★★MARRIOTT BLOOR YORKVILLE
90 Bloor St. E., Toronto, 416-961-8000, 800-859-7180; www.marriott.com

Situated in the fashionable Yorkville neighborhood, this hotel's creative and artistic décor makes it fit right in. Although it's located at perhaps the city's busiest intersection, the hotel feels tucked away and serene. In-room amenities abound, including 42-inch LCD high-definition televisions, swivel desks and roomy bathrooms with rain showerheads and Bath & Body Works toiletries.

258 rooms. Restaurant, bar. Business center. Fitness center. Pets accepted. $251-350

★★★MARRIOTT TORONTO AIRPORT
901 Dixon Road, Toronto, 416-674-9400, 800-905-2811; www.marriott.com

Both business and leisure travelers will like this property's proximity to Pearson International Airport and that a complimentary shuttle provides transportation to the airport. Plus, the hotel is about 20 minutes from downtown Toronto. The property offers a variety of dining options. Mikada serves traditional Japanese dishes, while the Terrace's menu is Continental. Toucan's Lounge & Patio is a nice place to meet up with friends for a quick drink.

424 rooms. Restaurant, bar. Business center. Fitness center. Pool. Pets accepted. $151-250

★★★MARRIOTT TORONTO EATON CENTRE

525 Bay St., Toronto, 416-597-9200, 800-905-0667;
www.marriotteatoncentre.com

In the Financial District and near the Theater District, this property attracts all types of visitors. Shopping at Eaton Centre and must-see sights like the CN Tower are just a short stroll away. If you want to take a swim or get a good view of Toronto, head to the top-floor pool overlooking the city. Guest rooms include custom duvets, comfy featherbeds and a choice of pillows to fit your preference.

459 rooms. Restaurant, bar. Business center. Fitness center. Pool. $151-250

★★★METROPOLITAN HOTEL TORONTO

108 Chestnut St., Toronto, 416-977-5000, 800-668-6600;
www.metropolitan.com

All of Toronto is within easy reach from the Metropolitan Hotel. Close to world-renowned shopping, art galleries and museums, the hotel has the services of a large property and the intimacy of a private residence. In the mornings, guests can hop in the complimentary limousine to go downtown, or start your day with a swim in the heated pool. The Lai Wah Heen is a serene setting for its luscious Cantonese cuisine, which is considered an excellent example of authentic dim sum.

422 rooms. Restaurant, bar. Business center. Fitness center. Pets accepted. Pool. $351 and up

★★★PANTAGES SUITES HOTEL AND SPA

210 Victoria St., Toronto, 416-362-1777, 866-852-1777;
www.pantageshotel.com

What makes this hotel stand out is its unusual amenities and services, such as a complimentary meditation channel, yoga mats, 400-thread-count Egyptian cotton linens and in-room European kitchens replete with a dishwasher, a fridge, a washer and dryer, and pots and pans. Rooms are sophisticated and modern with floor-to-ceiling windows, hardwood floors and oversized padded headboards; hues of maroon and tawny make the spaces inviting. The hotel is close to Eaton Centre mall and other city attractions and just two minutes from the subway and Toronto's underground walkway. But a fun place to hang out is the intimate onsite Martini Bar, which has a double-sided fireplace in a library, a glowing bar and sofas for lounging.

111 rooms. Bar. Complimentary breakfast. Business center. Fitness center. Pool. Spa. $251-350

WHAT ARE THE MOST LUXURIOUS HOTELS IN TORONTO?

Four Seasons Hotel Toronto
Guests get the all-star treatment that's synonymous with the Four Seasons brand. Rooms are elegant; the hotel provides luxe extras like gratis limo service; and the eatery caters to guests' needs, like a separate kosher kitchen to service Jewish diners.

The Hazelton Hotel
At the Hazelton, you'll almost get lost in the spacious rooms that come with dressing rooms and balconies. Check out the hotel's upscale movie theater. Instead of soda-stained seats typical at most theaters, the Hazelton puts you in comfy leather chairs.

Park Hyatt Toronto
The Park Hyatt aims to pamper, whether it be spoiling you with freebies like bicycle rentals and WiFi, or offering amenities like a 24-hour concierge and 42-inch TVs. The most pampering perk of all is the Stillwater Spa, one of the best in the city.

★★★★PARK HYATT TORONTO

4 Avenue Road, Toronto, 416-925-1234, 800-977-4197; www.parktoronto.hyatt.com

The Park Hyatt Toronto calls the chic Yorkville area home. Located at Avenue Road and Bloor Street, this hotel has some of the world's leading stores just outside its doors. If you want to further explore the area, borrow one of the hotel's complimentary bicycles to do some riding. In the hotel, a clean, modern look dominates the rooms and suites, and they come equipped with 42-inch televisions, free WiFi and luxe marble bathrooms. When you want the escape the demands of the world, visit the excellent Stillwater Spa. Get a blissful Swedish massage, and then revel in your relaxed state in the spa's tea lounge. For dinner, international dishes are the specialty at Annona, while the grilled steaks and seafood of Morton's of Chicago are always a treat.

346 rooms. Restaurant, bar. Business center. Fitness center. Spa. $251-350

★★★SHERATON CENTRE HOTEL

123 Queen St. W., Toronto, 416-361-1000, 800-325-3535; www.starwoodhotels.com

Though large in size, this hotel specializes in personalized service. Each guest room has the signature Sheraton Sweet Sleeper bed, a flat-screen TV and a nice view of the city. The 2-acre waterfall garden that runs through the lobby emphasizes the urban oasis that is Toronto.

1,377 rooms. Restaurant, bar. Business center. Fitness center. Pool. Pets accepted. $151-250

★★★SHERATON GATEWAY HOTEL

Toronto International Airport, Toronto, 905-672-7000, 800-325-3535; www.sheraton.com

Perfect for a layover, the hotel is connected to Terminal 3 at Toronto International Airport. But don't worry about the noisy jets keeping you awake; first-class soundproofing ensures a good night's sleep before an early flight. Even Rover will get a solid night's rest with the hotel's Sweet Sleeper dog bed. This glass-walled hotel is thoroughly modern. If you like plane spotting, request one of the rooms with great views of the runways. Before your flight, you can squeeze in a workout at the gym or do some laps in the pool.

474 rooms. Restaurant, bar. Complimentary breakfast. Business center. Pool. Pets accepted. $151-250

★★★SOHO METROPOLITAN HOTEL

318 Wellington St. W., Toronto, 416-599-8800; www.metropolitan.com

This boutique hotel earns high marks for its urban chic interiors, stylish food, central location and smart technology. The hotel really focuses on the details, like its entrance. Well-known glass artist Dale Chihuly created the hotel awning of colorful hand-blown glass sculptures. The accommodations appeal with clean, simple lines and light wood furnishings. You'll get pampered in the marble bathrooms, which have Molton Brown toiletries, multiheaded showers and heated floors. The SoHo Metropolitan's Senses Bakery & Restaurant offers the contemporary gourmet experience with its artfully designed and creatively prepared cuisine. But the delicious cakes and pastries may overshadow the restaurant's cuisine.

366 rooms. Restaurant, bar. Business center. Pool. Pets accepted. $251-350

★★★THE SUTTON PLACE
955 Bay St., Toronto, 416-924-9221; www.suttonplace.com

You get an old Europe feel from the hotel's rich surroundings, including mahogany trim in the meeting rooms and crystal chandeliers. Original art and antiques grace the comfortable guest rooms and suites. To kick back, grab a drink in the elegant lobby bar.

294 rooms. Restaurant, bar. Business center. Fitness center. Pool. Pets accepted. $151-250

★★★THE WESTIN BRISTOL PLACE TORONTO AIRPORT
950 Dixon Road, Toronto, 416-675-9444, 877-999-3223; www.starwoodhotels.com

Just five minutes from Pearson International Airport, this is a good choice for those on a short trip. The indoor pool and state-of-the-art workout facility will get you up and going in no time, and the proximity to downtown is convenient if you're looking to experience the city's nightlife. Rooms are inviting with dark wood, muted tones and dim, romantic lighting.

287 rooms. Restaurant. Business center. Pool. $151-250

★★★THE WESTIN HARBOUR CASTLE
1 Harbour Square, Toronto, 416-869-1600, 800-228-3000; www.westin.com

The striking towers of this hotel are among the most recognized landmarks in the city. The glass-walled foyer offers a wide, clear view of Lake Ontario. The hotel is close to a host of tourist attractions, including the Air Canada Centre, the CN Tower, the Eaton Centre and the Theater District. After hitting the town, you'll be happy to retreat in your calming forest green and white room with its waterfront view.

977 rooms. Restaurant, bar. Business center. Pool. Spa. Pets accepted. Tennis. $251-350

★★★THE WESTIN PRINCE, TORONTO
900 York Mills Road, Toronto, 416-444-2511, 800-228-3000; www.westin.com

Located in the center of downtown Toronto, this hotel is just minutes from both the Ontario Science Centre and the Ford Centre for the Performing Arts. Activity is paramount here, as the hotel's 15 acres include tennis courts, an outdoor pool and walking trails. Contemporary guest rooms, decorated in white, cream and gray, offer vistas of the city skyline and the surrounding greenery.

381 rooms. Restaurant, bar. Business center. Fitness center. Pool. Tennis. $151-250

★★★WINDSOR ARMS HOTEL
18 St. Thomas St., Toronto, 416-971-9666, 877-999-2767; www.windsorarmshotel.com

The accommodations in this intimate and stylish hotel are sleek, modern and sublime. Though there are vestiges of classic hospitality. Rooms have a cupboard where you can place dirty laundry and shoes, and a butler will clean and shine your items without ever disturbing you. The hotel offers plenty to do outside of your room. The Tea Room serves a traditional tea by day and at night is transformed into Toronto's only champagne and caviar bar. Club 22 entertains with piano players and live bands and the Cigar Lounge offers decadent treats.

28 rooms. Restaurant, bar. Complimentary breakfast. Pool. Spa. Pets accepted. $351 and up

WHERE TO EAT

HAMILTON
★★★ANCASTER OLD MILL INN
548 Old Dundas Road, Ancaster, 905-648-1827; www.ancasteroldmill.com

Built in 1792, this building was originally a gristmill. Today it's a great spot to grab consistently good American fare with many organic options and farm-fresh ingredients. Try entrées such as the maple-marinated Alaskan black cod in local soya sauce with bok choy, mushrooms and sweet-potato gnocchi, and desserts including rhubarb upside-down cake.

American. Lunch, Dinner, Sunday brunch. Outdoor seating. $36-85

RECOMMENDED

NIAGARA FALLS
THE WATERMARK
Hilton Niagara Falls Fallsview, 6361 Fallsview Blvd, 905-353-7138;
www.watermarkrestaurant.com

Located in the Hilton Niagra Falls Hotel, the Watermark restaurant is a fine-dining restaurant providing incredible views of the surrounding falls. Start with one of the many signature martinis before moving on to the menu. Though the view is the real draw, dishes such as coconut breaded shrimp and pan seared halibut are more than satisfying.

American. Dinner. $36-85

NIAGARA-ON-THE-LAKE
★★★CARRIAGES
Pillar and Post, 48 John St., Niagara-on-the-Lake, 905-468-2123, 888-669-5566;
wwwvintageinns.com

This cozy, candlelit dining room of the Pillar and Post hotel features exposed beams and a working brick oven. The rack of Australian lamb is superb, as are many of the seafood options, including the Marrakech salmon.

American. Breakfast, lunch, dinner, Sunday brunch. Outdoor seating. $36-85

★★★ESCABÉCHE
Prince of Wales, 6 Picton St., Niagara-on-the-Lake, 905-468-3246, 888-669-5566;
wwwvintageinns.com

The formal dining room of the Prince of Wales hotel makes the Victorian experience truly memorable. Enjoy afternoon tea or a long, elaborate dinner. Start off with ahi tuna ribbons with avocado, daikon radish and ginger dressing. Then move on to the Canadian beef tenderloin with truffled forest mushrooms, and end with the Absolut citrus cheesecake with rosemary-poached pineapple and lemon-ginger sorbet. The wine list is equally impressive.

International. Breakfast, lunch, dinner. Reservations recommended. $36-85

TORONTO
★★★360
301 Front St. W., Toronto, 416-362-5411; www.cntower.ca

As the name suggests, this restaurant completes a 360-degree rotation, offering a breathtaking view from the CN Tower. The scenery inside is attractive as well,

with colorful décor and fresh, seasonal dishes such as the Alberta peppered strip loin steak and hot smoked Peking duck breast with a plum-rhubarb chutney.
International. Reservations recommended. $36-85

★★★AUBERGE DU POMMIER
4150 Yonge St., Toronto, 416-222-2220; www.aubergedupommier.com
Located north of the city, this restaurant manages to transcend its industrial park environs and feel like it is in rural France. It's mostly because the restaurant is housed in the remains of two 1860s woodcutters' cottages. The stone walls give it a rustic feel, and the service is attentive. For a decadent meal, go for the chef's tasting menu. As far as à la carte options, the pommes frites are divine.
French, American. Lunch, dinner. Reservations recommended. $36-85

★★★BIAGIO
155 King St. E., Toronto, 416-366-4040; www.biagioristorante.com.
This modern Italian restaurant is situated in the historic St. Lawrence Hall near the Theater District and serves specialties from the north, including risotto with oysters, shiitake and cremini mushrooms or veal scaloppini with artichokes and capers in lemon sauce. An ornate ceiling and a lovely patio with a fountain add to the ambience.
Italian. Lunch, dinner. Outdoor seating. $36-85

★★★★CANOE
66 Wellington St. W., Toronto 416-364-0054; www.oliverbonacini.com
Canoe is a stunning venue in which to experience creative, satisfying regional Canadian cuisine. While dazzling ingredients tend to be sourced from wonderful local producers, many organic, the kitchen borrows flavors and techniques from the world at large, including Asia, France and the American South. The end product is inventive food such as lamb loin with a spring cassoulet, sweetbreads and roasted garlic, or the Cornish game hen with local asparagus, confit onion, peaches and cream-corn pone. The five-course tasting menu is a roller coaster of succulent flavors. The wine list is just as indulgent.
Canadian. Lunch, dinner. Reservations recommended. Bar. $36-85

★★★CENTRO GRILL & WINE BAR
2472 Yonge St., Toronto, 416-483-2211; www.centro.ca
A lot of tastes are rolled into one destination at this contemporary European restaurant with a downstairs sushi and oyster bar. A colorful, New Age-style dining room and a worldly menu means you'll never be bored with novelties like caribou chop with juniper berry oil, Alsatian spätzle and Arctic cloudberry sauce.
International. Dinner. Reservations recommended. $36-85

★★★★CHIADO
864 College St., Toronto, 416-538-1910; www.chiadorestaurant.ca
Paying homage to the old Portuguese seaside town after which it is named but updating dishes for a more modern sensibility, Chiado features what might best be described as "nouvelle Portuguese cuisine." The food is first-rate and fabulous, featuring an ocean's worth of fresh fish simply prepared with olive oil

and herbs, as well as innovative takes on pheasant, game and poultry. To add to the authenticity of the experience, Chiado has the largest collection of fine Portuguese wines in North America and a superb selection of vintage ports.

Spanish. Lunch, dinner. Reservations recommended. $36-85

★★★★THE FIFTH GRILL

225 Richmond St. W., Toronto, 416-979-3000; www.thefifthgrill.com

It takes work to make it to The Fifth. First, an alley entrance leads you to The Easy, an upscale nightclub and former speakeasy. Once inside The Easy, you are directed onto a Persian rug-lined vintage freight elevator. There, an attendant takes you to the fifth floor. Exit and you have finally arrived at The Fifth, a treasured contemporary French restaurant and supper club. The food is of the deliciously updated French variety, and the dishes are perfectly prepared, beautifully presented and easily devoured. Don't miss the sticky banana cake with rum butterscotch sauce for dessert—it's heavenly.

French. Dinner. Closed Sunday-Wednesday. Reservations recommended. Outdoor seating. Bar. $86 and up

★★★HEMISPHERES

Metropolitan Hotel, 108 Chestnut St., Toronto, 416-599-8000; www.metropolitan.com

Hemispheres elevates hotel dining to a whole new level with its stylish interior and international fusion cuisine. The menu includes European and Continental classics, many with an Asian bent. Order the corn-fed chicken brushed with Oriental barbecue glaze, lemongrass and citrus-infused jasmine rice. Wine lovers will appreciate the well-rounded and extensive cellar.

International. Breakfast, lunch, dinner. Reservations recommended. $16-35

★★★JOSO'S

202 Davenport Road, Toronto, 416-925-1903; www.josos.com

The walls are covered with the chef's racy art and celebrity pictures at this popular restaurant, which offers unique and excellent Mediterranean cuisine. Though they take 20 minutes to prepare, the delectable risotti are worth the wait.

Mediterranean. Dinner. Outdoor seating. $36-85

★★★LA FENICE

319 King St. W., Toronto, 416-585-2377; www.lafenice.ca

The stark, modern dining room of this downtown restaurant recalls the chic design aesthetic of Milan. The pink and orange hues complement the casual atmosphere and tasty Italian fare. Go for the risotto or the market-fresh whole fish presented tableside and drizzled with extra virgin olive oil.

Italian. Lunch, dinner. Reservations recommended. $36-85

★★★LAI WAH HEEN

108 Chestnut St., Toronto, 416-977-9899; www.laiwahheen.com

Lai Wah Heen, meaning "luxurious meeting place," is truly luxurious with its two-level dining room featuring black granite, 12-foot ceilings and a solarium-style glass wall. Exotic herbs and spices, skillful use of tropical fruits and seafood dishes make for a Cantonese menu rich with Pacific Rim flair. The

HIGHLIGHT

WHAT ARE TORONTO'S BEST OVERALL RESTAURANTS?

CANOE

A stunning venue, creative and satisfying regional Canadian cuisine and a great wine list easily make this one of Toronto's top restaurants.

CHIADO

The food at this Portuguese dining establishment is first-rate and fabulous, featuring an ocean's worth of fresh fish simply prepared with olive oil and herbs, as well as innovative takes on pheasant, game and poultry. The restaurant also boasts the largest collection of fine Portuguese wines in North America and a superb selection of vintage ports.

THE FIFTH GRILL

This French restaurant blends classic with contemporary. In the dining room, you'll see white-tablecloth-clad tables as well as exposed pipes and beams. The food also shows modern flair, particularly the Châteaubriand Rossini with foie gras and truffle butter.

NORTH 44

Chef-owner Mark McEwan expertly blends the bright flavors of Asia with those of Italy, France and Canada. The service is smooth, refined and in perfect harmony with the cool space and stellar cuisine.

ONE RESTAURANT

Housed in Toronto's grand Hazelton Hotel, the décor here is sharp, the energy is buzzing and the cuisine is and the cuisine is refined. You wont want to pass up dessert either.

SCARAMOUCHE

Locals flock to this institution for top-notch French fare. But don't fill up on entrées like Ontario filet mignon and Nova Scotia lobster. Save room for the restaurant's outstanding desserts, like its famous coconut cream pie.

SPLENDIDO

With interpretations of international cuisines and a focus on clean, flavorful sauces and local Canadian ingredients, Splendido has hit its stride to become one of Toronto's best restaurants. Several charming details like the champagne cart and the selection of petit fours make this a fun and enjoyable dining experience.

restaurant serves an excellent dim sum.

Cantonese, Chinese. Reservations recommended. $16-35

★★★MISTURA

265 Davenport Road, Toronto, 416-515-0009; www.mistura.ca

Contemporary, seasonal Italian cuisine and a stylish, upscale environment are the hallmarks of this elegant Toronto restaurant. Menu items like wild boar-filled pasta with dried cherries delight the palate along with fresh ingredients and artful presentation. Desserts are just as inventive, such as the coconut semifreddo with slow-poached vanilla rhubarb or the pine nut butter tart with a scoop of maple ice cream.

Italian. $16-35

★★★★NORTH 44

2537 Yonge St., Toronto, 416-487-4897; www.north44restaurant.com

Style, serenity and elegance infuse every aspect of North 44 Degrees. From the loft-like dining room to the world-class New Continental cuisine, North 44 is a sublime and sexy dining experience. A sophisticated crowd fills the restaurant, named for the city's latitude, on most nights. Chef-owner Mark McEwan expertly blends the bright flavors of Asia with those of Italy, France and Canada. The service is smooth, refined and in perfect harmony with the cool space and stellar cuisine, like pan-roasted Dover sole and Arctic turbot with tempura lobster.

International. Dinner. Reservations recommended. Bar. $86 and up

★★★OLD MILL

Old Mill Inn & Spa, 21 Old Mill Road, Toronto, 416-236-2641, 866-653-6455; www.oldmilltoronto.com

The main dining room of the Old Mill Inn & Spa, a charming, English-style inn along the Humber River, features a warm and romantic atmosphere with beamed ceilings, a roaring fireplace, brick walls and soft lighting. Reinventing old classics like beef Wellington nouveau and Australian lamb souvlaki keeps diners guessing and the kitchen on its toes. There is a cover charge (Friday-Saturday from 8 p.m.)

International. Dinner. Reservations recommended. Outdoor seating. Jacket required (weekend dinner). $36-85

★★★★ONE RESTAURANT

The Hazelton Hotel, 116 Yorkville Ave., Toronto, 416-961-9600; www.onehazelton.com

One Restaurant, housed in Toronto's grand Hazelton Hotel, means serious business. The main dining room caters to diners looking for quality food as well as sharp décor. Chocolate-brown leather booths line its walls, while the 16-seat Neil Young Room is reserved for those to discuss business, view presentations on the 52-inch plasma screen or just have an intimate meal with a small group. Red walls and mirrored doors make this room ooze sophistication. The menu is equally refined, thanks to chef Andrew Ellerby, whose roasted goose foie gras on warm toast will make you swoon, as will pastry chef Tony Accettola's apple charlotte with cinnamon ice cream.

American. Breakfast, lunch, dinner, Saturday-Sunday brunch. $86 and up

★★★OPUS RESTAURANT
37 Prince Arthur Ave., Toronto, 416-921-3105; www.opusrestaurant.com

This plush Yorkville restaurant is elegant, romantic and filled with the energy of Toronto's powerful and moneyed elite. They come to dine on complex dishes like bee pollen-rubbed magret of duck and lobster fritters on braised lentils with drunken cherry gastrique and to drink from the more than 50,000-bottle wine cellar.

International. Dinner. Reservations recommended. Outdoor seating. $36-85

★★★ORO
45 Elm St., Toronto, 416-597-0155; www.ororestaurant.com

This restaurant has changed hands and names many times since it opened in 1922. It's famous for its patrons, who have included Ernest Hemingway and Prime Minister Jean Chrétien. The décor is contemporary and elegant, as is the food. Order the pistachio-crusted Australian rack of lamb with pomegranate-glazed smoked ribs, purple carrots and a pea purée.

International. Lunch, dinner. Bar. $36-85

★★★PANGAEA
1221 Bay St., Toronto, 416-920-2323; www.pangaearestaurant.com

Vaulted ceilings and exotic floral arrangements set the stage for sophisticated Continental cuisine using the wealth of each season's harvest. Try the halibut with roasted salsify, fingerling potatoes, wild mushrooms, pancetta, leeks and oyster beurre blanc. Tired Bloor Street shoppers will find this a great place to break for lunch or tea.

International. Lunch, dinner. Reservations recommended. Bar. $36-85

★★★★SCARAMOUCHE
1 Benvenuto Place, Toronto, 416-961-8011; www.scaramoucherestaurant.com

Up on a hillside overlooking the dazzling downtown lights, Scaramouche is the perfect hideaway for falling in love with food or your dining companion. This modern, bi-level space is known for its fantastic contemporary French fare and is often filled with dressed-up, savvy locals. The restaurant is divided between a formal dining room upstairs and a modestly priced pasta bar downstairs. If you head upstairs, go for the elk with smoked bacon, leeks, mushrooms, hazelnut whipped potatoes, crispy shallots, red wine jus and triple-crunch mustard.

French. Dinner. Sunday closed. Reservations recommended. $86 and up

★★★★SPLENDIDO
88 Harbord St., Toronto, 416-929-7788; www.splendido.ca

Splendido has hit its stride to become one of Toronto's best restaurants, with interpretations of international cuisines and a focus on clean, flavorful sauces and local Canadian ingredients. Several charming details like the champagne cart and the selection of petit fours make this a fun and enjoyable dining experience. The extensive selection of cheeses also makes for a nice late afternoon snack.

International. Dinner. Closed Sunday-Monday, July-August. Reservations recommended. $36-85

SPAS

TORONTO

★★★★THE SPA AT THE HAZELTON HOTEL

The Hazelton Hotel, 118 Yorkville Ave., Toronto, 416-963-6307;
www.thehazeltonhotel.com

Toronto's prized hotel keeps up the second-to-none hospitality at its spa and health club. Leading the charge is Linda McDonald-Ferris, whose experience as a skincare specialist for the past 20 years shows in the quality treatments that are offered here. For utter relaxation, start with the lemon sea salt body scrub, followed by a shiatsu massage and an exfoliating session known as the Body Glow. Waxing, manicures and pedicures are also available. After you're done pampering and primping, end your spa day with a dip in the gorgeous indoor lap pool, which is outfitted in imported mosaic tile.

★★★★STILLWATER SPA

Park Hyatt Toronto, 4 Avenue Road, Toronto, 416-925-1234; www.parktoronto.hyatt.com

With its cool, crisp interiors—complete with a fireplace in the tea lounge and waterfalls and streams throughout the facility—and fabulous mind and body relaxation therapies, Park Hyatt Toronto's Stillwater Spa offers you an escape. The signature Stillwater massage customizes an aromatherapy blend to accompany a relaxing bodywork combination of Swedish massage, trigger-points pressure and stretching techniques.

WHERE TO SHOP

NIAGARA FALLS

CANADA ONE FACTORY OUTLETS

7500 Lundy's Lane, Niagara Falls, 905-356-8989, 866-284-5781;
www.canadaoneoutlets.com

This outlet sells discounted merchandise from stores such as The Body Shop, Club Monaco, Guess and Tommy Hilfiger.

TORONTO

DRAGON CITY SHOPPING MALL

280 Spadina Ave., Toronto, 416-596-8885

Located in the heart of Chinatown, the Dragon City Shopping Mall consists of more than 30 stores. Buy Chinese herbs, look at Asian jewelry, browse chic Chinese housewares and gifts, or admire Oriental arts and crafts. Afterward treat yourself to a meal at Sky Dragon Cuisine in the Dragon City tower, an upscale Chinese restaurant with a beautiful view of the Toronto skyline.

EATON CENTRE

220 Yonge St., Toronto, 416-598-8560;
www.torontoeatoncentre.com

This 3 million-square-foot building is a masterpiece of architecture and environment. Its glass roof rises 127 feet above the mall's lowest level, and under it a flock of fiberglass Canadian geese floats through the air. The large, open space contains glass-enclosed elevators; dozens of long, graceful escalators; and porthole windows. There are more than 230 retailers here, including

Abercrombie & Fitch, Banana Republic, The Gap, H&M and Pottery Barn. Even if shopping isn't a favorite vacation activity, Eaton Centre is worth a trip.

HOLT RENFREW

50 Bloor Street West Toronto, 416-922-2333; 25 The West Mall, Toronto, 416-621-9900; 3401 Dufferin Street, Toronto, 416-789-5377; www.holtrenfrew.com

This small department store had a well-edited collection of designer apparel, accessories and beauty items. Women can shop for the latest YSL bag and La Prairie skincare items, while men can pick up beautiful Penrose London shirts and bespoke suites. The café is a nice spot for a tartine after shopping. There are three locations within Toronto.

Monday-Wednesday 10 a.m.-7 p.m., Thursday-Friday 10 a.m.-8 p.m., Saturday 10 a.m.-7 p.m., Sunday 12 p.m.-6 p.m.

LILEO

55 Mill St., Toronto, 416-413-1410; www.lileo.ca

Grab a smoothie at the juice bar and browse the unique times at this fashion boutique/gallery/bookstore. This is a great spot to find unique items and gifts. Lileo houses many hard-to-come-by labels. Visitors also have fun with the cool light fountain.

Monday-Saturday 9 a.m.-6 p.m.

SOUTHWESTERN ONTARIO

The Southwestern Ontario region boasts a beautiful and diverse landscape. It has Carolinian forests as well as limestone cliffs, and in between you'll find small towns and some larger cities.

On the small-town front, Brantford offers world-class gardens, museums and cultural attractions, scenic trails and paddling—all just an hour's drive from Toronto. The twin cities of Kitchener-Waterloo were settled in the early 1800s by Mennonites, Amish and Germans, whose cultural heritages are still widely celebrated. A vigorous spirit of youth and industry pervades, and there's plenty of nightlife, restaurants, cultural facilities, more than 124 miles of trails and lovely golf courses.

Representing the bigger cities, London is a busy, modern hub with a charming small-town atmosphere. Located on the Thames River, its street names echo "the other" London, as does the contrast of Victorian architecture and contemporary skyscrapers.

In nearby Stratford, the names "Stratford" and "Avon River" can conjure up only one name—Shakespeare. And that is exactly what you will find in this lovely city. World-renowned, the Stratford Shakespeare Festival takes place here every year. For a relatively small town, Stratford offers up a wonderful variety of shows, concerts, plays, art galleries and spas—ideal for a weekend escape, and sealed with plentiful gardens and a Victorian city core.

Windsor is at the tip of a peninsula and is linked to Detroit by the Ambassador Bridge and the Detroit-Windsor Tunnel. Aside from its status as the Ambassador

City, thanks to its proximity to the United States, Windsor is also known as the City of Roses for its many beautiful parks. Of note is the Coventry Garden, which has the only fountain floating in international waters. A cosmopolitan and determinedly bilingual city with many French influences, Windsor enjoys a symphony orchestra, theaters, a light opera company, art galleries, nightlife and all the amenities of a large city.

WHAT TO SEE

BRANTFORD

GLENHYRST ART GALLERY OF BRANT

20 Ava Road, Brantford, 519-756-5932; www.glenhyrst.ca

The gallery at this 16-acre estate contains changing exhibits of paintings, sculpture, photography and crafts from both local and international artists. Don't skip the beautiful grounds and nature trails surrounding the estate.

Admission: free. Tuesday-Friday 10 a.m.-5 p.m., Saturday-Sunday 1-5 p.m.

HER MAJESTY'S ROYAL CHAPEL OF THE MOHAWKS

301 Mohawk St., Brantford, 519-756-0240; www.mohawkchapel.ca

The first Protestant church in Ontario, the Mohawk Chapel is the only Royal Native Chapel in the world belonging to the Six Nations people.

Daily 10 a.m.-5 p.m.

SANDERSON CENTRE FOR THE PERFORMING ARTS

88 Dalhousie St., Brantford, 519-758-8090, 800-265-0710;
www.sandersoncentre.on.ca

This 1919 vaudeville house has been restored and transformed to a theater featuring music, dance and dramatic performances. The stage has seen everyone from Mickey Rooney to the improv impresarios in the Second City comedy troupe.

WOODLAND CULTURAL CENTRE

184 Mohawk St., Brantford, 519-759-2650; www.woodland-centre.on.ca

This center preserves and promotes the culture and heritage of the First Nations of the eastern woodland area. There are education, research and museum programs, art shows and annual festivals. Check out the rotating display of contemporary art from those with First Nations ancestry.

Admission: adults $7, seniors and children 6-16 $5, children 5 and under free. Tuesday-Friday 9 a.m.-4 p.m., Saturday-Sunday 10 a.m.-5 p.m.

KITCHENER-WATERLOO

BINGEMAN PARK

425 Bingemans Centre Drive, Kitchener, 519-744-1555; www.bingemans.com

This recreation center on the banks of the Grand River includes a swimming pool, a water park, bumper boats, a go-cart track, an arcade, roller skating, miniature golf, a golf driving range, batting cages, cross-country skiing, picnicking, a restaurant, a playground and camping facilities.

Admission: varies. Hours vary.

BEST ATTRACTIONS

WHAT ARE THE TOP THINGS TO DO?

BROWSE THROUGH THE KITCHENER MARKET
This farmer's market has been around for more than 130 years. Check out the more than 100 stalls that sell everything from fresh produce and crafts. You can do your souvenir shopping here and pick up maple-syrup candies.

BRING THE KIDS TO STORYBOOK GARDENS
This family friendly theme park will keep kids entertained with rides, a sunken pirate ship and an animal-filled Enchanted Forest. When the winter hits, the park transforms into an ice-skating trail.

CATCH A SHOW IN THE STRATFORD SHAKESPEARE FESTIVAL
"Shakespeare" is in the company's name, so there will be productions of *As You Like It* and other Bard classics. But the festival also offers non-Shakespearean performances, including *Peter Pan* and *Evita*.

WALK AROUND COVENTRY GARDENS
These parts are known for having lovely verdant gardens. Coventry Gardens has its share of flowers and other greenery, but it also has a riverfront park and a 75-foot-high floating fountain.

GLOCKENSPIEL
King and Benton streets, Hamilton

Canada's first glockenspiel tells the fairy tale of Snow White. Twenty-three bells form the carillon. Performances last 15 minutes.

Four times daily.

JOSEPH SCHNEIDER HAUS
466 Queen St. S., Kitchener-Waterloo, 519-742-7752; www.region.waterloo.on.ca

The Joseph Schneider Haus Museum and Gallery is a community museum in downtown Kitchener that includes a Georgian-style frame farmhouse built by one of the area's first settlers, Joseph Schneider. Adjacent Heritage Galleries includes Germanic folk art and changing exhibits.

Admission: adults $2.25, seniors and students $1.50, children $1.25. Museum: July-September, Monday-Saturday 10 a.m.-5 p.m., Sunday 1-5 p.m.; September 2-December 24; also by appointment Wednesday-Saturday 10 a.m.-5 p.m., Sunday 1-5 p.m.

KITCHENER MARKET
300 King St. E., Kitchener, 519-741-2287; www.kitchenermarket.ca

At this more than 130-year-old farmer's market, more than 100 vendors sell fresh produce, meat, cheese and handicrafts. Mennonite specialties are featured. Pick up some maple syrup and maple-syrup candies for souvenirs.
Tuesday-Friday 9 a.m.-5 p.m., Saturday 7 a.m.-2 p.m.

PIONEER MEMORIAL TOWER
Pioneer Tower Road and Lookout Lane, Kitchener-Waterloo, 519-571-5684;
www.kwtourism.ca

This tower stands as a tribute to the industrious spirit of the pioneers who first settled Waterloo County. The cemetery on the grounds includes the graves of several of the original founders. It also offers an excellent view of Grand River.
May-October.

WATERLOO PARK
100 Westmount Road N., Waterloo, 519-725-0511; www.city.waterloo.on.ca

In this park, there is an 1820 log schoolhouse, which is surrounded by a picnic area, lake and playground. There is also a small zoo and band concerts in the summer.

LONDON

DOUBLE-DECKER BUS TOURS
300 Dufferin Ave., London, 519-661-5000, 800-265-2602; www.doubledeckertours.com

Take a two-hour guided tour aboard an authentic double-decker English bus with stops at Storybook Gardens in Springbank Park among other places. Tours depart from City Hall, Wellington Street and Dufferin Avenue. Reservations are recommended.
Admission: varies. July-Labor Day, daily.

FANSHAWE PIONEER VILLAGE
2609 Fanshawe Park Road E., London, 519-457-1296; www.fanshawepioneervillage.ca

This living history museum consists of 24 buildings and re-creates the life of a typical 19th-century crossroads community in Southwestern Ontario. There are log cabins, barns and a stable; blacksmith, weaver, harness, gun, woodworking and barber shops; a general store, church, fire hall, school and sawmill.
Admission: $5, children 3 and under free. Victoria Day Weekend-Thanksgiving, Tuesday-Sunday 10 a.m.-4:30 p.m.

GRAND THEATRE
471 Richmond St., London, 519-672-8800, 800-265-1593; www.grandtheatre.com

The contemporary façade houses a 1901 theater, built by Col. Whitney of Detroit and Ambrose Small of Toronto. The interior has been restored to include a proscenium arch, murals and cast plasterwork. The theater stages productions that range from *The Hobbit* to *Anything Goes*.
October-May.

MUSEUM OF ONTARIO ARCHAEOLOGY
1600 Attawandaron Road, London, 519-473-1360; www.uwo.ca

This museum traces the prehistory of Southwestern Ontario with more than

40,000 artifacts showing how indigenous people lived thousands of years before Columbus was born. There are archeological and ethnographic exhibits from Southwestern Ontario, as well as a gallery, theater and gift shop.

Admission: adults $5, seniors and students $4, children 5-12 $3, children 4 and under free. May-August, daily 10 a.m.-4:30 p.m.; September-December, daily 10 a.m.-4:30 p.m.; January-April, Saturday-Sunday 1-4 p.m.

STORYBOOK GARDENS

1958 Storybook Lane, Springbank Park, London, 519-661-5770; www.storybook.london.ca

Storybook Gardens is a family-oriented theme park featuring a children's playworld with rides and a zoo. During the winter, the park offers an outdoor ice-skate trail that's kept refrigerated from below to ensure consistently good skating conditions.

Admission: adults $7.50, seniors and children $6.50. Early May-mid-October, daily.

STRATFORD

GALLERY STRATFORD

54 Romeo St. N., Stratford, 519-271-5271; www.gallerystratford.on.ca

This public gallery is tucked inside the city's former pump house. There are three galleries and one studio space along with a shop to pick up a souvenir. The galleries showcase both historical and contemporary works from Canadian artists as well as changing exhibits. Guided tours are available on request.

Admission: adults $5, students and seniors $4. mid-April-mid-November, Tuesday-Sunday 10 a.m.-5 p.m.; mid-November-mid-April, Tuesday-Sunday noon-4 p.m.

SHAKESPEAREAN GARDENS

Huron St., Stratford, 519-271-5140; www.welcometostratford.com

Fragrant herbs, shrubs and flowering plants common to William Shakespeare's time are featured in this English garden.

STRATFORD SHAKESPEARE FESTIVAL

55 Queen St., Stratford, 519-273-1600, 800-567-1600; www.stratford-festival.on.ca

The distinguished actors who make up the Stratford Shakespeare Festival company perform a full slate of shows, everything from *Evita* to *The Tempest*. Contemporary, classical and Shakespearean dramas and modern musicals are put on at four local venues, the Festival, Avon, Studio and Tom Patterson theaters.

Admission: varies. April-November, matinees and evenings.

WINDSOR

ART GALLERY OF WINDSOR

401 Riverside Drive W., Windsor, 519-977-0013; www.artgalleryofwindsor.com

Collections at this art gallery consist of Canadian art, including Inuit prints and carvings. The emphasis is on Canadian artists from the past and the present. There is also a children's gallery and gift shop.

Admission: $5, free Wednesday. Wednesday, Saturday-Sunday 11 a.m.-5 p.m.; Thursday-Friday 11 a.m.-9 p.m.

COVENTRY GARDENS AND PEACE FOUNTAIN

Riverside Drive E. and Pillette Road, Windsor, 519-253-2300; www.citywindsor.ca

Coventry Gardens is a riverfront park and floral garden. A standout feature is the 75-foot-high floating Peace Fountain. There is also myriad 3-D water displays with spectacular nighttime illumination.

May-September, daily.

WILLISTEAD MANOR
1899 Niagara St., Windsor, 519-253-2365

This restored 36-room English Tudor mansion was built for Edward Chandler Walker, the son of famous distiller Hiram Walker, on 15 acres of wooded parkland. It has elegant interiors with hand-carved woodwork and furnished in turn-of-the-century style.

Admission: adults $5, seniors $4, children 3-13 $3, children 2 and under free. Year-round; call for tour reservations.

WHERE TO STAY

KITCHENER-WATERLOO
★★★LANGDON HALL COUNTRY HOUSE HOTEL & SPA
1 Langdon Drive, Cambridge, 519-740-2100; www.langdonhall.ca

You wouldn't guess that Langdon Hall Country House is a hotel as you approach the red-brick mansion with graceful tall white columns that face a vast, manicured lawn. Country-style décor and antique charm await visitors, who will appreciate the variety of room styles, from the Stable Terrace to the Rose Suite. The house, which was well-to-do Eugene Langdon Wilks' vacation home more than 100 years ago, was designed in the classic American Federal Revival style, much of which is maintained today. The hotel offers wedding services, a spa and high-end restaurant, but the best feature is its 200-acre "backyard" with four walking trails. Hoof it on either Maple Lane, which takes you through a canopy of maple trees, or the Deer Run, where there's frequent sightings of the creatures.

52 rooms. Restaurant, bar. Business center. Fitness center. Spa. $251-350

★★★WATERLOO INN
475 King St. N., Waterloo, 519-884-0220, 800-361-4708; www.waterlooinn.com

This hotel is close to the famous St. Jacob's Farmers Market, the Elora Gorge and the Stratford Festival. The rooms are charming and comfortable, with flat-panel LCD televisions, complimentary WiFi and 400-thread-count linens.

155 rooms. Restaurant, bar. Fitness center. Pool. Pets accepted. $61-150

LONDON
★★★HILTON LONDON ONTARIO
300 King St., London, 519-439-1661; www.hiltonlondon.com

An attached heated walkway makes access to the convention center easy from this hotel when the weather is less than cooperative. The indoor pool provides a great break to the winter doldrums. When it warms up, 15-acre Victoria Park is only two blocks from the hotel. The rooms are spacious and have little extras spread throughout, including Crabtree & Evelyn products, blackout curtains, Cuisinart coffeemakers and lap desks for your laptop.

322 rooms. Restaurants, bar. Business center. Fitness center. Pool. Pet accepted. $151-250

STRATFORD
★★QUEEN'S INN
161 Ontario St., Stratford, 519-271-1400;
www.queensinnstratford.ca

This lovely Victorian inn is on the main street of downtown, close to a variety of shops and restaurants. The inn has its own restaurant and English pub onsite. The family-owned hotel features uniquely decorated rooms that feel like a home away from home.

32 rooms. Restaurant, bar. Pets accepted. $61-150

★★★TOUCHSTONE MANOR
325 St. David St., Stratford, 519-273-5820;
www.touchstone-manor.com

This 1938 inn is in a quiet, residential neighborhood within walking distance of downtown and about a half-hour stroll to the Shakespeare Festival area. The rooms boast period antiques, deep colors and personalized detailing. Amenities include flatscreen televisions with DVD players, bathrobes and slippers and Aveda products. You can relax with a book in the mahogany-filled library, or take a seat in the proper parlor and play the baby grand piano, in case you want to tickle the ivories. A two-course breakfast, served on fine china, is included in your stay.

4 rooms. Complimentary breakfast. No children under 12. Closed late December-late January. $251-350

WINDSOR
★★★CAESARS WINDSOR HOTEL
377 Riverside Drive E., Windsor, 519-258-7878, 800-991-7777;
www.casinowindsor.com

An oasis from the frenetic casino activity, this hotel offers guest rooms with views of the Detroit skyline or the city of Windsor. The beige, black and cream rooms also offer HD flat-panel televisions, pillowtop mattresses and refrigerators. A constant line-up of major entertainers and a buzzing casino in the lobby will keep you busy.

758 rooms. Restaurant, bar. Fitness center. Pool. Casino. $251-350

★★★HILTON WINDSOR
277 Riverside Drive W., Windsor, 519-973-5555, 800-774-1500;
www.hilton.com

Whichever room you stay in at this waterfront hotel, you'll get a view of the river. The hotel is also conveniently interconnected to the Cleary International

---

WHICH RESTAURANTS HAVE THE MOST UNIQUE DÉCOR?

Church Restaurant and the Belfry
Your French meal will be a heavenly experience in this restaurant, which resides in a beautiful 19th-century Gothic church complete with wooden arches and stunning stained-glass windows.

Olde School Restaurant
School cafeteria meals don't conjure up the most delicious images, but that's not the case at this steak restaurant, which is housed in an 1850s schoolhouse. The attractive grounds also have a bell tower.

Convention Centre, which is good for business travelers, and close to other local attractions. The casual Park Terrace Restaurant serves breakfast, lunch and dinner. The River Runner Bar is a great place to catch the game.

305 rooms. Restaurant, bar. Business center. Pool. Pets accepted. $151-250

WHERE TO EAT

BRANTFORD
★★★OLDE SCHOOL RESTAURANT
Paris Road West at 687 Powerline Road W., Brantford, 519-753-3131, 888-448-3131; www.theoldeschoolrestaurant.ca

This steak and seafood restaurant, located in a relatively rural area, is housed in an 1850s schoolhouse with a bell tower and beautifully landscaped grounds. And its baked lobster tail and the veal rib chop with peppercorn sauce are much better than the meals you'd find in the typical school cafeteria. After dinner, stop in the piano lounge to hear the nightly live music.

Steak, seafood. Lunch, dinner. Children's menu. Bar. $36-85

KITCHENER-WATERLOO
★★★CHARCOAL STEAK HOUSE
2980 King St. E., Kitchener, 519-893-6570; www.charcoalsteakhouse.ca

Consistently delicious steaks and a relaxing, serene atmosphere have made the Charcoal Steak House a Kitchener favorite for more than 50 years. The menu highlights Canadian steaks, like the thick porterhouse, and fresh seafood, including the sashimi tuna niçoise. For a sweet ending, order the crème fraîche cheesecake with strawberry foam, sangria gelée and pistachio meringue. If you prefer a more potent meal capper, a number of cocktails choices are offered in addition to an award-winning wine list.

Steak. Lunch, dinner, Sunday brunch. Reservations recommended. Children's menu. $36-85

★★★★THE DINING ROOM AT LANGDON HALL
Langdon Hall Country House Hotel & Spa, 1 Langdon Drive, Cambridge, 519-740-2100; www.langdonhall.ca

Executive chef Jonathan Gushue heads this lovely restaurant, which features dishes made with fresh local ingredients. The Dining Room is also open for breakfast, brunch and lunch, but its true star is its dinner menu. Try the robust herb-basted rainbow trout or the dry-aged beef tenderloin. If you're really looking for an unforgettable dining experience, Gushue also prepares a $95 tasting menu with wine pairings, featuring poached Arctic char with local morels and a crispy St. Jacobs pig cheek, followed by delightful strawberry compote with lime sorbet.

American, French. Breakfast, lunch, dinner, Sunday brunch. Reservations recommended. Jacket required. $86 and up

STRATFORD
★★★CHURCH RESTAURANT AND THE BELFRY
70 Brunswick St., Stratford, 519-273-3424; www.churchrestaurant.com

Housed in a 19th-century Gothic church, with wooden arches and stained-glass windows, this restaurant makes dining an uplifting experience. Try opulent dishes such as Quebec duck three ways—breast, foie gras croquettes and pot pie—or spice-crusted elk loin with Niagara cherries. Follow it up with a sweet and savory dessert like chocolate bacon ganache with sorrel ice cream and pickled cherries.

French. Lunch, dinner, Sunday brunch. Reservations recommended. $86 and up

★★★RUNDLES

9 Cobourg St., Stratford, 519-271-6442; www.rundlesrestaurant.com

Located on the river at ground zero for the Stratford Festival, this longtime favorite affords the most elegant dining in the area. Like the environment, the chef's food is simple and thoroughly enjoyable. Try the sautéed Quebec foie gras with quail satay, pickled mushrooms and ginger-flavored sauce; and the pan-fried, organically farmed Irish salmon, braised with fennel and olive oil with vegetable-filled ravioli.

American. Lunch, dinner. Outdoor seating. $86 and up

WINDSOR
RECOMMENDED
COOK'S SHOP

683 Ouellette Ave., Windsor, 519-254-3377

Located in the basement of an old brownstone, this intimate restaurant—there are only 15 tables—with cobblestone walls has been around for three decades. Many consider it one of Windsor's most romantic restaurants and Detroiters drive across the border to dine here. Inside the dimly-lit space, many of the pasta sauces are made tableside and there are several grilled items.

Italian. Dinner. Closed Monday; also two weeks in August. Reservations recommended. $16-35

SPA

KITCHENER-WATERLOO
★★★THE SPA AT LANGDON HALL

Langdon Hall Country House Hotel & Spa, 1 Langdon Drive, Cambridge, 519-624-3220; www.langdonhall.ca

Along with the traditional body and facial treatments, the Spa at Langdon Hall offers hydrotherapy sessions, which include de-stressing, detoxifying or re-mineralizing baths. The private soaks are powerful, with 144 jets that promise to relax the tightest knots. A detoxifying seaweed wrap will leave you feeling rejuvenated, and the Vichy Aroma Rain Body Therapy—a sea salt and jojoba body scrub under rainfall—is an invigorating treatment that results in super-soft skin.

INDEX

MICHIGAN

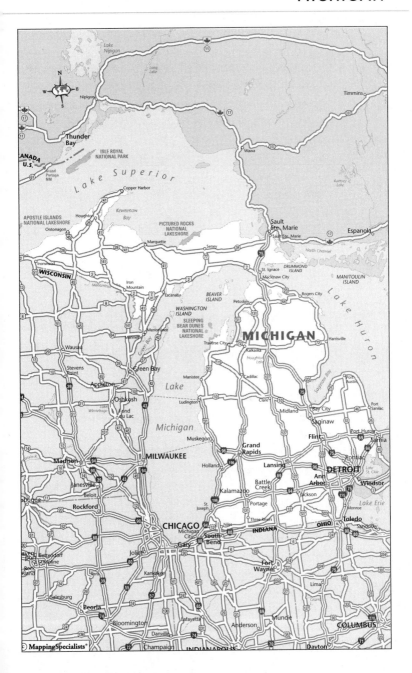

© Mapping Specialists®

MINNESOTA

WISCONSIN

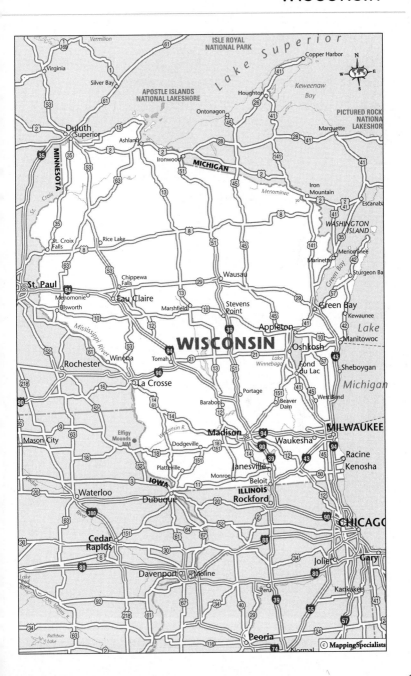

ONTARIO

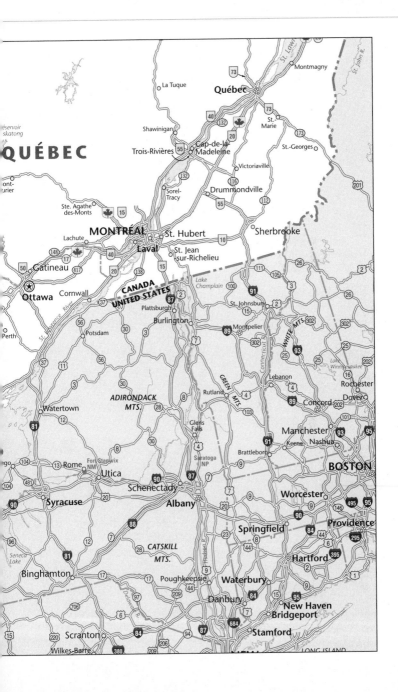

NOTES

NOTES

NOTES